FREE FROM THE LAW

An exposition of Galatians

FREE FROM THE LAW

An exposition of Galatians

by

NORMAN ROE
in a series of 26 sermons

WEST WELLS BOOKS

2024

WEST WELLS BOOKS
8 West Wells Crescent
Wakefield
West Yorks
WF5 8PL

Phone: 07918 656326

westwellsbooks.co.uk
westwellsbooks@gmail.com

incorporating:

Faith Books Ossett

ISBN: 978-1-7393295-1-8

First published 1991 in four photocopied volumes under the
CBO Publications imprint.

Printed by:

4edge Limited
22 Eldon Way Industrial Estate, Hockley, Essex
SS5 4AD

CONTENTS

Publisher's Note   ix

1   ACTS 14:21-23   1
And when they had preached the gospel to that city, and
had taught many; they returned again to Lystra.

2   ACTS 15:31   11
Which when they had read, they rejoiced for the
consolation.

3   GALATIANS 1:1-5   21
Paul, an apostle, (not of men, neither by man, but by
Jesus Christ, and God the Father, who raised him from
the dead).

4   GALATIANS 1:6-9   31
I marvel that ye are so soon removed from him that hath
called you into the grace of Christ unto another gospel.

5   GALATIANS 1:9-24   42
As we said before, so say I now again, If any man preach
any other gospel unto you than that ye have received, let
him be accursed.

6   GALATIANS 2:1-5   53
Then fourteen years after I went up again to Jerusalem.

7   ROMANS 14   62
Him that is weak in the faith receive ye, but not to
doubtful disputations. For one believeth that he may eat
all things: another, who is weak, eateth herbs ...

8   GALATIANS 2:6-21   71
       They who seemed to be somewhat in conference added
       nothing to me.

9   GALATIANS 2:15-21   81
       Knowing that a man is not justified by the works of the
       law, but by the faith of Jesus Christ, even we have
       believed in Jesus Christ..

10   GALATIANS 3:1-2   91
       O foolish Galatians, who hath bewitched you, that ye
       should not obey the truth.

11   MATTHEW 5:20   100
       Except your righteousness shall exceed the righteousness
       of the scribes and Pharisees, ye shall in no case enter into
       the kingdom of heaven.

12   GALATIANS 3:6-9   110
       Abraham believed God, and it was accounted to him for
       righteousness.

13   GALATIANS 3:10-14   121
       For as many as are of the works of the law are under the
       curse..

14   GALATIANS 3:15-18   130
       Brethren, I speak after the manner of men; Though it be
       but a man's covenant, yet if it be confirmed, no man
       disannulleth, or addeth thereto.

15   GALATIANS 3:19-26   140
       Wherefore then serveth the law? It was added because of
       transgressions, till the seed should come to whom the
       promise was made..

16   GALATIANS 3:26-29   150
       For ye are all the children of God by faith in Christ Jesus.

17   GALATIANS 4:1-3   158
       Now I say, That the heir, as long as he is a child, differeth
       nothing from a servant, though he be lord of all.

18   GALATIANS 4:4-7   167
*But when the fulness of the time was come, God sent forth
his Son, made of a woman, made under the law, to
redeem them that were under the law, that we might
receive the adoption of sons.*

19   GALATIANS 4:8-20   176
*Howbeit then, when ye knew not God, ye did service unto
them which by nature are no gods. But now, after that ye
have known God, or rather are known of God, how turn
ye again to the weak and beggarly elements, whereunto
ye desire again to be in bondage?*

20   GALATIANS 4:21-31   186
*Tell me, ye that desire to be under the law, do ye not hear
the law? For it is written, that Abraham had two sons, the
one by a bondmaid, the other by a freewoman. But he
who was of the bondwoman was born after the flesh; but
he of the freewoman was by promise. Which things are an
allegory.*

21   HEBREWS 10:38-39   195
*Now the just shall live by faith: but if any man draw back,
my soul shall have no pleasure in him.*

22   GALATIANS 5:1   204
*Stand fast therefore in the liberty wherewith Christ hath
made us free, and be not entangled again with the yoke of
bondage.*

23   ROMANS 9:30-33   213
*What shall we say then? That the Gentiles, which
followed not after righteousness, have attained to
righteousness, even the righteousness which is of faith.*

24   GALATIANS 5   222
*Behold, I Paul say unto you, that if ye be circumcised,
Christ shall profit you nothing. For I testify again to
every man that is circumcised, that he is a debtor to do
the whole law.*

25   GALATIANS 6:1-10   234
      Brethren, if a man be overtaken in a fault, ye which are
      spiritual, restore such an one in the spirit of meekness;
      considering thyself, lest thou also be tempted.

26   GALATIANS 6:11-18   246
      Ye see how large a letter I have written unto you with
      mine own hand. As many as desire to make a fair shew in
      the flesh, they constrain you to be circumcised; only lest
      they should suffer persecution for the cross of Christ.

PUBLISHER'S NOTE

This series of twenty-six sermons expounds the epistle of Paul to the Galatians. They were preached by Norman Henry Roe on Friday evenings between 4th December 1989 and 27th July 1990 at Ebenezer Strict and Particular Baptist Chapel, Ossett where he was the pastor.

We first published them under the same title in 1996 as four photocopied booklets each containing six or seven sermons. Reprinting them now in a single hardback volume we have taken the opportunity to carry out a little further editing to improve ease of reading. Bible quotes are all from the Authorised Version and capitalisation in the general text is as the A.V. Hymn quotes are from Gadsby's hymnbook.

This book reflects the apostle's deep concern over the heresy which had made inroads in the Galatian churches. False teachers were insisting on obedience to the Mosaic law as an essential accompaniment to faith in Jesus. They said that without it, believers could not be saved. This amounted to a rejection of Christ's righteousness and atoning death as the *only and all-sufficient* means of salvation. The law demands perfect obedience. No person, before or after conversion, can perform one such act. Therefore none can *ever* obtain God's favour by any such supposed but imperfect works of righteousness. Jesus Christ was made under the law to fulfil to perfection all the obedience it requires of his people and to fully suffer the curse and punishment demanded for all their sins. Since all debts have been paid, the law can require nothing more of the saved sinner. They are thus made free from the rule of law and live according to the gospel rule. "The life which they now live in the flesh they live by the faith of the Son of God, who loved them, and gave himself for them." In "faith which worketh by love" they embrace his will as supremely and conclusively revealed through the promised outpouring of the Holy Spirit on the apostles. "The law was given by Moses, but grace and truth came by Jesus Christ." Moses foretold that, "The LORD thy God will raise up unto thee a Prophet from the midst of thee, of thy brethren, like unto me; unto him ye shall hearken; according to all that thou desiredst of the LORD thy God in Horeb in the day of the assembly, saying, Let me not hear again the voice of the LORD my God, neither let me see this great fire any more, that I die not."

These vital principles of the faith are strongly expressed repeatedly in this book, in love and faithfulness to Christ and to the souls of his redeemed people today. As is often stated by the preacher, the desire is that all be to the praise of the glory of the Lord's great and holy name.

.

1

ACTS 14:21-23

And when they had preached the gospel to that city, and had taught many; they returned again to Lystra, and to Iconium, and Antioch, confirming the souls of the disciples, and exhorting them to continue in the faith, and that we must through much tribulation enter into the kingdom of God. And when they had ordained them elders in every church, and had prayed with fasting, they commended them to the Lord, on whom they believed.

On these Friday evenings at times in the past I have preached a series of sermons on particular portions of holy scripture. We looked at the book of Job over a number of weeks, and another time at the first epistle to Corinthians. Though I have not done things in this way for a while, I have felt for some weeks my mind drawn to the epistle to the Galatians and I want, as the Lord may help me, to look at this epistle over the coming months. I do not want to confine myself absolutely to looking at Galatians on Friday evenings if I feel another portion of God's word laid on my mind. But the Lord willing, I want as helped, to look particularly at this epistle in our weeknight services.

I believe what is brought out in it is most important. It certainly was so in the days when it was written by the apostle and sent to the churches at Galatia. And I am increasingly convinced that it is as important and necessary that the essential vital truths for which the apostle contends in this epistle be still set forth. We need to be continually reminded of them and be led and established in these truths by the Holy Spirit.

Now obviously this evening I have not turned directly to the epistle to the Galatians, and I shall have very little to say this time with respect to it. We will leave that to another week. I have read this chapter in the Acts of the Apostles as I believe it is distinctly bound up with the epistle to the Galatians. For it is generally reckoned that these cities that are spoken of in this chapter, such as Derbe, Lystra, Iconium and Antioch (not the Antioch in Syria) formed a part of the region that was known as the Roman province of Galatia. I know that there has been some dispute over this, for these cities did not actually form a part of Galatia proper. That was more to the north of where these cities lay. There is no record in the Acts of the Apostles that Paul ever visited the northern part of Galatia proper. It is generally reckoned that Paul wrote his epistle to these cities of Galatia very early on in his ministry. Certainly that which was recorded in chapters 13 and 14 of this Acts of the Apostles comprises the first missionary journey on which Paul and Barnabas were sent, as we read in the opening part of chapter 13. "Now there were in the church that was at Antioch certain prophets and teachers; as Barnabas, and Simeon that was called Niger, and Lucius of Cyrene and Manaen, which had been brought up with Herod the tetrarch and Saul. As they ministered to the Lord, and fasted, the Holy Ghost said, Separate me Barnabas and Saul for the work whereunto I have called them. And when they had fasted and prayed, and laid hands on them, they sent them away."

So we see that even with respect to Paul's first coming among these towns in the Roman province of Galatia, as recorded in this fourteenth chapter, he and Barnabas did not come there of their own accord. They were commissioned of the Holy Spirit to that work and they were guided by him in it. And it is evident that the Holy Spirit blessed their work and ministry in those places in spite of all the opposition they met.

We find in chapter 13 they sailed first from Syria to Cyprus and after they had ministered for some time there, they passed over into Asia and came to these towns recorded in this fourteenth chapter. I was saying there is evidence that the epistle to the Galatians was written early on in Paul's ministry, particularly following the council that took place at Jerusalem as recorded in chapter 15. It is evident that the Galatian epistle deals with those things that were considered by that gathering of the elders and apostles in Jerusalem. There, the whole church confirmed the glorious gospel of sovereign grace and mercy, *that salvation is by grace through faith alone in the Lord and Saviour Jesus Christ.* All the apostles faithfully and distinctly taught and preached this gospel for which Paul contends in his epistle to the Galatians. For what was settled at that council in Jerusalem, what they set aside as *not* according to the truth as it is in Jesus, was the very thing being advocated in Galatia by the teachers and false apostles as Paul calls them. As helped by the Holy Spirit, he faithfully and boldly contends against those who were troubling the church with their heretical teachings.

And as I have said, the glorious truths brought out in the epistle to the Galatians need to be contended for, advocated and set forth as much today, that our souls may be truly led into gospel liberty. As Paul says in that well known verse, "Stand fast therefore in the liberty wherewith Christ hath made us free, and be not entangled again with the yoke of bondage" (Gal. 1:5). But we will speak more on those things when we come particularly to the epistle.

As helped, let us consider in some little detail this evening, Paul's first coming among those places in the Roman province of Galatia. We find that he visits Iconium, Antioch, Lystra and Derbe and at each of these places he preaches the gospel. And though there were those that through sovereign grace were brought to hear and receive the word of the truth of the gospel, yet much opposition was stirred up against him.

Let us look at this chapter. "And it came to pass in Iconium, that they went both together into the synagogue of the Jews, and so spake, that a great multitude both of the Jews and also of the Greeks believed." It was the general practice of Paul when he came to a new place, to first preach in the synagogue of the Jews if the opportunity arose. We must bear in mind that the Jews, or colonies of them, lived in many parts of the Roman Empire. It is not surprising then that at such places as Iconium, Lystra, Derbe and Antioch there should be colonies of Jews who even in such places far from the land of Israel, still cleaved to the traditions of their fathers.

So Paul preached in the synagogue of the Jews. Notice the importance of this, as it has particular bearing upon what we will consider in the epistle to the Galatians. In verse 7 we read, "And there they preached the gospel." A very brief, emphatic statement! What a fulness is in it! *"They preached the gospel."* They did not come with a refined form of Judaism to those places and the synagogues of the Jews. The gospel of Jesus Christ that they preached, though rooted and grounded in the old testament scripture and what the prophets had declared, was not a form of Judaism. It was that which was essentially new. It was startling. As faithfully set forth, it provoked much controversy as well. For we see that the gospel of free and sovereign grace in Jesus Christ which Paul preached (as did the other apostles as well), was not willingly received by fallen man. It never has been received and it is not today. The gospel is utterly contrary to the ideas and concerns of men and women dead in trespasses and sins. It is the very reverse of the natural religion of the human heart.

Now what is the natural religion of the human heart? The religion which is so dear to fallen human nature is grounded on works, men's works. The centre of it is man himself—what he has to do or what he has to strive to attain to. As I have said on other occasions, you look at all the religions abroad in the world today, including the many sects within supposed Christendom, and what is the one thing common to them all? They all have distinctive things connected with them. In their outward manifestations they may well differ in many things, but one thing is common to them all. Every one is a religion of works, works being so dear to the natural heart of fallen sinful man. It is very evident that the gospel Paul preached, the true gospel given us in the holy scriptures, is the very opposite of natural religion. If it was not so, it would not be the gospel. For what does the gospel, or the word *gospel,* essentially mean? It means the great and good news from heaven itself. Remember, at the birth of the Lord Jesus Christ in Bethlehem, what those shepherds who were keeping their flocks by night heard the angel of the Lord say. "I bring you good tidings of great joy, which shall be to all people. For unto you is born this day in the city of David a Saviour which is Christ the Lord" (Luke 2:10-11).

The gospel then, is essentially the great and good news from heaven, that which God himself has made known in the person and work of the Lord Jesus Christ. It speaks of what God in Christ has done. As the angel said, "Unto you is born this day in the city of David, a Saviour which is Christ the Lord." As the angel said to Joseph, "Thou shalt call his name JESUS: for he shall save his people from their sins" (Matt. 1:21). It is the gospel which speaks of salvation accomplished and applied, not through what man is or what men can do, but what Jesus Christ himself is and has done. Ah, I repeat, *the gospel speaks of salvation accomplished and applied, not by what man is or can do, but by what Jesus Christ himself is and has done*. It is that which speaks of salvation through the sovereign grace and mercy of God to wretched, ruined, guilty, needy sinners brought into saving knowledge of this gospel under the gracious mighty working of God the Holy Spirit. The gospel then, and what is essentially found in it, is the very opposite to what is the religion of a natural heart. The religion of the natural heart likes nothing better than to think that in some way or other it can placate the justice of God to obtain his favour. But as I have said, the gospel speaks of what God in Christ has done.

"And there they preached the gospel." And oh, behold the wonder of this. "A great multitude both of the Jews and also of the Greeks believed." Yes, that word had effect. Many that heard it were brought to receive it and why was this? What was this the result of? Was it the personality of Paul that accomplished those things? You know there is often a great deal placed upon the personality or the persuasiveness of the minister. Great emphasis is often laid on those things as being vitally important when it comes to the preaching of the gospel. But was it so with Paul? Was it because he was so eloquent and persuasive a preacher that so many were brought to believe? He says to the Corinthians when he came among them, "I determined not to know any thing among you, save Jesus Christ, and him crucified" (1 Cor. 2:2). It was not with wisdom of words that he sought to persuade them, not with the powers of oratory he sought to influence them. No. It was the unction and power of the Holy Spirit that accompanied the word.

Look at this as brought out in the Acts of the Apostles when Peter and the others preached on the day of Pentecost. Ah, men were amazed, not only at what they heard but at the power of that word. And who were the preachers on the day of Pentecost? Many of those whom the Lord had called to be his immediate disciples were but poor fishermen. They were not men that had had a great education. They were not those that had great powers of oratory and utterance, so that by their own abilities and gifts they could persuade multitudes to receive what they said. No. Look at the sermon of Peter on the day of Pentecost. What essentially was it? It was a faithful stating of the truth of the person and work of the Lord Jesus Christ. And see how that was mightily used of the Holy Spirit.

It was so in the ministry of Paul. True, he had been brought up at the feet of Gamaliel. Paul had had a good education, as it might be termed today. And I have heard it said by some that those were the things that fitted and equipped Paul for the future work God had for him to do. I do not believe that was so for one moment. I do not believe what some people think, that his good education which he learned at the feet of Gamaliel prepared him for the future work that God had for him to do. No. Did he learn the truth as it is in Jesus at the feet of Gamaliel? Did he receive there the grace of God and faith in Jesus Christ? No. And we do not find that Paul ever put emphasis on his upbringing or the education that he had received. He does not even seem to feature these things in his work of the ministry. No, what fitted and prepared Paul for the work of the ministry was what he heard and received from the Lord Jesus himself, during those three years that he spent in Arabia. We are not told what took place, but without question, there was opened up to him the depths of the fulness of truth in the Lord Jesus Christ which he afterwards preached.

"They preached the gospel" with astounding effect as many were brought to saving faith through the gracious mighty operations of the Holy Spirit. But that was not all. We find there was opposition raised up as well. "Long time therefore abode they speaking boldly in the Lord, which gave testimony unto the word of his grace, and granted signs and wonders to be done by their hands. But the multitude of the city was divided; and part held with the Jews and part with the apostles." We see the effect of faithful preaching. Some believed not. The word had an effect in every case. It was either used by the Holy Spirit to the saving of the soul or there was bitter opposition to the truth as it is in Jesus. Opposition was the sad evidence of the sin rooted in the fallen nature of man. And wherever the gospel is faithfully set forth, then we may be assured that similar effects will follow. If it is not used of the Holy Spirit to the saving of the soul, there will be sadly evidenced the stirring up of the corruption and antagonism of the natural heart against the truth. Satan is ever active where the gospel is faithfully preached and set forth. We shall find opposition arising in one form or another. It is so with the individual believer.

I remember years ago now when I was first baptised, a servant of God wrote to me and said, 'Where God works graciously there the devil will seek to work maliciously.' That is invariably so. The believer finds it so in his own experience in the daily workings of his innermost being. Where there is the life of God in the soul, so the opposition to that work of grace will manifest itself as well.

Here in these cities of Lystra, Iconium, Derbe and Antioch, the apostles found opposition in a very overt way. In particular, Paul was stoned and left for dead at Lystra. The unbelieving Jews in other parts stirred up great opposition against him. And yet let us notice this. Did all this discourage the apostles? Did they run away from the work they were given? True, as opposition became very great in one city they moved to another, but they didn't desert the work. We find in the words of our text, that when they had preached the gospel in Derbe and taught many, they returned again to Lystra, Iconium and Antioch—the very places where they had been so evilly entreated.

We see here the effect of the grace of God in their faithfulness and love to that work. It arose from the love of the Lord Jesus that had been made known to them, and in their love and deep concern for the brethren who had heard and received the word through grace in those places. They returned again to Lystra and to Iconium and Antioch. But just let me notice this as well. They experienced great opposition, physical violence upon their persons, for the gospel that they preached. But that outward persecution never did so much harm to the church as did the heresies which afterwards troubled the churches, and against which Paul contends in his letter to the Galatians. Where the church has been subject to outward persecution, instead of the church diminishing, it has often grown and increased. The more they were persecuted, the more the church increased. When the church at Jerusalem was scattered through the persecution that arose upon the death of Stephen, the brethren went everywhere preaching the gospel, and numbers were added to the church. We see churches springing up in all parts and places as it was here in the regions of Galatia. Outward persecution never seemed to really harm the church. But oh, what grievous trouble was caused by those that brought and taught doctrines contrary to the truth as it is in Jesus.

No wonder the apostle John warns the church in his epistles, against false teachers who bring a doctrine contrary to what they had received. The apostle Paul does the same in his epistles. See the harm and distress wrought in the churches of Galatia by those judaizing teachers, those false apostles which came, as Paul said, with another gospel which was not a gospel, not the true gospel of Jesus Christ. The activity of the enemy of souls is seen in this just as much, if not more so, than in the outward persecution that was raised against the church. We ever need to watch and pray against it.

We read, "They returned again, to these cities, confirming the souls of the disciples, and exhorting them to continue in the faith and that we must through much tribulation enter into the kingdom of God." Three things are particularly brought before us. Firstly, *confirming the souls of the disciples*. This is the strengthening and encouraging of them. And by what was this encouragement? Was it just the presence of the apostles that was so advantageous to the churches here in Galatia? No doubt they did appreciate very much the times that the apostles spent among them, as did other churches. But Paul didn't remain in those places long. You know, if the continuance of them in the faith was dependent on the presence of the apostles with them, then how soon would their faith have evaporated. Soon after they had left, the churches would have completely fallen away from the faith. No, it was not to himself and the other apostles that Paul directed the believers in those places. It was to their Lord and Saviour Jesus Christ, the one on whom they believed, assuring them of his power, love and faithfulness. He speaks to them of the Lord, that he was still the living one who was even then present with them according to his promise, the one that was able to do "exceeding abundantly" above what they could ask or think.

We then read, secondly, of his *"exhorting them to continue in the faith."* Now let me just briefly touch upon this point for it is very important. "To continue in the faith" not only relates to the importance of their personal believing what they had heard and received. That was important and he sought to confirm the souls of the disciples in it. But he exhorted them to continue in the faith, in the sense of those things that are believed and received as the truth that is in Jesus. Now this raises a very important point, something that is so often overlooked and I fear to a greater part forgotten in the days in which we live. That is, *how essential is right and true doctrine as it concerns the church of Jesus Christ.* People put great emphasis on believing. We are not belittling that, but friends the important thing is, *what* is believed? The issue here is not so much the strength of the faith in its subjective sense, but the importance of the objective faith, *the truth that is believed.* You know, we find even in all false religions an essential element is what might be termed very strong faith, *but* it is the things that are believed and received that are important.

"And he exhorted them to continue in the faith." Remember that faith which is the true work and gift of God the Holy Spirit, the faith of God's elect, brings us to believe, receive and cleave in love to *the truth as it is in Jesus.* See how Paul contends for this in his letter to the Galatians, as we shall notice in due course. Paul doesn't say that sound doctrine doesn't matter, and that as long as people are sincere, what they actually believe is of little account. Far from it. Those false apostles and teachers that had come to the churches of Galatia and who were causing so much trouble, were very sincere. They were very zealous. They sought to persuade many to receive what they were saying and teaching.

But see how Paul contends there for right doctrine. And that is vital for the true welfare, the peace and comfort of the church, the living family of God.

"Exhorting them to continue in the faith, and that we must through much tribulation enter into the kingdom of God." Here, thirdly, he reminds them that even the oppositions and persecutions to which they were subject, were to be looked for and expected. They were part of that which is involved in the true believing and receiving and walking out of the truth as it is in the Lord Jesus Christ. Be not surprised that these things are so. It is the path that the Lord has appointed for his church and people. It is through much tribulation that we enter the kingdom. True, these things are in the way but what a glorious object is set before us! There is the entering into the kingdom of Jesus Christ. There is the glorious end and prospect of the full and final victory over all these afflictions. Does not Paul write in his epistle to the Romans, "We are more than conquerors through him that loved us"? (Rom.8:37). The apostle here sounds the very note of victory, even to these believers in the church in Galatia.

But I will leave the remarks there this evening. May the Lord add his blessing. Amen.

2

ACTS 15:31

Which when they had read, they rejoiced for the consolation.

I said last Friday that subject to the Lord's will I want to direct your attention to the epistle to the Galatians on these Friday evenings during coming weeks. In doing so, first of all I looked last week at chapters 13 and 14 of this Acts of the Apostles where there is the record given of Paul's first preaching the gospel in the region of Galatia. We saw the effect it had, the fruits it produced in the hearts of those men and women who heard and received the word by divine grace.

Now this evening, in looking at this fifteenth chapter, I want to draw your attention to the matter that was dealt with and settled at this assembly of the apostles and elders at Jerusalem. It forms the very basis of all that Paul is setting forth in the epistle to the Galatians. It is important that we lay the groundwork for the consideration of the vitally important matter that the Galatian letter deals with. Paul refers to this gathering or council at Jerusalem particularly in the second chapter of his epistle. We find that he attended this meeting which took place some seventeen or eighteen years after he had been first called by divine grace, called to be an apostle and put by the Lord Jesus Christ into the ministry. He tells the Galatians that he went into Arabia very shortly after the Lord had met with him on the Damascus road and he had preached in Damascus that Jesus was the Christ. After three years he made a brief visit to Jerusalem,. We find that he then entered more particularly on the ministry to which the Lord had called him. It was fourteen years later that this council at Jerusalem took place, at which the matter Paul handles in his epistle to the Galatians was dealt with in the gathering of the brethren, elders and apostles. So then, it was some seventeen or eighteen years after Paul had first been called by grace that this council at Jerusalem took place.

What tremendous happenings had come to pass in those few years! How the gospel had been taken so rapidly from the day of Pentecost through great tracts of the known world of those days! How vast had been the expansion of the church under the power, unction and blessing of God the Holy Spirit! True, great opposition had been raised against the church. But persecution, instead of causing the work to cease, was the very instrument in God's hand for the brethren to be scattered abroad. The word of the truth of the gospel was thereby taken into many places. Ah, though this book is called the Acts of the Apostles as it records the work and ministry of the apostles, yet we can surely say that in their acts we see the mighty operations of God the Holy Spirit. We see the wonders of divine grace as men and women whom God had ordained to eternal life are brought to hear and receive the word of truth and to repentance and saving faith in the Lord and Saviour Jesus Christ.

It was not the zeal or eloquence of the apostles that accomplished those things. True, they were the instruments that the Holy Spirit used and yet look at what many of them were. They were poor ignorant men as far as this world views matters. Though we might say Paul was one of the most educated among them, yet he never claimed that his education was the vital cause of his ministry being used to the salvation of so many. No, he ascribes all to the glory of God's grace. He says he laboured more abundantly than all the other apostles, yet he immediately adds, "Yet not I, but the grace of God which was with me" (1 Cor. 15:10). He claims no glory for that work on account of his own efforts as an apostle. He lays all the glory at the feet of the Lord Jesus Christ. It is all the work of God's grace. The joy and delight of his heart was to see the work go forward in others being called by grace *and* in their being established in deeper knowledge, understanding and walking out of the blessed truths of the gospel they had received. That was why he contended so vigorously and emphatically against the pernicious errors that had appeared and were making headway in the churches of Galatia and elsewhere in the new testament church at that time. We find that they even surfaced here in the church at Antioch.

We read, "And certain men which came down from Judaea taught the brethren, and said, Except ye be circumcised after the manner of Moses, ye cannot be saved." Now it is evident that these men which came down from Judaea were Jews. You say, well, so was the apostle Paul. Indeed he was. But these Jews were still rooted in, and cleaved to what may well be termed their Judaism. That is, they did not preach and teach the pure gospel of the grace of God as it centres in the person and work of the Lord Jesus Christ. No, they were stipulating that men and women must be conformed to, and keep the law of Moses, as well as have faith in Jesus Christ, if they were to be saved. That is, to obtain the favour of God as they were sinners they must believe in Jesus Christ but that in itself was *not sufficient*. They must keep the law of Moses, for that is what is embodied in their advocating circumcision. It was not just the basic rite of circumcision itself but what that embodied in it. Paul emphatically brings this out in his epistle to the Galatians. And it is also clearly stated in this chapter in the matter here dealt with by this council at Jerusalem.

We read in verse five, "But there rose up certain of the sect of the Pharisees which believed, saying, That it was needful to circumcise them, and to command them to keep the law of Moses." They were saying that the law of Moses was binding on all Gentile believers and there was no hope of salvation for them unless they were circumcised and kept the law. Surely did not this seem a very plausible thing? Who can object to such a statement as that? Was not Moses indeed the faithful servant of God—one of the greatest old testament prophets? Without question he was. How glorious were those things made known by God to Moses on mount Sinai. Was there not the giving of the law in all the moral principles of it, in all the ceremonial aspects of it, in all the judicial implications of it to Israel as a people and nation? Ah! Remember that the children of Israel were a people specially chosen of God from all other nations of the earth to be his own distinct people to whom he gave the great things of his law. Surely then, does not the argument run—can those things be overlooked and dismissed? Can we turn our back on such great and glorious revelations as were given by God to Moses? Those things had been binding on the children of Israel down to that time. What then had changed to suggest for one moment that they were no longer binding on all who profess to be in a right relationship with God?

Here was no dealing with a mere academic point. It was not just dealing with peripheral things of a secondary nature which did not really matter whether they were received or not as far as the salvation of the soul was concerned. This is the point. There are things which can well be described as of a secondary nature. Whether we attend to them or not is left to the individual liberty of the believer. They do not bring any real harm to his spiritual life or to his standing before a holy heart-searching God. But here it was not secondary things that were being dealt with but first principles. Paul could see only too clearly that what these men were advocating undermined the very gospel itself. If what they were saying was true, if those things were needful, then what he taught with respect to salvation by grace through faith alone in Jesus Christ was of no value. Indeed such was the seriousness of this matter, that if what they said was true, then Christ had died in vain, and all Paul had been preaching and teaching during the past eighteen years was of no value whatsoever. That is why he so emphatically declared as he did, "But though we, or an angel from heaven, preach any other gospel unto you than that which we have preached unto you, *let him be accursed"* (Gal. 1:8).

But as I said, I want this evening to lay the foundation in leading up to what the epistle to the Galatians essentially brings before us. I feel it very important that we have a clear understanding of the issues dealt with by the apostles, elders and church gathered together at Jerusalem. For, brethren, they are matters that are as vital today as they were then. We find that what may well be termed the Galatian error is still prevalent in the professed church of Jesus Christ. There is still the sad tendency to be deluded, to be drawn aside by the very things advocated by these "certain men which came down from Judæa"—that they must keep the law of Moses to be saved.

What then is the issue here? It was not just over the rite of circumcision but what that implied. As Paul says, "For I testify again to every man that is circumcised, that he is a debtor to do the whole law" (Gal. 5:3). What we must not forget either is that when the scripture here speaks of the law of Moses, I am fully persuaded it means all that God made known to Moses. I know some are ready to divide what is termed the law of Moses into three distinct parts. They speak of the moral law, the judicial law and the ceremonial law. The moral law they say embodies the ten commandments that were specifically given on mount Sinai. The judicial law is considered to be that which had respect to the rule of law in the nation of Israel—how they were to act in their relationships one with another and with the Lord their God. The ceremonial law is defined as that which had to do particularly with all the ordinances, sacrifices and offerings of the worship of God, first within the tabernacle and then afterwards in the temple.

But I say that though the law of Moses had those three distinct parts, yet it must always be viewed as a whole, for that is how it is set before us in the word of God. It is no use saying that certain parts have been done away, yet other parts remain. We find how that argument prevails in many circles today. They say that the issue dealt with here by the church at Jerusalem and in the epistle to the Galatians, only concerns the ceremonial element of the Mosaic law. The liberty we have as believers through grace in Jesus Christ is liberty from the ceremonial law. Friends, I say the argument goes far deeper than that. The matters the epistle deals with are *not* just related to the ceremonial aspect of the law God gave Moses. No. The whole law is addressed—moral, ceremonial and judicial.

Now the important thing to bear in mind is this. True, what was given to Moses was indeed given to him of God. It was a glorious revelation. It is spoken of as being a holy and a fiery law. Ah, there is no question that there is no fault or failing in the things God gave to Moses. But I want to come to this question: *Is the law of Moses in the whole of it, or even in part of it, binding on the new testament church, on believers, now that Christ has come and finished the work of redemption for his church?* That is the great matter. Are those things still binding on the new testament church—on believers in the Lord Jesus Christ? These

that came down from Judaea said that they *were* binding, that
new testament believers were subject to that Mosaic law and *must
be so* if they are to be saved. Paul says, and not only Paul but the
other apostles also, by the authority of the Holy Spirit, that the
Mosaic law whether in whole or in part, *is no longer binding on
the new testament church, the new testament believer.* The
redemption in Jesus Christ, the very truth the gospel proclaims,
is complete deliverance from all those things. It *doesn't* say that
the revelation given to Moses was of no account. Indeed, it
emphasises the glory of that revelation.

We find that when the brethren at Antioch heard the decision
reached by the council at Jerusalem according to the mind and
will of the Holy Spirit, they rejoiced for the consolation that was
in it! Their liberty in Christ was not undermined! It had not been
removed! They rejoiced for the consolation that the gospel brings
to needy, guilty sinners. It delivers from all the curse and guilt of
a broken law. It brings us into a right relationship with God, into
the kingdom of our Lord Jesus Christ and into fellowship and
communion with him through rich divine grace.

Friends, look at this in the light of the epistle of Paul to the
Hebrews. See how he shows that all the law is fulfilled in the
person and work of the Lord Jesus Christ. The statement in the
epistle to the Romans that "Christ is the end of the law for
righteousness to everyone that believeth" is surely emphatic
enough (Rom 10:4). Are we to say that Christ is the end of the
law for righteousness but that only includes the ceremonial or the
judicial aspects of the law of Moses? Does it not fully embody
even the moral law in all its implications and in its binding
authority on all men as they are the descendants of Adam? That
Christ is the end of the law for righteousness, that he has himself
fulfilled it, is the great teaching of the gospel. It was the teaching
of Paul. It was what he himself gloried in as taught by the Holy
Spirit, he a sinner without any righteousness of his own. As he
said, if any could claim to be righteous on the ground of law, that
is, in keeping and obeying what God required in the law of
Moses, then he could put a claim in there. Ah! He says, 'I have
credentials as good as any other.' Why, he could even say that
touching the righteousness which is in the law he was

blameless—that is, until his eyes were opened to see the solemn implications in that law.

Bear in mind the main purpose of the Lord Jesus Christ in his sermon on the mount. I fear many misunderstand the main purpose of what Jesus was setting forth in that sermon. He has much to say there with respect to the law of Moses, but the emphasis is on the holiness and spirituality of that law and the utter impossibility of any man or woman ever keeping that law and meeting its demands in themselves. He says, "Except your righteousness shall exceed the righteousness of the scribes and Pharisees, ye shall in no case enter into the kingdom of heaven" (Matt. 5:20). The scribes and Pharisees, and Paul as Saul of Tarsus was one himself, were looked to with esteem. Surely if ever any were holy men, any keepers of the law, then they were these people who were so religious and very strict in their lives. But oh, Jesus said your righteousness must exceed that. That of itself sadly and solemnly is abomination in the sight of God. It never met the requirements of God's law. No, the righteousness which exceeds the righteousness of the scribes and Pharisees is never a righteousness which is produced by men, either before or after the Lord has called us by his grace. No, the righteousness that *exceeds,* is the righteousness of Jesus Christ, the obedience *he* has rendered to the law. And it is his righteousness that the gospel so gloriously makes known, which the grace of God reveals, which faith indeed receives. The righteousness of Jesus Christ is imputed to us as we are sinners in all our sin, and in all our ruin through our sin.

That is where grace brings us as sinners. By the Holy Spirit we are truly taught in every aspect of our lives to look away from self and all that is in self, whether good or bad, and to look alone to Jesus Christ. He is my righteousness and your righteousness if through grace we are brought as sinners to saving faith in him. It is his obedience alone with which God is well pleased. It is his atoning blood that cleanses us from all sin. Except there is a righteousness that exceeds the righteousness of the scribes and Pharisees, except our righteousness exceeds theirs, oh, we are utterly lost and undone. The Lord Jesus then brings out the holiness and spirituality of the law. And his gospel reveals the glorious truth of the complete deliverance from those things for the believer in him. This is what was clearly set forth in the decision by this council at Jerusalem under the clear leading of the Holy Spirit.

Now another point. I believe we always need to look at these things in this way. As I said, the law of Moses was a glorious revelation from God as the scripture makes known. It was what might well be termed a dispensation from God clearly given by him to Moses. Yet friends, in the coming of Jesus Christ those things have been fulfilled and that dispensation has come to an end. Christ in that sense is the end of the law. He has brought in a wholly new dispensation. The gospel is the greatest revelation that God has given of himself. It supersedes in every aspect of it even what was known to Moses and established in old testament days. Now that principle is clearly taught in all the writings of the new testament and see how it is particularly brought out in the epistle to the Hebrews. Ah then, for the new testament church the law of Moses is done away in Christ. It is no longer binding on the new testament church. The believer through divine grace is brought into the kingdom of our Lord Jesus Christ. The new testament church is under an entirely new administration and dispensation where Jesus Christ is set forth as its great and glorious head.

Now when we speak of the law being finished and completed, as it surely is in the person and work of the Lord Jesus Christ, when we say those things are no longer binding on the new testament church, what is the reaction of men who do not see these things clearly? Paul dealt with this issue very distinctly in his epistles. They immediately say, 'Well then if the law is done away, that implies there is no law for the believer, for the new testament church. Believers can do what they want. They can live as they like. It makes no difference. There's no law. They are under no obligation to God.' Paul shows that *that* view is an utterly travesty of what the gospel of Jesus Christ reveals. Yes, says the apostle, we do joy, we do glory in the fact that the law is done away and that in this sense we are without law. Yet as brought by divine grace into a true relationship with God through faith in Jesus Christ, what is the believer called unto? They are called to be saints. They are called to holiness. Where the grace of God is made known and a sinner is brought to saving faith in the Lord Jesus, can there be any doubt that the fruit of the work of the Holy Spirit will be seen in lifelong concern to know and do the will of their Saviour? The very principles which the gospel sets forth are fully consistent with the holiness of God. The glory of God's grace which delivers his people, through the redemption in his Son, from all the curse of the law, *also* brings us to walk in the light, life and liberty of the truth as it is in Jesus.

I say then how important it is to see that the law of Moses and that old dispensation is in this sense *finished*. It is done away. It is superseded by the glorious revelation of the gospel into which sinners are brought through divine grace. It is for these things, even the full true liberty of the believer through the redemption that is in Christ Jesus, that Paul so earnestly contends.

Friends, do not overlook this either. You know, even from the very time of man's fall these truths were wonderfully set forth. It is true that all men, including ourselves, as we are the descendants of Adam born into this world, come under what the scriptures speak of as the covenant of works. The holy law of God with all its just demands is binding on all of us without exception. That law requires complete obedience and unless we render it then the law curses us. It condemns us. It tells us that the wages of sin is death. The solemn truth is this: we cannot escape from the condemnation of the law of ourselves. We can never free ourselves from its obligations. Living and dying without true saving faith in Jesus Christ, then the solemn implications of what the law of God demands will be solemnly realised by us.

As I said, right from the very time of Adam's fall, the whole of the human race, all men and women as born into this world, come under that covenant of works. Its demands are upon them. They are under the holy law of God with all it requires. And yet you know, from the very time of Adam's fall not only was the covenant of works clearly revealed, but also the word of promise. This word spoke of a salvation which is not according to men's attempts to keep the law of God to obtain his favour. In that way there is no salvation. It is utterly impossible for men and women to obtain the favour of God by their own works. Sinners—how can they ever begin to meet the requirements of God's law? But the promise spoke of salvation by grace. It pointed to that which was to come, which in due time God himself would reveal.

We might say that in what was delivered to Moses on mount Sinai, there was the embodying in a more formal way the covenant of works. It showed the awful reality of what a holy God demands of sinful men and women, and yet the utter impossibility for those requirements to be met by the sinner. Yet even in that dispensation there was the promise, the word of truth and grace, that set forth a glorious hope for poor sinners taught by the Holy Spirit. Their expectation was fulfilled in the person of the Lord Jesus Christ. Ah, old testament believers lived by grace through faith in the promise. Indeed, they not only lived but they died in faith and were saved by faith and entered into the glory prepared for them on the ground of what was set forth in the promise.

And the Lord Jesus being come, the gospel makes known the fulness and freeness of grace to sinful men and women. As it says here, when the believers read the letter sent by the apostles "they rejoiced for the consolation." They rejoiced for the confirmation that was given to them and to us, that though we are sinners, yet as through grace I am brought to faith in Jesus Christ, then the law has nothing to say to me. Its demands have been fully met in the person and work of the Lord Jesus Christ. True, the law curses and condemns the transgressor. But as taught by the Holy Spirit and blessed with living faith in the Saviour the believer proves that though the law condemns him as a sinner, yet all its requirements have been met for him by the Lord Jesus Christ. As one many years ago well said, and it is a very important and precious truth that is set forth in those simple words:

"I'm a sinner and nothing at all.

But Jesus Christ is my all and in all."

But I will leave the remarks there this evening. May the Lord add his blessing. Amen.

3

GALATIANS 1:1-5

"Paul, an apostle, (not of men, neither by man, but by Jesus Christ, and God the Father, who raised him from the dead;) and all the brethren which are with me, unto the churches of Galatia: Grace be to you and peace from God the Father, and from our Lord Jesus Christ, who gave himself for our sins, that he might deliver us from this present evil world, according to the will of God and our Father: To whom be glory for ever and ever. Amen.

On the last two Friday evenings I spoke from two passages in the word of God, in seeking to lead us into this epistle to the Galatians. Here Paul rightly contends, in all faithfulness and love, for the vitally important and blessed truth of the gospel. Last Friday we looked at Acts chapter 15, where the very matter that Paul deals with in this epistle, was considered by the gathering of the apostles, elders and brethren in Jerusalem. They drew up an emphatic letter which was delivered by Paul and Barnabas to the church at Antioch and which was published in all the other churches as well.

Now this evening I do not want to go over the same points I have already made, particularly concerning the main issue dealt with by the apostle. That will come out in more detail as we go through the epistle. This evening, I want to look at these introductory remarks of Paul in this first chapter. Now bear in mind that this letter was not directed to one particular church but to those that were in the region of Galatia. It is evident there were a number of local churches in that area which had been sadly affected by the false teaching that Paul so emphatically condemns and contends against in this letter to them. In these opening remarks he very distinctly states his authority and apostleship. Now Paul does not do this with any idea of calling attention to himself as if he was greater or more influential than any of the other apostles. He states his apostleship in the way he does because of the fact that he *was* an apostle of Jesus Christ and was under attack by these judaizing teachers who had so affected those churches.

If we read the epistles to the Corinthians and particularly his second one, we see there were similar false teachers in that church, and they also attacked the authenticity of Paul as an apostle of Jesus Christ. They were saying he was not equal to the others. He had not been an immediate disciple of the Lord and Saviour Jesus Christ as John and Peter had been. Their aim was to belittle Paul's claim as an apostle of Jesus Christ. But in that second epistle he very vigorously defends his apostleship. As I said, this was not to call attention to himself. We see how the grace of God was evident in Paul, that though he laboured abundantly in the work of the ministry and could say that he laboured more abundantly than them all, he immediately adds, "Yet not I, but the grace of God which was with me" (1 Cor. 15:10). As he emphasised again and again, he owed everything to the free sovereign grace of God. He ever affirmed that wherever that work was owned and used, all the praise and glory must be given to the Lord Jesus Christ, the great head of the church, and to the triune God.

But a point I would just notice is this. Paul will not have that belittled which he had received from the Lord Jesus Christ. In a real sense, and rightly so, there was a godly jealously with Paul over his call and appointment to the apostleship. To attack that, was to attack the appointment of the Lord Jesus Christ himself. As he states here, "Paul, an apostle, (not of men, neither by man, but by Jesus Christ, and God the Father, who raised him from the dead)." The apostleship of Paul and his call to that work was unique. True, he had not been a disciple of Jesus Christ. He had not in that way seen the Lord when he had been here on earth. He had not been a literal eyewitness of the resurrection of Jesus Christ as had the others. That was one of the important credentials for the apostleship. But as Paul himself so emphatically states, he was no whit behind the other apostles, for he had seen the Lord in a unique, very distinct and remarkable way. The Lord Jesus Christ had manifested himself to Paul. He had called him and appointed him to that work and Paul had seen the risen and ascended Saviour. And he bears witness to the truth of those things which he had heard and received. As he says later on in this chapter, "When it pleased God, who separated me from my mother's womb, and called me by his grace, to reveal his Son in me." I will not pursue that point any further this evening, as it will come before us again as we look at this chapter in a little more detail.

"Paul, an apostle, (not of men, neither by man, but by Jesus Christ, and God the Father, who raised him from the dead)." It is not without significance that we find the Lord Jesus Christ and God the Father linked together again and again in the word of God. There is an important truth unfolded to us in these things. As he says in this first verse, "Jesus Christ and God the Father." And again in verse 3, "from God the Father, and from our Lord Jesus Christ." What is the important significance of such statements as these concerning God the Father and our Lord Jesus Christ? I believe the importance of it is that with us as sinners— and each one of us is a sinner, as are all men—there are no dealings with a holy God, *no* acceptance by him, except through the Lord and Saviour Jesus Christ. It is a solemn truth, as true today as it ever has been, that out of Christ, God is a consuming fire.

Many have much to say of God as if they can come before him and are accepted, even though they ignore the Lord Jesus Christ altogether. Every religion that claims to have a knowledge or understanding or acceptance before a holy God, which leaves out the Lord Jesus Christ, is erroneous and is a most dangerous deceit. And you know, it is so even still in professing Christianity. It was so with respect to the teaching which Paul so contends against in this epistle to the Galatians. The idea in this teaching was that there could be dealings with a holy God on the ground of law, and not through Jesus Christ alone. It was a case of themselves *keeping the law as a ground of acceptance by God.*

Unless they did so, even faith in Jesus Christ would not avail.

But the point I want to make is that there are no dealings with a holy God for us as sinners with respect to access and acceptance before him, outside and apart from Jesus Christ. Oh the solemn and awful reality of sin is no light matter, indeed it is not. The holiness of God is such a glorious thing. Can ever a sinner stand accepted before him? Is there any access into the presence of God for that which is polluted and defiled by sin. No, the holiness of God repels it, and the righteousness of God utterly forbids it. For men and women to think they can find access and acceptance before God, while ignoring Jesus Christ, is vain and foolish. I say it is a grievous error and one of the deceits of Satan himself. The joining together then, of God the Father and our Lord Jesus Christ, ever reminds us of that which is the way of access unto God for us sinners. It is through the person and work of the Lord Jesus Christ. He is the "one mediator between God and men, the man Christ Jesus" (1 Tim. 2:5). This also emphasises the glorious reality of God manifest in the flesh. As one says, and we shall sing that verse at the close of this service if the Lord will:

> "Till God in human flesh I see,
> My thoughts no comfort find;
> The holy, just, and sacred Three,
> Are terrors to my mind."

Oh let us beware of vain speculation upon the holiness and majesty of God, outside and apart from the person and work of Jesus Christ. In him all the glory of God's grace is revealed. As the Lord told Moses, "Thou canst not see my face: for there shall no man see me, and live" (Exod. 33:20). As John says, "No man hath seen God at any time; the only begotten Son, which is in the bosom of the Father, he hath declared him" (John 1:18). Here is that which alone meets the need of the sinner. Here is the way of access unto and acceptance by God, as he is revealed in the person of Jesus Christ, as Emmanuel, God with us. Oh, the glory of God's grace in the person of Jesus Christ! This is no figment of the imagination. See how glorious, and I put it this way, how tangible is the revelation God has given of himself in the person and work of the Lord Jesus Christ, that which is so suitable to the sinner and which so glorifies his great and holy name. *God in*

Christ! See it friends, in all the wonder of it, as set forth in the words and works of the Lord Jesus Christ as recorded in the gospels.

One other thought I would set before you regarding these words, "God the Father and our Lord Jesus Christ." Oh, the wonder of the grace and truth here revealed. Through a living and true relationship by grace with Christ Jesus, his people are brought, indeed sinners are brought, into a living vital relationship with God the Father. Is not that made known in the truth of the gospel and by the Spirit's teaching in the hearts and lives of sinners called by divine grace? It is as Jesus said to Mary Magdalene, and may he speak those truths afresh to your soul and mine this night, "I ascend unto my Father, and your Father; and to my God, and your God" (John 20:17). Friends, there is the reality of reconciliation between God and men. There is all the unfolding of that glorious relationship—God our Father "through the redemption that is in Christ Jesus" (Rom. 3:24).

He says here, "Who raised him from the dead." Ah, why the emphasis on the resurrection of Jesus Christ from the dead? Never overlook the vital importance of this as set forth in the truth of the gospel. "Who raised him from the dead." Herein as well, we see brought before us the glorious reality of the divinity of our Lord Jesus Christ, that he was truly God as well as really man. As he himself said with regard to his life, "I have power to lay it down, and I have power to take it again. This command-ment have I received of my Father" (John 10:18). And therein is seen the mighty power of God in the raising of Jesus Christ from the dead, with all that implied for the salvation of the church, all that is found therein to meet the deep needs of the sinner. We read of him, "Who was delivered for our offences, and was raised again for our justification" (Rom. 4:25). How important is Christ's resurrection for the church and people of God, for time and eternity!

"And all the brethren which are with me." Paul writes here not only from himself but from all the brethren that were with him. These churches in Galatia had been greatly influenced by the false brethren, those that came with their pernicious doctrines, those that would belittle, isolate and sideline the apostle Paul as if he were only a mere individual who spoke the things that he did. There was no need to take any notice of him. They questioned his authority as an apostle. They were saying he was in a minority as well. But Paul says, "And all the brethren which are with me." He did not stand alone. There were many that stood with him and witnessed with him to the same glorious truths of the gospel. Now friends, this is an important point. It is true that to the greater part the church is always a minority. It is but a remnant in the earth, and there may well be times in the experience of the people of God when they feel they stand alone against so many things. Yet are we really alone? There have been figures in the history of the church that have stood forth boldly, as witnesses to the truth as it is in Jesus, who appeared to have stood alone for the truth. But has that really been so? You know, Elijah thought that was so with himself. As he said to his God, "I, even I only, am left; and they seek my life, to take it away" (1Kings 19:10). But was he the only one left? Did not the Lord tell him there were seven thousand in Israel that had not bowed the knee to Baal nor kissed him. And so here with Paul. In one sense he did stand alone but he says, "The brethren which are with me."

Friends, what a mercy is this. None of the Lord's people ever stand alone. The Lord himself is with them. And so it was with Paul. Even when he was isolated in a prison cell, did he not thank God for those brethren that remained faithful and loyal to the truth and who were prayerfully concerned for him in the situation in which he was found? In writing to the Philippians, how he thanks God, "For your fellowship in the gospel from the first day until now" (Phil. 1:5). Often the people of God are called to walk a very lonely path, as they feel. But friends, there's a real blessing in the fellowship of the gospel. They are not altogether isolated. There are those also that know the same power of the truth in their own hearts and lives, and love the same Saviour and friend of sinners, who has revealed himself to them by grace.

"And all the brethren which are with me, unto the churches of Galatia: Grace be to you and peace from God the Father, and from our Lord Jesus Christ." Notice how often in the word of God, grace and peace are linked together. And friends, how true it is that there is no real peace apart from grace. We never come to any realisation or enjoyment of true peace—that is, peace of conscience and peace with God—apart from grace. Oh, where can we, as sinners, look for and expect to know and enjoy peace with God in the full and free forgiveness of our sin, and deliverance from all its curse and condemnation? Where can we look for and expect such a peace as that apart from grace? Can we of ourselves earn it? Do we deserve it for any reason? No. As utterly condemned by the law of God, as under the curse and guilt of our own sin, peace with God is so far from us, altogether beyond our reach, and ever must be so, apart from grace—the free, undeserved love and favour of God.

See the wonderful reality of the grace and peace which Paul desires these brethren in the churches of Galatia might know in all its fulness! "Grace and peace from God the Father and from our Lord Jesus Christ, *who gave himself for our sins.*" In that statement is the wonderful unfolding of grace and the blessed reality of peace as well. Oh, pause and rightly consider this wonderful statement of divine truth. May we not overlook the importance of the pronoun in this statement here: "who gave himself for *our* sins." May we not rest short of that blessed truth. That Christ died for sinners, that Christ gave himself for sinners is a glorious truth, but friends, how important is this as it concerns ourselves. "Who gave himself for *our* sins," that is, *my* sins, *your* sins. We find the apostle is not resting short of this. He says in the following chapter, "Who loved *me* and gave himself for *me.*" Surely, here is the real blessedness in true religion. It is the personal realisation of this tremendous grace.

He says, *"Who gave himself* for our sins." Just look at one or two points in this statement, full as it is of glorious and blessed truth. See what a price, what a cost is opened up to us here, and what was involved in the redeeming of his people from their sins. *He gave himself.* Ah, surely friends, here the glory and blessedness of Jesus Christ is set before us! Oh he is not set forth here as a stern judge, as an hard and austere master. No. Here we have unfolded the wonderful love of his heart. He gave himself. What more could he give? Look at the dignity of his person, the one who gave himself. Here is no mere mortal man. Here is not one that could even be described merely as a good man. Here is the Lord of heaven and earth, God manifest in the flesh. Great is the dignity of his person, in that he is the only begotten, the eternal Son of God. He is God manifest in the flesh. *He gave himself.*

You know it will require eternity itself to fully understand the wonder of redeeming love and grace. He gave himself for whom? Those that deserved it, those that endeavoured to please him? No, he gave himself for those that are sinners, those lost and ruined in the fall, those that are rebels against God. Oh, what divinity is here. It says, "Who gave himself for our sins." Yes, let us never forget what this sets forth. *Our sins.* Not sins of little significance. No, but for great sins, grievous sins, black and vile sins, he gave himself. You know, how little we truly understand or appreciate or really receive these things. We sometimes sing:

"Christ is the Friend of sinners;
Be that forgotten never;
A wounded soul, and not a whole,
Becomes a true believer."

How hard it is to get away from the attitude of mind that we can understand how the Lord could have given himself for such characters as Paul and Peter or the other disciples. They were surely worthy of such grace. But such ideas and thoughts are totally contrary to the truth of the gospel. Any supposed worthiness in those for whom Christ gave himself never enters into it. For friends, none are worthy. No. "He gave himself for our sins," not for our good works or our endeavours to please him or our walking in obedience to his revealed will. "He gave *himself* for our sins," as he himself testified.

You remember the case of Zacchaeus. What a sinner was that man. He was a publican, one of the Roman tax gatherers, and a thorough rogue as well, who had enriched himself by falsifying his accounts and practicing fraud in a big way. As such, though protected by the Roman authorities, he was despised and hated by the Jews. See the wonders of grace here. When the Jews cavilled saying Jesus had gone to be the guest of a man that was a sinner, he says, "the Son of man is come to seek and to save that which was lost" (Luke 19:10). There are no qualifications here, in those who are recipients of this grace. The devil would ever have us look for qualifications, saying, 'well, yes, he gave himself for sins, but can you think for such great, grievous sins, such provoking sins as yours, such a life totally contrary to the law of God, sins of thought and word and deed?' How has it been with you who have good ground for trusting that he has called you by his grace? Even since then, what has been your life? Has it been free of defilement through sin? Can you come before God this evening and say, 'Lord, look what I have done; see how I have endeavoured to behave myself; see what efforts I have put in to follow thee?' No. I believe the language of a child of God is ever this: 'I am an unprofitable servant.'

Here, in our text, is the whole ground and source of consolation to those who are poor, needy, guilty and defiled sinners. "Who gave himself for our sins." Is there a greater wonder of love and grace than this? I say, we do not half believe these things. We have not yet entered into the fulness of the wonder of these truths. Says one:

> "Wonders of grace to God belong,
> Repeat his mercies in your song."

"Who gave himself for our sins." And you know, that is where the gracious teaching of the Holy Spirit will bring us. See how contrary this statement was to what was being advocated at this time among the churches of Galatia. They were directing sinful men and women to what? To the free, sovereign grace of God, to the one offering and sacrifice of Jesus Christ? No. They were directing men and women to their own works, to their own efforts and endeavours. They were telling them to do something which was utterly impossible for them to do. You must keep the law to be saved. Paul says, Christ *"gave himself for our sins."* Oh that this may be indelibly written on your heart and mine by the Spirit of truth and grace, and may we know more of the fruit that follows. "Who gave himself for our sins, that he might deliver us from this present evil world, according to the will of God and our Father."

See the purpose for which he gave himself for our sins. What Paul states here is utterly contrary to what these influential teachers in the Galatian church were teaching. They were saying, 'You must believe in Christ and keep the law to be saved.' The implication was that if you preach free and sovereign grace, that sins are freely forgiven through the redemption that is in Christ Jesus, then may we not continue in sin that grace may abound? Paul emphatically denies that is the logical consequence of what he says, "Who gave himself for our sins, *that he might deliver us from this present evil world.*" The fruit of this grace is ever to draw the believer into those ways of obedience to his Lord and Saviour.

Here is real full deliverance from this present evil world, in the gracious reality of the forgiveness of sins. Wonderfully bound up in this is deliverance from the guilt and curse of sin and all the consequences of sin as well. To believers, there is through grace deliverance from sin and all its curse, upon the ground of the person and finished work of the Lord Jesus Christ. There is deliverance from this present evil world and from all the working of sin and Satan which surrounds and besets us. The victory is sure to the believer because it has been obtained for us by the grace of our Lord Jesus Christ. He lives and reigns at the Father's right hand. We sometimes sing:

"He lives triumphant o'er the grave."

He lives to what purpose? To bring his people where he is. And neither sin, Satan, nor hell itself can ever frustrate those purposes of God, for it is "according to the will of God and our Father: to whom be glory for ever and ever. Amen."

But I will leave the remarks there. May the Lord add his blessing. Amen.

4

GALATIANS 1:6-9

I marvel that ye are so soon removed from him that called you into the grace of Christ unto another gospel: which is not another; but there be some that trouble you, and would pervert the gospel of Christ. But though we, or an angel from heaven, preach any other gospel unto you than that which we have preached unto you, let him be accursed. As we said before, so say I now again, If any man preach any other gospel unto you than that ye have received, let him be accursed.

Last Friday evening we looked at the first five verses of this chapter which formed the introduction of the apostle in this letter to the churches in Galatia. We saw his prayerful desire that grace and peace from God the Father and the Lord Jesus Christ might be with them. We considered his opening up of the wonderful truth that the Lord Jesus "gave himself for our sins, that he might deliver us from this present evil world, according to the will of God and our Father." And for this he truly gives thanks and ascribes honour and glory to God, "To whom be glory for ever and ever. Amen." He ascribed glory to God for such great grace manifest to sinful men and women, that grace which had been preached by him among those people in the region of Galatia. They had not only heard that grace in the word of the truth of the gospel, but they had also received it under the Spirit's blessing.

The greatness of God's grace ever filled the apostle with wonder and amazement, knowing himself to be the subject of it. You notice how often he refers to what the Lord had done for him, calling him so remarkably by grace on the road to Damascus. Oh, the remembrance of how the love and grace of the Lord Jesus Christ had been first manifest to him when the Lord stopped him on that road, ever remained with the apostle. We find him referring again and again in his epistles to what the Lord had done. Ah, he says, as we shall notice later in this chapter, "who called me by his grace." Oh, the wonder of this, as one could well say:

> "Oh why did Jesus show to me
> The beauties of his face?
> Why to my soul did he convey
> The blessings of his grace?"

Ah, why? Paul ever ascribed it to the sovereign, distinguishing grace and mercy of God:

> "But 'twas because he loved my soul,
> Because he died for me;
> Because that nothing could control,
> His great, his wise decree."

And we find that the reality of the love of God in Christ, that had so laid hold of the apostle, was ever the motivating principle for Paul in the work of the ministry to which he was called. And is it not out of the realisation of this grace, that he writes as he does here to the churches of Galatia and says in verse 6, "I marvel that ye are so soon removed from him that called you into the grace of Christ unto another gospel?" "I marvel." He is saying that it appeared astounding to him that they should be so soon removed from the gospel, from the wonderful reality of the grace of God which had been preached to them. And they had turned to what he describes as another gospel, which in fact was no gospel at all. How can this be! Ah, Paul says, 'I find it astounding that you should leave the fulness and freeness of the grace of God revealed in the gospel which so meets the deep needs of sinful men and women and should be turned to that wherein is no profit.' Yet the apostle well knew the deceitfulness of the human heart and what men and women are when left to themselves. We find the same true of Israel of old, even as God had taken them as a people into a covenant relationship with himself. By the mouth of his servant Jeremiah, he sets forth the same thing.

"They have forsaken me the fountain of living waters, and hewed them out cisterns, broken cisterns, that can hold no water" (Jer. 2:13). They had turned from the one and only living God, the God of all their mercies. They had not only forsaken him but had been taken up with things of no profit whatsoever to their souls, but which rather brought them under condemnation.

Well does he call them "foolish Galatians" (Gal. 3:1). And friends, men and women are fools of themselves, and you and I no different apart from upholding grace and mercy. Truly he writes to these that had been sadly drawn aside, who had backslidden from the grace of Christ that had been preached and received among them. But though the apostle writes to these churches in this way, "I marvel that ye are so soon removed from him that called you into the grace of Christ unto another gospel," he puts the blame chiefly where it was to be laid. He reserves his strictest censures and condemnation for men who had crept in among them and led them away by teaching and preaching what he described as another gospel which was no gospel. And these are not only the words of the apostle but of the Holy Spirit himself. We shall notice more of this in a moment.

"I marvel that ye are so soon removed from him that called you into the grace of Christ unto another gospel." Oh, how this is surely a very salutary word for us as well. Let us not overlook who was working in these things. What was it that so troubled the churches in Galatia? You know it was not outward persecution. It was not threat by pagan or even religious rulers that brought the problems and troubles into the churches in Galatia. No, these things arose from within them. And you will find that not only was this true here, but it has been so throughout the history of the church of Jesus Christ. And as I say, here are salutary words of warning for ourselves also. It is things which have arisen from within that have caused the most harm and havoc within the church. And as here in the churches of Galatia, this is particularly through the bringing in of teachings contrary to the truth as it is in the Lord Jesus Christ. You know, the devil is the master of subtlety. Has he not proved down the generations that he gains little when he comes as a threatening roaring lion against the church and people of God? The devil and his agents have done their worst in the history of the church in outward persecution. But those attacks have invariably ended, not in the church being annihilated or even weakened, but by the church growing and increasing in a most remarkable way. It is true what has been well said that the blood of the martyrs is the seed of the church.

But I say that the devil is a very cunning and subtle adversary. We find the greatest havoc has been caused in the church when he comes, as the apostle warns us in another place, as an angel of light, and his agents come as ministers of light as well. You notice here in Galatia, that these teachers did not come totally denying the truth as it is in Jesus. They did not come and say directly that Paul was utterly wrong, totally mistaken in what he had preached among them. No. If they had come in such a bold way as that, many may not have been taken in as easily as it appears they were. They came as angels of light. The errors that were introduced into the church at Galatia were dressed up in the guise of truth. Ah, as I have mentioned before and we shall notice more as we go on in this epistle, they were not denying the necessity of faith. They were saying *faith was not sufficient, that believing in the Lord Jesus Christ could not save a sinner unless it was accompanied with obedience to the law.* As I have said before, this had such a guise of truth about it and yet it was the most pernicious error that has ever been set forth. It was introducing poison, as it were, into the truth of the only salvation for sinful men and women.

Look how heinous was the error. What Paul contends against so vigorously in this epistle, and what he and the other apostles stood for so firmly in that council at Jerusalem was no unimportant secondary matter. As I have said before, this struck at the very foundations of the truth as it is in Jesus, so that if this point be carried, then the whole ground of salvation for sinful men and women is utterly taken away. Paul writes later in this epistle, "If righteousness come by the law," that is, if men and women are to be accepted and justified before God upon the ground of their own doings, their own obedience to the law of a holy God, "then Christ is dead in vain." There was no need for the person or work, the life, obedience, death and resurrection of our Lord Jesus Christ. No, those things were totally unnecessary if what these false brethren were teaching in Galatia was true.

We see then how serious were the errors being propagated under the guise and semblance of truth, having some apparent authority, even rooted we might say, in the scriptures. For what did they appeal to? Did they not appeal to the old testament scripture, to the law of Moses? Could not they claim this was the revelation that God had given from heaven, which indeed was true? But, friends, we see how so often when error is propagated under the guise of truth, scripture is taken in a very selective way. There is the overlooking of other parts of holy scripture as well. It is the same old thing, the failure to consider matters in the light of what the scripture as a whole sets forth. You know, if we over-emphasise any section of holy scripture at the expense of another, then we can become at the least very unbalanced in our understanding of the word of God. And at the worst there can be the propagating of the most grievous errors under the guise of a supposed foundation in scripture. You will see that this is at the root of all error. What has caused the rise of so many different sects within the professed Christian church? These things have arisen because there has been the taking of a part of scripture totally out of its context and advocating particular things, while neglecting the general teaching of God in his word. But never forget this—the Holy Spirit in the scripture never contradicts scripture. *The whole of the old testament scripture must always be considered and interpreted in the light of the new. The key to the understanding of the law and the prophets and the psalms is Jesus Christ.*

You remember what Paul writes in that second chapter of his first epistle to the Corinthians, where he says, *"I determined not to know anything among you, save Jesus Christ, and him crucified."* He goes on to set forth there what is the wisdom which is from above, that is, the glorious reality of the grace of God revealed in the gospel. And he says that "the natural man receiveth not the things of the Spirit of God: for they are foolishness unto him: neither can he know them, because they are spiritually discerned." He speaks of the spiritual man, the person born again, the person who is under the gracious teaching of the

Holy Spirit. And he writes there of "comparing spiritual things with spiritual." So many misquote what the apostle says there. They will say that it is comparing scripture with scripture. But that is not what Paul says. He says it is "comparing spiritual things with spiritual." True, there is a comparing of scripture with scripture, but it is spiritual things with spiritual. The spiritually minded person under the gracious teaching of the Holy Spirit is not just concerned with what I might term the bare letter of scripture.

You know, there are many that profess to be great bible students. You take, just to illustrate this point, Jehovah's Witnesses. They claim to be great bible students, and in some respects, they are well-versed in their particular version of holy scripture. We have had contact with people in the past who have come out from the Jehovah's Witnesses and one thing that marked them was the great emphasis they put upon bible study and their searching the scripture. Yet what I came to realise with some that I had contact with, was that with all their great emphasis upon the study of scripture, they were time and again missing the main point that the scriptures were setting forth. They would be taken up with certain aspects of it in one way or another, but they seemed utterly blind to the spiritual truth which was there revealed. So much effort was put into seeking to interpret and understand what might be termed more dark and difficult passages of holy scripture, and yet their eyes seemed blinded to what was plainly and clearly revealed. I realise more than ever that it is not just the studying of scripture that is needful. Oh, in a right sense let us indeed be students of the holy scripture. Let us be well-versed in the word of God. But how we need *the spiritual illumination and the gracious unction of the Holy Spirit.* May that prayer ever be, not only upon our lips but in our heart, "Open thou mine eyes, that I may behold wondrous things out of thy law" (Ps. 119:18).

I was saying then that here we see error dressed up in the guise of truth, apparently having scripture support for it as well. Yet there was the neglecting of what the Holy Spirit had revealed. And Satan is a past master at these things. As I said, what a salutary word there is for us here. How we need grace to watch and to pray. Paul says he marvelled, he was amazed that they were "so soon removed." It was only a short while after they had received the word of the truth of the gospel, that they were now seemingly moved away from it, drawn aside by these false teachers. As I said, he leaves his severest censures and condemnations for those that led the churches astray. But those who were led astray were not without blame. Ah, how we ever need to pray, "Lord, hold up my goings in thy paths, that my footsteps slip not" (Ps. 17:5). Let us not fondly think we are proof against temptation. Let us not rest in saying: 'I know the scripture. I am well versed in these things. I have a depth of experience of them. I've been many years in the way. Ah, surely then to think I could be deceived or drawn aside by those that bring things contrary to the truth in Jesus Christ, oh, this does not seem possible.'

But friends, may we ever be diffident of ourselves and conscious of our dependence upon the Lord Jesus Christ. May we lean upon him day by day. "Lean not unto thine own understanding, but in all thy ways acknowledge him and he shall direct thy paths" (Prov. 3:6). May we never lose sight of the fact that we are daily dependent on the Lord. He himself says, "Without me, ye can do nothing" (John 15:5). O for grace to know the true spiritual daily abiding in the Lord and Saviour Jesus Christ. He says, "Abide in me, and I in you. As the branch cannot bear fruit of itself except it abide in the vine; no more can ye, except ye abide in me" (John 15:4). Is not this an important spiritual fruit—the keeping close to the vine, cleaving not only to the word but to the Lord Jesus himself, who is indeed the incarnate Word? Here is the real place of safety for the Lord's people. It is not to stand boldly in the sense of our own strength and abilities. It is to be kept daily at the feet of the Lord Jesus Christ, conscious of our sins and needs, and that our all is bound up in Jesus, he being precious to our souls.

"I marvel that ye are so soon removed." If these who had been under such a ministry as the apostle Paul were so soon moved away, how we need to realise our dependence on the Lord's upholding and keeping. You know, the greatest privileges we may be under, will not of themselves secure us against being led away with the error of the wicked. Oh, may we not only be under the sound of the truth, but may the love of the truth be found in our own souls.

"I marvel that ye are so soon removed from him that called you into the grace of Christ unto another gospel." What a comparison is here. Yet when rightly viewed, is there anything to be compared to the grace that is in Christ Jesus? Why, I say, there is nothing to be compared with the fulness and freeness of the grace that is in Christ Jesus. That they should be removed from the true gospel of God's grace to this false teaching which he describes as another gospel, and yet which was no gospel at all—how amazing! Well may we ask the question: what is any man, even the best of men, left to himself? What is any man where Satan is active? Can any man of himself stand against those subtle ways and insinuations of the enemy? Not even Adam in his innocency could stand against the powerful temptation of the enemy, and much less can we who are fallen sinful creatures. Well may the warning be given, as Peter writing his epistle says, "Your adversary, the devil, as a roaring lion, walketh about, seeking whom he may devour: whom resist steadfast in the faith" (1 Pet. 5:8). What is this steadfastness in the faith? It is our daily knowing our need as a sinner, and being kept looking to Jesus, the author and finisher of our faith. The hymn writer sweetly illustrates this point:

"Keep close to me, thou helpless sheep,
  The Shepherd softy cries;
  Lord, tell me what 'tis close to keep,
  The listening sheep replies.
  Thy whole dependence on me fix;
  Nor entertain a thought,
  Thy worthless schemes with mine to mix,
  But venture to be nought."

Paul continues, "Which is not another; but there be some that trouble you, and would pervert the gospel of Christ." As I have already indicated, they didn't come denying the gospel. They came perverting it. How true it is that Satan is more active oftentimes in seeking to pervert the gospel, than he is in denying the gospel. More have been led away with the perversions of the gospel than ever have been led away when the gospel has been completely denied.

He says, "Which is not another." See the heavy censure he brings against those that so pervert the gospel. Now it is evident that these false teachers had very pleasing ways looked at from the human standpoint. It seems their personalities carried many along with them. But people failed to consider *what they were saying.* They were rather more taken up with the way in which it was said and the personality of these teachers. That is always attractive to human nature. You take how it has been seen that many can be swayed by the force of a man's personality. You take Hitler before the last war, how he swayed the whole of the German nation with the force of his oratory. We see what dangerous things these are, what evil can be bound up in them.

The point I just want to make is this. We need to look deeper and beyond the personality and persuasiveness of the preacher. We need to look at what is actually being said. Is it according to the truth as it is in Jesus Christ? They may come with pleasing manners. But look carefully at how the apostle speaks of himself on more than one occasion, as to how he went forward in the ministry. You never find he sought to influence people by the power of his personality or by persuasive oratory. He says he particularly avoided such things. In his epistle to the Corinthians he says that when he came amongst them preaching the gospel, it "was not with enticing words of man's wisdom, but in demonstration of the Spirit and of power" (1 Cor. 2:4).

The apostle lived in times when the power of oratory and rhetoric was greatly esteemed. You look at how it was with ancient Greece and their orators and what Athens itself was renowned for. Paul says that if he had so wished he could have used those things as well as any other. There were few who could have compared with him if it had really come to it. But he studiously avoided all such things in the preaching of the gospel. "And I, brethren, when I came to you, came not with excellency of speech or of wisdom, declaring unto you the testimony of God" (I Cor. 2:1). He refers to those that said of him that "his bodily presence is weak, and his speech contemptible" (1 Cor. 10:10). Many despised his outward appearance, because he studiously avoided using the things by which men are so often greatly influenced. Paul looked to and relied upon the word of truth alone, accompanied by the power and unction of the Holy Spirit, to influence the hearts and lives of men and women.

And friends, it is only the word of the truth of the gospel accompanied with the power and unction of the Holy Spirit, that will ever have real effect in the hearts and lives of men and women. It cannot be produced by men. Paul always preached with a consciousness of utter dependence on the Lord the Holy Spirit. He looked to the Holy Spirit alone to use the word to the ends which he has appointed, to the praise of the glory of God's grace. And so may we ever be found in utter dependence upon the operations of the Holy Spirit.

He says, "Which is not another." No, what they preached was no gospel for sinful men and women, whatever they might call it. It was that which may well have been alright if they were not sinners, but being sinners it is no gospel to them. For the lost, the ruined, the utterly bankrupt soul, for the person who is spiritually destitute and unable to do anything for themselves, was it a gospel? Is it good news to tell them that they must do this, that or the other and unless they do so, they cannot be saved? Ah friends, that is no gospel, no good news to the ruined, wretched, hell-deserving sinner, the one who is conscious that he cannot even produce a good thought to merit heaven. To tell such a one he must do this and the other, when he is utterly helpless and ruined, is no good news. It adds to the anguish and distress of the soul rather than alleviates it. It might sound alright in the ears of the self-righteous. It may well be favourably received by those who are utterly ignorant of their lost and ruined state and think that they can please God by their own works and ways.

That was the problem with so much of the religious world in those days. There was a failure to realise, on the one hand, the holiness of God, the righteousness and justice of his holy law, and on the other hand what man is of himself as an utterly lost and ruined creature. And we still see how prevalent is the failure to truly recognise what was involved in the garden of Eden, that man's fall there affected every part and particle of his being, body and soul. It is failure to recognise that man is a totally fallen creature. And it is failure also to recognise what was effected at Gethsemane and on the cross of Calvary. For it is what the gospel sets forth concerning those sufferings, death and resurrection of the Lord Jesus Christ, that is really good news to ruined, wretched men and women.

He says, "Which is not another; but there be some that trouble you, and would pervert the gospel of Christ." See the solemn censure that such come under. No stronger language can be used than this, "But though we, or an angel from heaven, preach any other gospel unto you than that which we have preached unto you, let him be accursed." And that there be no mistaking what he means, the apostle repeats this, "As we said before, so say I now again, If any man preach any other gospel unto you than that ye have received, let him be accursed."

Oh, the solemnity of those things! Well might sinners fear and tremble. Well might false teachers and prophets, whatever name or guise they come under, tremble at those solemn words. But friends, we find that such is the hardness of man's heart, such is the boldness of false teachers, that Paul's words seem to have little effect. But of this we may be assured, they shall not escape the condemnation spoken by Paul, unless brought to repentance through sovereign grace.

But I will leave the remarks there this evening. May the Lord add his blessing. Amen.

5

GALATIANS 1:9-24

As we said before, so say I now again, If any man preach any other gospel unto you than that ye have received, let him be accursed. For do I now persuade men, or God? Or do I seek to please men? For if I yet pleased men, I should not be the servant of Christ. But I certify you, brethren, that the gospel which was preached of me is not after man. For I neither received it of man, neither was I taught it, but by the revelation of Jesus Christ. For ye have heard of my conversation in time past in the Jews' religion, how that beyond measure I persecuted the church of God, and wasted it: And profited in the Jews' religion above many my equals in mine own nation, being more exceedingly zealous of the traditions of my fathers. But when it pleased God, who separated me from my mother's womb, and called me by his grace, to reveal his Son in me, that I might preach him among the heathen; immediately I conferred not with flesh and blood: neither went I up to Jerusalem to them which were apostles before me; but I went into Arabia, and returned again unto Damascus. Then after three years I went up to Jerusalem to see Peter, and abode with him fifteen days. But other of the apostles saw I none, save James the Lord's brother. Now the things which I write unto you, behold, before God, I lie not. Afterwards I came into the regions of Syria and Cilicia; And was unknown by face unto the churches of Judæa which were in Christ: but they had heard only, That he which persecuted us in times past now preacheth the faith which once he destroyed. And they glorified God in me.

At our last week-evening service I spoke particularly from verses

6-8, where the apostle takes up the main purpose for which he wrote this epistle to the churches in Galatia, under the teaching of the Holy Spirit. It was because of the sad evidence that they were turning away from the gospel which he had preached to them, and which they had received and believed, and had turned to what he declares was another gospel. In fact, it was no gospel at all. We find how he utters in verse 8 and confirms again in verse 9 his solemn condemnation of those that preached this other gospel. He says, "Let him be accursed." It matters not with what authority they come. Though they were an angel from heaven, if they bring that which is contrary to the things he had preached and taught and that they had received, he says, "Let him be accursed." Now in his using such strong terms, it was evident that the matter he dealt with was no insignificant point, no secondary matter. It was vital and fundamental to the truth as it is in Jesus. It greatly concerned the glory of God. It deeply concerned the true welfare, the salvation, of men and women.

Now I do not want at this juncture to further pursue the apostle's condemnation of what he describes as "another gospel." That will come out as we continue our consideration of this epistle. I want, this evening, to concentrate on one or two points that come out particularly from these verses that I have now read in the rest of this first chapter. We find Paul here positively states that the gospel he preached was what he had received and he speaks of the very real effects it had had upon himself. One of the main points I want to deal with is what Paul meant when he said 'the gospel that *he* preached,' rather than what being taught at Galatia which was no gospel.

Now this word *gospel* we often hear mentioned and it is set forth in various contexts but what is meant by this word? What are we to understand when Paul speaks of the gospel that he preached and that which he had received? Before coming, as helped, to answer that question, let us here consider firstly how Paul declares he had come by the gospel. Oh he declares that this was not a work of man but it was the sovereign work of God himself in his dealings with Paul.

He says, "For do I now persuade men, or God? or do I seek to please men? for if I yet pleased men, I should not be the servant of Christ." Paul's means that if his whole concern was just to please unregenerate men, to stand high in their estimation, to be a popular speaker, then he says, "I should not be the servant of Christ." For what Paul had to preach did not meet with the popular acclaim of men and never does, for it cuts right across the pride of the human heart. It sets forth the situation that men are in, as lost, ruined, guilty, helpless sinners, unable to do anything towards their own salvation. And what is more, they have no desire left to themselves to do anything about it even if it were possible, which it is not. Paul is saying, 'The message that I bring is truly a message from heaven, but it is not with the idea of pleasing men. For if I did so, if that was my purpose, I would not come preaching the gospel that I have received.' It was evident that these men who had come from Judæa and were causing such havoc in the churches in Galatia, brought a very popular message, as Paul could see,. What they had to say went down very well with the natural inclinations of the human heart, but it was not the gospel of Jesus Christ. In fact, as I have said, it was no gospel at all. For he says, "I certify you, brethren, that the gospel which was preached of me is not after man."

"I certify you, brethren." The apostle makes a most emphatic and positive statement, but he still looks on the people in the churches of Galatia as brethren. O indeed, they were being led astray. He has some strong condemnation of those who were leading them astray, but those that were being led astray he still considers as brethren. His whole concern here, as led and taught by the Holy Spirit, was that they might be recovered from the error into which they had been drawn. As we find him saying in another place later on in this epistle, oh how he travails in birth again for them. There is the drawing out of the very desires of his soul after their real spiritual welfare, that they might be delivered from the snare in which they had become entangled. His desire was that they be truly established upon the one foundation of Jesus Christ and him crucified, as their only hope of salvation in all the reality of his person and finished work.

He says, "But I certify you, brethren, that the gospel which was preached of me is not after man. For I neither received it of man, neither was I taught it, but by the revelation of Jesus Christ."

The gospel which he preached was not something he had learned of men. It was not something he had received from man, but it was what the Lord Jesus himself had directly and distinctly revealed to him. Now I want to emphasise that the experience that Paul is outlining here was unique to him, as he was a true apostle of Jesus Christ. Remember, one of the important qualifications for an apostle was that they were eyewitnesses of the resurrection of the Lord Jesus Christ. Now Paul had not had that experience in the same way as the other apostles. When the Lord was crucified and rose again from the dead the third day and made himself known during the following forty days before his ascension into heaven, Paul was not one of the disciples. At that time, as Saul of Tarsus, he was a very rigid strict Pharisee, one who had no sympathy whatsoever, to put it mildly, towards the truth as it is in Jesus. And he soon evidenced how deep was his enmity against those things. So, as Saul of Tarsus he had not seen the risen and ascended Lord. But he had a unique experience when God called him by his grace and revealed Jesus Christ in him. It was the risen Lord that encountered him on that Damascus road. There he saw the risen and ascended Lord. There, even in that experience, was delivered unto him the gospel that he preached. I say that this experience was unique to the apostle.

We do not receive the gospel in the same way as Paul. We receive it through the instrumentality of those whom God has raised up and sent forth in the ministry of the word. We have the testimony to the truth as given us in the holy scriptures. We cannot claim to have had the unique experience that Paul had, of which he speaks here. We receive the gospel through the ministry of the Lord's servants. Yet let us not overlook that the gracious unction and power of the Holy Spirit is essential to make the preached word effectual in the hearts of sinful men and women. Oh, the vital importance of the sovereign unction of the Holy Spirit accompanying the word that is preached. Paul knew this as well as any other. What was it that made his ministry effectual in the hearts and lives of men and women? Was it because Paul was a very persuasive speaker? No. Paul knew that his preaching of the gospel he had received in such a remarkable way, required the power and unction of the Holy Spirit to accompany it, to be

effectual in the hearts of sinners. He gloried in the fact that the
gospel is the power of God unto salvation to everyone that
believeth, and that the work is the sovereign, gracious work of
God the Holy Spirit in the sinner's soul. It is the Holy Spirit alone
who imparts spiritual life to those dead in trespasses and sins and
brings them to repentance and faith in the Lord and Saviour Jesus
Christ. Paul could say that he may plant, and Apollos water, but
it is God alone that giveth the increase (1 Cor. 3:6). So it is still.
The application of the word is of God alone.

As Paul says then, the gospel that he preached was what he
had received of the Lord in a very direct and unique way. He
emphasises this point because those men that were troubling the
church in Galatia were actively seeking to belittle his ministry.
They were saying he was not like the other apostles, for he had
not seen the Lord as they had. Not only in Galatia but also in
Corinth, Paul had the same problem to face. As he records in his
second epistle to the Corinthians, he there had to seek to vindicate
himself in a sense. Not that he desired to call attention to himself,
but what he made plain was that he was truly an apostle called
and appointed of the Lord, and he had received of the Lord the
gospel he preached,. He goes on to emphasise this point, showing
that nothing in his background gave any credence to the idea that
he had received this gospel of men or that he had come by the
knowledge of these things though some natural process. Why, he
calls attention to how they had heard that, instead of being
favourable to this gospel that he now preached, he was active in
contention against it. He says, "For ye have heard of my
conversation," that is, my manner of life, "in time past in the
Jews' religion." It is not without significance that the apostle uses
the term "the Jews' religion," for it was that religion which these
men who had come from Judæa were seeking to propagate in the
churches in Galatia. Oh, we might say it was religious
knowledge. It had some teaching in it with regard to God, but it
was, as Paul describes here, "the Jews' religion." It was not the
religion of Jesus Christ. There was a great difference between
these two, which will be apparent as we go on through this
epistle.

He says they had heard "how that beyond measure I

persecuted the church of God, and wasted it: and profited in the Jews' religion above many my equals in mine own nation, being more exceedingly zealous of the traditions of my fathers." He says, 'You surely know that I took a leading part in opposing this gospel that I now preach. Why, I did everything in my power to persecute those that called upon the name of Jesus Christ. Are these who are troubling the church, zealous of the traditions of my fathers? So was I, and I even went beyond them in my zeal for the traditions of my fathers.' And he is not referring here just to the many practices that had grown up around the traditions of the Pharisees. He says, "the traditions of my fathers" embracing, I believe, what is termed the law of Moses and its practices, which these troublers of the church of Galatia were seeking to impose on Gentile believers. 'For all those things I was exceedingly zealous,' says Paul.

But oh, what he brings our attention to is this: what made the difference? What brought about the change with him? Was it of men or was it of God? Was there a time when Paul came to the decision of himself that he was not really doing right and therefore he changes direction? Nothing of that whatsoever. The point I here want to make is that Paul gives all the glory to God and nothing unto men. He shows how it was in his own experience. It was of God, not of men, that he was a changed character and now preached the gospel he once sought to destroy. All the glory was due to the Lord alone. In preaching out of his own experience what that gospel essentially is, his whole emphasis is on the work of God and not of man. It glorifies God and ever abases the sinner.

What does he say caused the difference? What made such a change? In the ninth chapter of the Acts with which you are all surely familiar, we read that he was going to Damascus. He was zealously intent on the purpose of his mission to destroy if possible all who professed the name of Jesus in Damascus. Here was a man that was not even seeking after the gospel or after the knowledge of the Lord Jesus Christ. Here was one who was bitterly opposed to it—in arms against God. *"But when it pleased God, who separated me from my mother's womb, and called me by his grace."* This is the great theme. Paul is not here setting forth a God that is helplessly dependent on men. He never does preach such a God. It is a God who is a sovereign God, in whose hands were all the ways of Paul, and whose eye was upon him from his very birth and even before that. It is the God who, according to his own sovereign purposes, was ordering, controlling and bringing all things to pass in the personal life of the apostle. And not only was that true of Paul but it is true of everyone whom the Lord calls by his divine grace.

'But when it pleased God. Not in my time, but in God's time. Not what I did, but what God sovereignly and graciously did, as he stopped me in my mad career.' He did not put a proposal to Paul. He did not come to Paul on that Damascus road with an offer of salvation to him. But he says, "Who called me by his grace." How not only here, but throughout the epistles of Paul, this glorious truth shines forth. It is the sovereignty of grace, the mighty operations of divine grace. And cannot this which is so humbling to men, yet so glorifying to God, be traced out in the Lord's dealings with each one whom he calls by his divine grace? With ourselves, if we know anything of saving mercy in our own souls, from whence did this salvation arise? What were the beginnings of it? Was it because I sought the Lord or because he sought me? Was it because I decided for him, or rather that he in sovereign grace stopped me in my mad career and brought me as a sinner to the feet of the Saviour? Oh, friends, Paul says here, "But when it pleased God."

Where did the grace of God find Paul? It found him dead in trespasses and sins, a rebel to God and in opposition to the gospel. But see the power here of sovereign grace. It is the Lord alone that can give life, that can raise the dead. So it was in the case of Paul. Ah, God here raiseth the dead. It is the sovereign work of God the Holy Spirit to impart spiritual life to those dead in trespasses and sins. And where that spiritual life is imparted, where the work of God the Holy Spirit is begun, see what an opening up there is of the glorious truth as it is in the Lord Jesus Christ.

He says, "But when it pleased God...to reveal his Son in me, that I might preach him among the heathen; immediately I conferred not with flesh and blood: Neither went I up to

Jerusalem to them which were apostles before me; but I went into Arabia, and returned again unto Damascus." Here he goes on to show that it was God who called him by his grace, who revealed his Son in him. The point he is making is that he didn't learn of men the gospel that he received. He didn't even receive it from those who were apostles before him. He showed he had little contact, only a brief acquaintance, with those that were apostles in Jerusalem. After his Damascus experience, or not long after, he was in Arabia for three years. Those that have been called the silent years of the apostle in Arabia, were no doubt when he was led deeper by the Holy Spirit into the glorious truths that he afterwards preached and taught. But the essence of the gospel was revealed to him when the Lord met with him on that Damascus road.

What then is this gospel that Paul had received, which he preached, and which was not of men, neither did he receive it by man, but from God alone? What are the essentials of this gospel? This is by no means an unimportant matter to consider. We often hear the word *gospel* used, but what do we mean or what rather is meant by *the gospel*? Now I do not have time to go into the many ideas which men call the gospel. What was the gospel *Paul* preached? We know that the word *gospel* in the simple meaning of it is *good news*. It is that which has been revealed from heaven. It is that which is the revelation of God unto men. It is always set forth in the word as glorious, as most blessed, and which meets the deepest needs of sinful men and women.

The gospel that Paul preached is the revelation from heaven of God's sovereign grace and mercy as it centres in the person and work of the Lord and Saviour Jesus Christ. It is as Paul writes in his epistle to the Ephesians, "For by grace are ye saved through faith; and that not of yourselves: it is the gift of God: not of works, lest any man should boast" (Eph. 2:8). The gospel sets before us the sovereign gracious work of God himself in the rich and full provision that he hath made in the person and work of the Lord Jesus Christ. For whom? For guilty, ruined, needy sinners. It speaks of salvation for them in all its fulness and freeness. The emphasis in the gospel is on what God has not only *provided,* but what God *himself* has *done* in the person and work of the Lord Jesus Christ. Paul sums it up in this way. He says, "For I delivered unto you first of all that which I also received, how that Christ died for our sins according to the scriptures; and that he was buried, and that he rose again the third day according to the scriptures" (1 Cor. 15:1-2). He puts the whole emphasis on the person, work, life, death and resurrection of the Lord Jesus Christ. Central to the gospel that he preached was *the cross of the Lord Jesus Christ. There* the Lord Jesus is set forth as the atonement, the propitiation, the one great sacrifice for sins, the just for the unjust, that he might bring us to God.

When we come to the consideration of what Paul describes as the gospel, oh, what a fulness is here! What a subject! How vast it is! Paul doesn't bring it down to some mere simple formula. It contains everything that he taught. If there is a simple statement of it, it is surely in the words he writes in his epistle to Timothy, "This is a faithful saying, and worthy of all acceptation, that Christ Jesus came into the world to save sinners; of whom I am chief" (1 Tim. 1:15). He says that the gospel he preached is what he had received of the Lord. The whole emphasis is on the grace of God as it centres in the person and work of the Lord and Saviour Jesus Christ. Friends, I want to highlight this great point.

> "Christ is the Friend of sinners,
> Be that forgotten never,
> A wounded soul, and not a whole,
> Becomes a true believer."

The gospel of God's grace is truly revealed from heaven to sinful, guilty, needy men and women. Let us never forget that. As Paul could say, "Christ Jesus came into the world to save sinners; of whom I am chief." The whole emphasis is on the fact that *he saves sinners.* But shall not some then say, surely is not this grace for *all* sinners? "For there is not a just man upon earth, that doeth good, and sinneth not" (Eccl. 7:20). It is true that all are sinners in God's sight, all are under the curse and condemnation of the law. But does the gospel that Paul preached tell us that as all are sinners, therefore Christ died for all, he atoned for the sins of all indiscriminately? Friends, if we deal honestly with the scriptures that can never be the conclusion we reach. But that Christ is the Saviour of sinners *is* a glorious truth. I believe it is summed up in the language of the hymn writer. He speaks there of the grand distinction that must always be maintained:

> "Though all are sinners in God's sight,
> There are but few so in their own."

The hymnwriter is saying that all men are sinners and, as sinners, are dead in trespasses and sins. And though the gospel is preached to them, yet left to themselves there is no response, no hearing, no receiving, no life evidenced in them whatsoever. And never will there be life, apart from the sovereign working of God the Holy Spirit. The gospel Paul preached is a gospel for sinners. But he did not come saying that God loved all and sundry. He did not come saying that the Lord Jesus died for the sins of everyone. In his preaching of the gospel he set forth the state that men are in by nature—dead in trespasses and sins, and under the curse of a broken law.

You see how this comes out in Peter's sermon on the day of Pentecost when he bare witness to the truth of the gospel. What did he say to those on the day of Pentecost? He said that they had crucified the Lord of life and glory. Yes, he charged their sin upon them. The apostle showed to them their sins, that they were guilty before a holy, heart-searching God. And we see the discriminating grace of God there evidenced. There were those to whom the word came with convicting power. They cried, "Men and brethren, what shall we do?" And to what does the apostle direct sinners thus convicted and made aware of their need, through the sovereign grace of God alone? Oh, how he sets forth the fulness of divine grace and mercy that meets the deepest needs of the guiltiest of sinners. As the hymn writer well says:

> "The vilest sinner out of hell
> Who lives to feel his need,
> Is welcome to a Throne of Grace,
> The Saviour's blood to plead."

What a vast subject is this gospel that Paul had received and which he preached. Oh, the fulness of God's grace and mercy revealed therein. Its sum and centre is in Jesus Christ and him only. It is that which in every aspect of it, brings glory to God and lays the sinner and all of human worth and merit in the very dust.

But we will leave the remarks here this evening. May the Lord add his blessing. Amen.

6

GALATIANS 2:1-5

Then fourteen years after I went up again to Jerusalem with Barnabas, and took Titus with me also. And I went up by revelation, and communicated unto them that gospel which I preach among the Gentiles, but privately to them which were of reputation, lest by any means I should run, or had run, in vain. But neither Titus, who was with me, being a Greek, was compelled to be circumcised: and that because of false brethren unawares brought in, who came in privily to spy out our liberty which we have in Christ Jesus, that they might bring us into bondage: to whom we gave place by subjection, no, not for an hour; that the truth of the gospel might continue with you.

As we come into this second chapter of the epistle to the Galatians, we find the apostle Paul pursuing the same theme. He is setting before the church at Galatia the things that concerned himself with respect to the gospel he had received, not of men, neither by man, "but by the revelation of Jesus Christ." He goes on to show that this gospel which he had received and which he had preached among the Gentiles, and which they had believed in the churches of Galatia, was indeed the true gospel of the grace of God. He showed that he differed in no way from the other apostles. Like them, he fully and truly preached the gospel. As I mentioned before, false teachers were troubling the Galatian church, teaching that for salvation, sinners must not only believe in Jesus Christ, but must keep the law of Moses. The apostle emphatically contends against and denounces their pernicious teaching.

One of the points these false teachers were raising was that
Paul was inferior to the other apostles. The Galatians had no need
to take heed to him because he was not like the others who had
been with the Lord Jesus when he was here on earth and had been
eyewitnesses of his resurrection. Not only in the churches of
Galatia but also in the church at Corinth, Paul had on more than
one occasion to contend with false teachers and the aspersions
they cast on his call and authority as a true apostle of Jesus Christ.
As I have said before, Paul did not desire to call attention to
himself. Oh, as the grace of God was with him, and as the Holy
Spirit was upon him, Paul was jealous for the honour and glory
of the Lord and Saviour Jesus Christ. He vigorously withstood
those that would belittle the call that the Lord Jesus had given
him when he appointed him to be a true apostle and preacher of
the gospel.

But I want as helped this evening to notice one or two points
in particular that Paul brings out in these first five verses of this
second chapter. He spoke in chapter one of his first brief visit to
Jerusalem, and now says here, "Fourteen years after I went up
again to Jerusalem with Barnabas, and took Titus with me also."
He is referring to the gathering of the apostles and elders
recorded in Acts chapter 15. A few weeks ago, when speaking on
matters leading up to this epistle to the Galatians, I spoke on that
passage. They had gathered to deliberate on this matter that
troubled the churches, not only in Galatia but in other places as
well. And they fully confirmed that what Paul preached was the
true gospel of the grace of God. They considered the question:
Did believers in Jesus Christ have to keep the law of Moses to be
saved? Not only Paul but also Peter and the other apostles,
showed that this was wholly contrary to the revelation of grace
and truth given to them. They confirmed that salvation was by
grace through faith alone in the Lord and Saviour Jesus Christ. It
was not the work of men. It was the work of God the Holy Spirit,
the gracious reality of his saving grace. The law of Moses and all
the implications of it were done away for the believer. They had
been fulfilled and satisfied in the person and work of the Lord
Jesus Christ. As Paul says later on in this chapter, "I through the
law am dead to the law, that I might live unto God." In his epistle

to the Romans he writes, "Know ye not, brethren (for I speak to them that know the law,) how that the law hath dominion over a man as long as he liveth?" (Rom. 7:1). He says it is like a woman that has a husband. She is under the dominion of the law of her husband as long as he liveth, but if the husband dies then she is released from the law of her husband. She is at liberty to be married to another. The law of her first husband has nothing more to do with her. And he says, "Wherefore, my brethren, ye also are become dead to the law by the body of Christ; that ye should be married to another, even to him who is raised from the dead, that we should bring forth fruit unto God." Ah, glorious truth!

This he contended for in the council at Jerusalem and was fully supported by the other apostles. He shows clearly and plainly that he had not arrived at these things by collusion with the other disciples or the apostles. In fact, he had had little contact with the apostles such as Peter and John and James. He had met them on only brief occasions. Also, as he says, "I went up by revelation," that is, by the direct teaching of the Holy Spirit. It was of the Lord that he and Barnabas, and Titus with them, went at that time to Jerusalem, "and communicated unto them that gospel which I preach among the Gentiles, but privately to them which were of reputation, lest by any means I should run, or had run, in vain." We are not to think by this statement that the apostle had some doubt about the things he had preached. I believe there is no question of that. But as he says, he communicated privately to them which were of reputation, that is the elders and other apostles in Jerusalem, the things that he preached. They fully agreed with him that the gospel he preached was the gospel of God's grace, the same that had been given by revelation to them.

Let us first of all just attend to this point. He says, "I communicated unto them that gospel which I preach among the Gentiles." Now I said something last week with respect to the gospel that Paul preached and I want to refer to that matter again. In doing so, I would just direct your attention to chapter 13 in the Acts of the Apostles. I believe that therein is clearly defined the gospel Paul preached among the Gentiles, the gospel of the grace of God. I said last week there is much confusion as to what the preaching of the gospel really is, not only in professed religious circles generally but even in what are described as reformed evangelical churches as well. There are those who will insist that preaching the gospel is offering the gospel. Wherever the gospel is preached, it is to be offered to men and women indiscriminately, for them to receive or reject it. True, the claim is made that only those that are the elect will believe. And yet, I say, is that not only inconsistent with the gospel Paul preached, but with *how* he preached that gospel among the Gentiles?

The thirteenth chapter of the Acts of the Apostles is very instructive. We find that he and Barnabas, under the direct guidance of the Holy Spirit, had been set apart by the church at Antioch in Syria for the work to which the Holy Ghost had called them. And they went forth with the blessing of the church at Antioch in Syria. They went first to Seleucia and then to Cyprus and we read the account of what happened in those places as Paul preached the gospel. There was that conflict with Elymas the sorcerer and the manifestation of the power of God by the apostles. They then departed from Perga and came to Antioch in Pisidia. Now this is obviously a different Antioch to the one in Syria from where they had started out on their journey. This was in Pisidia. They went into the synagogue there on the Sabbath day and sat down. It was the usual practice of Paul in the places to which he went as directed by the Holy Spirit, to attend the synagogue of the Jews, and as opportunity arose, to speak the word of God.

Now, bear in mind that in such a synagogue of the Jews as at Antioch in Pisidia, the word of God, the old testament scriptures, the books of Moses and the prophets, were read in the hearing of the people. Some gave expositions of those scriptures and Paul is here invited to speak, if he has any word of exhortation for the people. And so he does. What is the substance of what Paul has to say to them in that synagogue? He shows to them that God himself had fulfilled what Moses and the prophets declared in the scriptures they had just read. The one of whom Moses and the prophets wrote had come and there had been done to him all that the prophets had declared would be done. He proclaimed that the one of whom the prophets spoke was indeed Jesus of Nazareth, the very one whom the Jews had taken, crucified and slain. The point here to notice is that Paul very plainly shows that the one whom the prophets foretold, was the one who had come and the Jews had crucified. But God had raised him from the dead. This same Jesus was indeed the Saviour who had been promised and had thus come in the fulness of time.

And he says to them "Be it known unto you therefore, men and brethren, that *through this man is preached unto you the forgiveness of sins.*" Now was not this a great and glorious truth, great and good news indeed? He whom God had promised in the writings of the prophets had come. The salvation of which the prophets had spoken was now manifested in the person and work of this one whom Paul preached, even Jesus Christ, the one and only Saviour of sinners. "Through this man is preached unto you the forgiveness of sins." What great and glorious truth is this— the forgiveness of sins! Why, friends, here is the greatest blessing that can ever be known and realized—the forgiveness of sins! It speaks to the deepest needs of wretched, ruined, sinful men and women. It is as one says:

"If sin be pardoned, I'm secure,
Death has no sting beside."

Ah, how those words of Paul must have sounded in the ears of the people in that synagogue! "That through this man is preached unto you the forgiveness of sins"! See the great contrast to what the Jews with all their privileges were looking to and resting upon, apart from those graciously and savingly taught of the Holy Spirit. Ah, they looked to and rested on the offerings and sacrifices of the levitical law, as that which they thought put away their sins. True, it brought them ceremonial cleansing, but it never spoke to their hearts, never gave them true peace and satisfaction. It never brought them into a real living relationship with God. For those things could never put away sin. They were not designed to do so. By the Spirit's gracious sovereign teaching, they were designed to direct sinners to what was contained in the promise God had spoken. They pointed to the one of whom Paul is here saying that he has come and "through this man is preached unto you the forgiveness of sins: and by him all that believe are justified from all things, from which they could not be justified by the law of Moses."

I come back to this point. What is the gospel which Paul preached? It is the gospel of the grace of God. It is that which speaks of salvation for sinners, by grace, through faith alone in the Lord and Saviour Jesus Christ. It is that which speaks, not of what man has to do, but what God in Christ has done. It was a full and finished salvation that Paul preached. It was not directing Gentiles, or even Jews, to the ceremonies of the levitical law. It was not even directing them to the fuller aspects of the law of Moses. It was the setting forth of the things fulfilled in the Lord and Saviour Jesus Christ—that by him there is real forgiveness of sins for sinners. "By *him* all that believe are justified from all things, from which they could not be justified by the law of Moses."

The gospel which Paul says he preached is the gospel of God's grace. It sets forth salvation for sinners by grace through faith alone in the Lord and Saviour Jesus Christ. In no way does Paul indiscriminately offer the salvation set forth in the gospel, to men and women dead in trespasses and sins. There is none of that whatsoever. He preached the gospel. He set forth the truth as it is in Christ Jesus. He declares what God in Christ has done. He sets forth the truth that all that believe are justified from all things. But friends, *believing* is a vital matter here in the receiving of these blessings. Indeed it is. The believing which Paul has in view is without question the believing to the saving of the soul. As he says, "by him all that believe are justified from all things, from which ye could not be justified by the law of Moses." Believing to the saving of the soul—*saving faith*—is a vital element, a key part, of the gospel that Paul preached.

But I say that not only the gospel that he preached but *how* he preached that gospel is vitally important as well. See how it comes through very clearly that he in no way infers that believing to the saving of the soul is either the work of man or within the ability of the sinner himself. For what does he say? "Beware therefore, lest that come upon you, which is spoken by the prophets." What do we find? As Paul preached these truths in the synagogue at Antioch in Pisidia there was evidently a rising antagonism against them. And I say, friends, it is as true today as it was then, "The natural man receiveth not the things of the Spirit of God: for they are foolishness unto him: neither can he know them, because they are spiritually discerned" (1 Cor. 2:14). The true gospel of the grace of God is never conducive to the natural inclinations of the human heart. Men and women dead in trespasses and sins will always, left to themselves, evidence a deep antagonism to the true gospel that Paul preached. He says, "Beware, therefore, lest that come upon you which is spoken of in the prophets; behold, ye despisers, and wonder, and perish: for I work a work in your days, a work which ye shall in no wise believe, though a man declare it unto you."

I believe we have here the fact that faith which is *saving* faith, which is the believing to the saving of the soul, is not the work of men. It is not the product of the natural heart, of fallen human nature. It is the rich gift of God, the blessed fruit and effect of his grace. For though there were those who rose in enmity against what Paul preached, the sovereign working of the Holy Spirit was evidenced in that there *were* those who believed, not only Jews but many Gentiles as well. How that word of the truth of the gospel *spoke* to them of a full and free salvation which God in Christ had done! Oh, how it came as a sovereign saving balm to many a distressed and burdened soul. To the sinner quickened and convicted under the power of the Holy Spirit, that word was a word of truth with power.

But we read later on, that Paul, on account of the antagonism of many in the synagogue against him, turns from them with those solemn words, "It was necessary that the word of God should first have been spoken to you: but seeing ye put it from you, and judge yourselves unworthy of everlasting life, lo, we turn to the Gentiles for so that the Lord commanded us, saying, I have set thee to be light of the Gentiles, that thou shouldest be for salvation unto the ends of the earth. And when the Gentiles heard this they were glad and glorified the word of the Lord: and as many as were ordained to eternal life believed."

Now just a few thoughts upon this important matter of gospel liberty. He says that when he went up to Jerusalem he took Titus with him. Now Titus was a Greek. He had not been circumcised and Paul made a point about this. Paul says, "But neither Titus, who was with me, being a Greek, was compelled to be circumcised." It is evident that when he went up to Jerusalem with Barnabas and Titus there were those who were insisting that Titus, even though he was a believer, yet being a Greek he must be circumcised. And they endeavoured to compel that to be done, such was their insistence upon it. But Paul says, 'We resisted, we stood firmly against them.' He says, "And that, because of false brethren unawares brought in, who came in privily, to spy out our liberty which we have in Christ Jesus, that they might bring us into bondage. To whom we gave place by subjection, no, not for an hour, that the truth of the gospel might continue with you." It is important to note that the council at Jerusalem dealt very thoroughly and effectively with this matter. They showed in no uncertain way that Gentiles who believed were not under bondage to the law of Moses, nor were they to be brought into submission to that law either. They showed that through faith in Jesus Christ there was complete deliverance from the law of Moses.

But evidently many of the Jewish believers, to some extent, still cleaved to what that law enjoined. That was permitted them because it was not always possible for them to immediately break from their upbringing in the law. Indeed, the law had been delivered to them *from God,* through the instrumentality of Moses. The important point here is that as they were true believers those matters were to be reckoned as things indifferent, and gospel liberty was allowed to those Jews to so continue for a time. But Paul strongly contends against imposing those things on Gentile believers, or to setting up matters that were indifferent as being vital and essential to salvation. He would not for one moment allow anything to hold place with the grace of God wherein true salvation is alone found. As I said, salvation is by grace through faith alone in Jesus Christ.

Friends, there are many matters in religion which can be looked upon as indifferent, as secondary things with respect to the observing or non-observing of them. They are to be left to the individual liberty of the believer. We must always bear in mind the importance of being guided by the teaching of scripture and walking in the spirit of Jesus Christ with real love and concern for the welfare of the church. And we are to bear in mind the needs of weaker brethren in the faith. But how we find, not only then but still today, there are those who are very ready to take what may be termed secondary indifferent matters and elevate them to a position they should never be allowed to occupy. They say that such things are necessary for salvation and that unless you do these things you cannot be a true believer. Or they say that if you are doing other secondary things with which they disagree, that evidences that you are not a believer in the Lord Jesus Christ. When it comes to compelling Titus to be circumcised, Paul resists that with every fibre of his being. He contends for the glorious truth that salvation is *by grace alone* through faith in the Lord and Saviour Jesus Christ. Oh, may we ever realise this vital distinction. May we know the *true unity* of the faith in being grounded and established on the truth as it is in the Lord Jesus Christ. May we cleave to him alone, and in that true sense to "earnestly contend for the faith which was once delivered to the saints" (Jude 1:3). We know that verse is often on the lips of many who think they are contending earnestly for the faith. But so much of the contention is not about vital truths essential to salvation. It so often revolves around secondary matters. How such things have plagued the true church of Jesus Christ over the generations. How Satan has sought thereby, as he did with the Galatians and the early church, to get an advantage over them. How important it is to daily seek grace to be established by the Holy Spirit's teaching in the vital truths of the gospel and to differentiate indifferent matters for which gospel liberty can be allowed.

But I must leave the remarks there this evening. May the Lord add his blessing. Amen.

7

ROMANS 14

Him that is weak in the faith receive ye, but not to doubtful disputations. For one believeth that he may eat all things: another, who is weak, eateth herbs. Let not him that eateth despise him that eateth not; and let not him which eateth not judge him that eateth: for God hath received him. Who art thou that judgest another man's servant? to his own master he standeth or falleth. Yea, he shall be holden up: for God is able to make him stand. One man esteemeth one day above another: another esteemeth every day alike. Let every man be fully persuaded in his own mind. He that regardeth the day, regardeth it unto the Lord; and he that regardeth not the day, to the Lord he doth not regard it. He that eateth, eateth to the Lord, for he giveth God thanks; he that eateth not, to the Lord he eateth not, and giveth God thanks. For none of us liveth to himself, and no man dieth to himself. For whether we live, we live unto the Lord; and whether we die, we die unto the Lord: whether we live therefore, or die, we are the Lord's. For to this end Christ both died, and rose, and revived, that he might be Lord both of the dead and living. But why dost thou judge thy brother? or why dost thou set at nought thy brother? for we shall all stand before the judgment seat of Christ. For it is written, As I live, saith the Lord, every knee shall bow to me, and every tongue shall confess to God. So then every one of us shall give account of himself to God. Let us not therefore judge one another any more: but judge this rather, that no man put a stumblingblock or an occasion to fall in his brother's way. I know, and am persuaded by the Lord Jesus, that there is nothing unclean of itself: but to him that esteemeth any thing to be unclean, to him it is unclean. But if thy brother be grieved with thy meat, now walkest thou not charitably. Destroy not him with thy meat, for whom Christ died. Let not then your good be evil spoken of: for the kingdom of God is not meat and drink; but righteousness, and peace, and joy in the Holy Ghost. For he that in these things serveth Christ is acceptable to God, and approved of men. Let us therefore follow after the things which make for peace, and things wherewith one may edify another. For meat destroy not the work of God. All things indeed are pure; but it is evil for that man who eateth with offence. It is good neither to eat flesh, nor to drink wine, nor any thing whereby thy brother stumbleth, or is offended, or is made weak. Hast thou faith? have it to thyself before God. Happy is he that condemneth not himself in that thing which he alloweth. And he that doubteth is damned if he eat, because he eateth not of faith: for whatsoever is not of faith is sin.

I want this evening, as helped, to deal with what I believe is a very important subject in the word of God and yet one that is much neglected and little understood in the professed churches of Jesus Christ today. It is what Paul is teaching in this fourteenth chapter of his epistle to the Romans. So that I may not be misunderstood on the points that I want to bring before you, I have brought some extensive notes on this subject, for which I make no apology. This fourteenth chapter relates to what we were dealing with last Friday evening out of the epistle to the Galatians. You remember, in the second chapter in that epistle, the apostle speaks of the case of Titus. When Paul and Barnabas took Titus with them to Jerusalem, some were very concerned that Titus was a Greek who had not been circumcised. Paul said they "came in privily to spy out our liberty which we have in Christ Jesus," and to see whether Paul would circumcise Titus or not. He said, "To whom we gave place by subjection, no, not for an hour." The apostle, most strongly and emphatically, resisted the pressure that some were ready to put on him to circumcise Titus.

It is this important matter of *Christian liberty* which I touched upon last Friday evening, that I want to consider tonight. Now, if

we read the Acts of the Apostles and the epistles of Paul, we find
there were times when he apparently very readily submitted to
various Jewish customs and such like matters. Yet there were
other times when he vigorously stands out against them as in his
epistle to the Galatians. Now some have suggested there was
inconsistency in Paul. If he contended against those who were
advocating Jewish customs which had no place in the new
testament church he should surely have always been consistent
in his opposition. But what Paul resisted with every fibre of his
being was the teaching in the Galatian churches that unless you
observe the Jewish customs and keep the law of God you cannot
be a saved believer. He would not have those things imposed as
necessary to salvation. His whole emphasis was on the true
gospel of salvation which is by grace through faith alone in the
Lord Jesus Christ. Nothing was to be allowed to take the place of
that gospel or be held alongside it. As soon as people begin to say
that such and such practices are necessary for salvation, then we
are to resist that teaching and attitude. This is the point I am
wanting to bring out this evening.

There were many, particularly among the Jews, who during
that time of transition in the early church still cleaved to the
things God had given through Moses. The conclusions of the
council at Jerusalem were clear and plain that those Jewish
observances were not to be enforced on Gentile believers. With
respect to the Jews they were to be left as matters indifferent,
matters of personal liberty. They were never to be brought into
the position that the keeping of them was necessary for salvation.
Paul often treated those Jewish observances in that way. He
respected believers from amongst the Jews who could not finally
separate themselves at that time from the customs in which they
had been brought up and had esteemed from their youth. As those
things were not sinful or evil in themselves, Paul left them as
matters of indifference. He respected the individual's observance
of those things so long as they were not exalted to being
considered vital for salvation.

Just to illustrate this point. You remember when Paul was
going to Jerusalem, as recorded in Acts 21, many warned him
and begged him not to go there when they heard what the

unbelieving Jews would do to him. We read, "Then Paul answered, What mean ye to weep and to break mine heart? for I am ready not to be bound only, but also to die at Jerusalem for the name of the Lord Jesus. And when he would not be persuaded, we ceased, saying, The will of the Lord be done." We read that when he came to Jerusalem the following day, "Paul went in with us unto James; and all the elders were present. And when he had saluted them, he declared particularly what things God had wrought among the Gentiles by his ministry. And when they heard it, they glorified the Lord, and said unto him, Thou seest, brother, how many thousands of Jews there are which believe; and they are all zealous of the law: and they are informed of thee, that thou teachest all the Jews which are among the Gentiles to forsake Moses, saying that they ought not to circumcise their children, neither to walk after the customs. What is it therefore? the multitude must needs come together: for they will hear that thou art come. Do therefore this that we say to thee: We have four men which have a vow on them; Them take, and purify thyself with them, and be at charges with them, that they may shave their heads: and all may know that those things, whereof they were informed concerning thee, are nothing; but that thou thyself also walkest orderly, and keepest the law. As touching the Gentiles which believe, we have written and concluded that they observe no such thing, save only that they keep themselves from things offered to idols, and from blood, and from strangled, and from fornication." Paul did not refuse to comply with that suggestion of the elders, though as it turned out it did not protect him from the rage and enmity of the unbelieving Jews in Jerusalem. They were determined to lay hands on Paul, and we know the lengths to which they went in their endeavours to do so. But here we see that Paul accounted laws and customs such as purification to be matters of indifference, so long as they were not insisted upon as being essential for salvation.

Now it is with such things as these that this fourteenth chapter in the epistle to the Romans deals. As I said, I have some extensive notes which I just want to read during our meeting this evening. Firstly, "We find that this fourteenth chapter is entirely occupied with a matter that gave rise to many difficult problems in the early years of the church's history. The Jewish converts carried with them pretty naturally their views and feelings about matters of eating and drinking, about observance of days and customs and the like. Their thoughts were partly based on the law of God and partly on the traditions of the elders, but at any rate their feelings were very strong. The Gentile converts had no such feelings and were inclined to regard it all as so much obstinate stupidity on the part of their Jewish brethren. There was a cause for endless friction. The whole question is raised here and settled with that admirable simplicity which characterises divine wisdom." I believe that statement sums up the matter very well. We can see how these observances to which so many of the Jews still cleaved and which the Gentiles were not prepared to observe, were not needful for salvation but caused much friction in the early church.

Now the matter dealt with in this fourteenth chapter is not just an academic point. It is not something that was of interest in the early days of the church but has no practical importance now. The very opposite is true. It has real practical implications for the church and the people of God today. "It is rather of very living and pressing importance. Though the exact questions that agitated and divided first century Christians may have largely faded away, there are many others of a like nature taking their place and much distress and harm is caused today when the instructions of this chapter are not observed." How true that is! There are many practical situations that arise in the individual lives of believers within the church which are covered by what Paul brings out in this chapter. It is important that we give due attention to this teaching and seek to walk in the light of it, by the grace of God.

There are then particular principles brought out in this chapter. The first of them we can call the principle of *Christian liberty*. Now what does this extend to? Let me state this before I go further. We are not at liberty to have different ideas on what may well be termed the essential truths of the faith. There is one faith that is delivered to the saints. There is one way of salvation that is made known in the gospel. To be a Christian, there are essential things which we must truly believe and receive. These include belief in the Godhead of God, the adorable Trinity, Father, Son and Holy Spirit—one God, yet three persons in that Godhead. And we must believe there is one Lord Jesus Christ, God manifest in the flesh. We must believe the facts of his birth, life, vicarious death, resurrection and ascension into heaven. Without going into these matters in greater detail, the point I am making is that there are essentials of the faith on which there can be no debate. We cannot be a Christian, a true believer, without receiving those things in faith and love. Let me also make this point. Where the Lord gives us a clear direction in his word, a distinct commandment on any matter then, without question, our path is humble obedience to his teaching.

Concerning Christian liberty I want to read this: "In these matters that have to do with personal behaviour and con-scientious service to the Lord, we are set free from the lordship of our brethren by being set under the over-Lordship of Jesus Christ. We may be right or wrong in our judgment but the thing of prime importance is that we each, with a single eye for our Master, do what we believe to be pleasing to Him. The exhortation concerning this is, *Let every man be fully persuaded in his own mind.* God intends us to be exercised as to such matters each for himself. Where there is a definite command in scripture there need not be exercise. Then, simple obedience is the only course pleasing to God. But there are other matters (and how many there are) such as: should I go here or there? Should I partake of this or that? May I enjoy this pleasurable recreation or not? Ought we to carry out this service or this ordinance in this way or that way? What acrimonious and harmful controversies have raged around such questions, and the answer is so simple— let the wrangling cease, hands off each other, each man to his own knees in the presence of his own Master, that he may get, as far as in him lies, the knowledge of his Master's will." And it is this important principle that Paul brings out in the chapter here before us. Let us look at it in some little detail.

With all such questions Paul says, "Him that is weak in the faith receive ye, but not to doubtful disputations." He brings out what he means by those that are weak in the faith. They are ones who have not the discernment, the depth of understanding and spiritual experience that some others may have. He says, "For one believeth that he may eat all things: another, who is weak, eateth herbs. Let not him that eateth despise him that eateth not; and let not him which eateth not judge him that eateth: for God hath received him." Here is a vital principle. We see how a problem so easily arises in matters which we can say are indifferent. For example, should we eat or abstain from certain foods? Should we enjoy this recreation or not? And there are many other such issues. Some may have very strong feelings and say that they feel it would be wrong to do certain things. Well, it is their right to say that. If they have a judgment in a matter, are persuaded in their conscience that it is right before God and can act with a single eye to his glory, then all very well. Let them observe those things. But let them not judge brethren who do not see the issue in the same way. This is the practical implication and outworking of Christian liberty.

As you know, the Jews had various days appointed for religious observance. With the new testament church no such days exist. True, there is the Lord's Day, the first day of the week when we are to gather together to worship God in remembrance of the resurrection of our Lord Jesus Christ from the dead. There is general agreement among believers that this is according to the mind and will of God. In that we would willingly agree. But observations of other days and times are things of indifference. If one brother or sister feels that for them it is important that they observe a certain day, then let them do so. But let them observe it to the Lord. If they are sincere in that matter, seeking to do so with a single eye to the Lord's glory, then all well and good. But let them not judge others who are not prepared to join with them because they see not the need for it. Likewise, those that see not the necessity of it, let them not despise their brother or sister who do those things out of a conscientious desire to serve the Lord. The matters themselves, whether observed or abstained from, are not sinful because they are matters of indifference. The brother or sister is at liberty to observe those things or not, as they are persuaded in their own consciences before God. Here you see the principle that applies to many areas of the individual lives of the Lord's people. Not only do we have this Christian liberty, but we are not to judge one another in these things. As Paul says in verse 13, "Let us not therefore judge one another anymore: but judge this rather, that no man put a stumblingblock or an occasion to fall in his brother's way."

As I have said, this Christian liberty applies to issues that are indifferent, not vital to the faith and for which there is no clear commandment in the word of God. Believers are at liberty to observe or not observe such matters as they feel led of the Lord. Now Paul brings out a further important point about this at the end of the chapter. He says, "Hast thou faith? have it to thyself before God. Happy is he that condemneth not himself in that thing which he alloweth. And he that doubteth is damned if he eats, because he eateth not of faith: for whatsoever is not of faith is sin." What are we to understand from that statement in connection with what I have been saying concerning matters of indifference? Paul says the important thing for the believer in his partaking or abstaining, his observing or not observing, is that *"whatsoever is not of faith is sin."* Friends, so often a problem is caused where brethren seek to press home matters of indifference upon the consciences of others. If a brother or sister cannot do something with a single eye to the Lord's glory, and without violating their own conscientious scruples, then for them to engage in such a thing is sin. Defilement of conscience is brought upon them. They should not have been so pressed in such matters. "Whatsoever is not of faith is sin." But where there is the observing or not observing, with a conscientious concern for the Lord's glory and the real good of his people, then "happy is he that condemneth not himself in that thing which he alloweth."

A further important principle here is that our personal preferences are not to condition our observing or ignoring of anything. So many want to exercise their own personal preferences, irrespective of what effect it may have on another. Paul says here, *"None of us liveth to himself, and no man dieth to himself."* As a believer, I am not merely to be concerned to exercise my own personal preferences in these matters of indifference. I seek to commit a thing prayerfully to the Lord to ascertain whether it is right for me to go in a certain way or do a thing or not. But I am not only to be concerned for my personal preferences. I am also to be concerned for the welfare of others. Friends, so often the pride of our hearts can arise in the matters Paul is dealing with here. What havoc this causes. Oh for the grace of true humble-mindedness and concern wherein each one is brought to seek his brother's or sister's welfare above his own. Paul in effect says here, that if I believe it my liberty to eat all manner of meats, I will in no way seek to bind that liberty on the conscience of my weaker brother. Why, I would rather abstain from the use of them than hinder his weak conscience in such a matter. Oh, does not this bring out the reality of brotherly love, as fully exemplified in our Lord Jesus Christ of whom it could be truly said, "He pleased not himself." He always had in view the glory of God and the welfare of his people.

But I will leave the remarks there this evening. May the Lord add his blessing. Amen.

8

GALATIANS 2:6-21

But of these who seemed to be somewhat, (whatsoever they were, it maketh no matter to me: God accepteth no man's person:) for they who seemed to be somewhat in conference added nothing to me: but contrariwise, when they saw that the gospel of the uncircumcision was committed unto me, as the gospel of the circumcision was unto Peter; (for he that wrought effectually in Peter to the apostleship of the circumcision, the same was mighty in me toward the Gentiles:) and when James, Cephas, and John, who seemed to be pillars, perceived the grace that was given unto me, they gave to me and Barnabas the right hands of fellowship; that we should go unto the heathen, and they unto the circumcision. Only they would that we should remember the poor; the same which I also was forward to do. But when Peter was come to Antioch, I withstood him to the face, because he was to be blamed. For before that certain came from James, he did eat with the Gentiles: but when they were come, he withdrew and separated himself, fearing them which were of the circumcision. And the other Jews dissembled likewise with him; insomuch that Barnabas also was carried away with their dissimulation. But when I saw that they walked not uprightly according to the truth of the gospel, I said unto Peter before them all, If thou, being a Jew, livest after the manner of Gentiles, and not as do the Jews, why compellest thou the Gentiles to live as do the Jews? We who are Jews by nature, and not sinners of the Gentiles, knowing that a man is not justified by the works of the law, but by the faith of Jesus Christ, even we have believed in Jesus Christ, that we might be justified by the faith of Christ, and not by the works of the law: for by the works of the law shall no flesh be justified. But if, while we seek to be justified by Christ, we ourselves also are found sinners, is therefore Christ the minister of sin? God forbid. For if I build again the things which I destroyed, I make myself a transgressor. For I through the law am dead to the law, that I might live unto God. I am crucified with Christ: nevertheless I live; yet not I, but Christ liveth in me: and the life which I now live in the flesh I live by the faith of the Son of God, who loved me, and gave himself for me. I do not frustrate the grace of God: for if righteousness come by the law, then Christ is dead in vain.

The last time I was with you I did not speak directly from the epistle to the Galatians. I endeavoured to deal with the important point of gospel liberty and its practical implications as Paul brings out in his epistle to the Romans. The last time we looked at this second chapter to the Galatians I dealt particularly with the first five verses. Now as helped this evening I want to continue with the things that are brought before us in this second chapter and particularly from verse 6 onwards.

We have noticed how the apostle would not for one moment put up with those who came in privily, as he says, "to spy out our liberty which we have in Christ Jesus, that they might bring us into bondage." This issue arose as Paul and Barnabas went up to Jerusalem, taking with them Titus who was a Gentile who had not been circumcised. Paul would not allow circumcision to be enforced on Titus. Bear in mind, as I have mentioned before, that the main reason for which Paul and Barnabas visited Jerusalem at that time was over this very matter of circumcision and adherence to Jewish ceremonies and the law of Moses. We read a few weeks ago, in that fifteenth chapter in the Acts of the Apostles, of the resolution reached as the brethren gathered to consider this matter as the Holy Spirit guided them. It was made plain that though Jewish believers were still to be allowed to observe some of the things in which they had been brought up, yet their observation was not to be enforced on Gentile believers. Not even with the Jews were those observances of the Mosaic law to be considered needful in any way for the salvation of the soul, for the justifying of the sinner before God. The plain fact was emphatically stated, which Paul is so concerned to defend and set forth in this epistle as the sum and substance of the gospel he preached, that *"by grace are ye saved through faith; and that not of yourselves: it is the gift of God: not of works, lest any man should boast" (Eph. 2:8-9).*

We see how zealous the apostle Paul was in a right way. Remember that as Saul of Tarsus he had been zealous for the traditions of the fathers and we know to what that zeal led. Friends, this is a point to notice. We can be very zealous. We can be very sincere. There is no denying that Paul, as he was Saul of Tarsus, was truly zealous and utterly sincere in what he was doing. But he was brought to realise that he was sincerely wrong. His zeal was that which was not directed, as he had fondly thought, to the promotion of the glory of God but to fighting against God. We know the great change that was wrought in him by sovereign grace. Then we see his zeal according to knowledge, a zeal that is embodied in the love that he has to the truth, and especially the love that he has to the Lord Jesus Christ through divine grace. Oh, he holds the truth very zealously but he holds that truth *in love.* How vital is that. Paul contends very vigorously against those that denied the truth, those who were adulterating the gospel that he had preached. He reproves even Peter himself in a very open and public way when Peter did not act according to the spirit of the gospel. Yet in all these things Paul not only contends for the truth, but he does so in love. As he contends for the truth there is none of that bitterness which is the fruit of the working of our fallen carnal nature.

Notice here this important distinction. It is very necessary to be reminded of this again and again. Jude writes those words that are so well known to us. "It was needful for me to write unto you, and exhort you that ye should earnestly contend for the faith which was once delivered unto the saints" (Jude 1:3). How many take up that word of Jude, "earnestly contend for the faith." And what do we find their contending for the faith in many respects amounts to? Sadly, if they are not careful, it amounts to abusing those who oppose their particular views. It is the denouncing of opponents of the truth. It is a contending which often shows far more of the working of the old nature than it ever does of the new nature. Is that the manner of contending that Jude was advocating? Is that the spirit which actuated the apostle Paul? We find that Paul makes very strong statements about the doctrine that was being promoted among the churches in Galatia. Yet his main emphasis is not to contend for the truth in a merely negative way but to set forth positively the truth as it is in Christ Jesus. This should always be our main concern also.

I remember reading, a good number of years ago, a definition of Protestantism. I believe this is a very important point. It defines its true nature. Protestantism, the writer says, is not just a protest against error. It includes that, but it is not just a negative thing. It is a positive thing. It is a protest for the truth. By the gracious enabling of God the Holy Spirit, it is a positive setting forth of the truth, not in word only, but also in deed. Ah, friends, so many that apparently contend for the truth ruin the whole of their position by the spirit in which it is done. And there can be the sad evidence in their lives, that they do not live according to the principles they are supposedly advocating. The witness of the true church of Jesus Christ is not just a witness against evil. It is a positive setting forth of the truth, not in word only but also in life. That was one thing that distinguished the new testament church. Oh what did men particularly notice about the believers? They noticed how they had been with Jesus and how they loved one another. They had to admit that they were law-abiding people in the community in which they lived. The only thing they could find against them was the truth they believed and by which they lived.

You remember the case of Daniel in the exalted position he held in the court of the Persian kings. There were those that hated him because of his being promoted to that position and they sought to undermine him and bring him down. Yet they had to say they could not find anything against him unless it was connected with the worship of his God. You remember the scheme they devised to entrap Daniel and to destroy him by having him cast into the den of lions. But see how the scheme they devised solemnly ended in their own destruction. They themselves fell into the very pit they had dug for Daniel.

But to come back to what is before us here. These false

teachers that were troubling the churches of Galatia sought to set the apostle Paul at nought. They claimed that he had no authority as an apostle of Jesus Christ for he had not the same credentials as the other apostles. He had not been with the Lord when he was here on earth. He had not been an eyewitness to the Lord's resurrection, therefore what was his authority as an apostle? Paul clearly shows that his authority as an apostle was that which he had received, not of men, but of the Lord. He had the credentials of an apostle for he had seen the Lord in a very distinct and remarkable way. Paul also goes on to show that the gospel he preached was not unique to himself. Though he had received it by the revelation of Jesus Christ, yet it was the same gospel that the other apostles preached. There was no difference between them in the things they preached. And he says that as he had come to Jerusalem and had communicated to the elders and the apostles in Jerusalem the gospel that he preached, they gave him and Barnabas "the right hands of fellowship." They agreed that he preached the same gospel as they did. He had been taught by the same Holy Spirit. There was no difference between them. The only difference between Paul and Peter was that Paul's ministry, as he was led by the Holy Spirit, was directed more to the Gentiles, the uncircumcision. With Peter, the sphere of his ministry fell more among the Jews and those who had been circumcised. But the same powerful working of the Holy Spirit that wrought through Peter in his ministry to the Jews, wrought through Paul in his ministry to the Gentiles.

You will remember how the Holy Spirit had clearly shown to Simon Peter that the middle wall of separation between Jew and Gentile had been taken away through the person and work of the Lord Jesus Christ. As recorded in Acts chapter 10, the Lord sovereignly and graciously heard and answered the prayers of Cornelius the Roman centurion. An angel appeared to Cornelius bidding him to send to Joppa and ask for one, Simon, who would tell him the things that concerned the salvation of his soul. When Cornelius sent messengers to Joppa to find Peter, the Holy Spirit also spoke to Peter in that vision which was given him. He was clearly shown that he was *to make no distinction between Jew and Gentile.* He was not to call any man common or unclean. The distinction that had existed was removed. The grace of God, the salvation revealed in the gospel of the Lord Jesus Christ, *was to be preached in all the nations of the earth.* God, through the preaching of the gospel and the operations of the Holy Spirit, would call those whom he had chosen before the foundation of the world, not only from the Jews but also from the Gentiles. Now Paul goes on here to speak to the Galatians of the case of Peter himself and of what happened on one occasion when they were in Antioch. But before coming to this point let me just notice this point.

Let us not fondly think that the early church was without its troubles, difficulties and trials. We have only to read these epistles of Paul to find that the new testament churches were not only harassed by opposition from without but they were also troubled and distressed by many things within the churches. We see the real strength and reality of their faith and love in how these things were handled. While here on earth, the church of Jesus Christ shall have trials, tribulations, temptations and distresses. As I have said many times, as surely as the Lord works graciously then the devil will seek to work maliciously. That they have no troubles, no temptations, nothing that distresses them, is not an indication that the Lord is with his people and is working graciously among them. Oftentimes the very opposite is true. Where the Lord is working graciously, the devil will not be far behind in seeking to disrupt the peace and fellowship of the true people of God. Here the true unity of the church is seen. As the members of the church are one in Jesus Christ, as blessed with the grace of God and true living faith, they seek to walk together in bonds of love and union. And the more the devil harasses, the closer are they drawn to the Lord Jesus Christ and to true fellowship with one another.

You look at a flock of sheep when danger threatens. Take a flock of sheep in a field and a strange dog comes into the field. What do the sheep do? You see the whole flock huddle together and the closer the danger comes the closer do they cling together. What an example is that. Should it not be so with the Lord's people as they walk together in church union and fellowship? The more the wolves of Satan howl, the more his dogs bark, the more should the true sheep of Christ cling closer together and essentially to him who is the great and good shepherd. For friends, let us not lose sight of this, using still the analogy of the shepherd and the flock—who do the flock belong to? Who is responsible for the care of the flock, for its provision and protection? Oh, we are thankful for this. It is not on the shoulders of men that these things are placed, but upon the shoulders of him who is God manifest in the flesh, he who is described as the great and good shepherd that "giveth his life for the sheep."

Notice that even when Paul rebukes Peter here, it is in a spirit of love and faithfulness. For true love does not exclude reproof when those things are needful. As I have said, the important point always to bear in mind is that these things are to be done in love. Let us look closer at this conduct of Peter at Antioch and why Paul so reproves him. Here was Peter, an apostle of Jesus Christ, yet he was not without his faults and failings. Even the best of men are but men at best. We would not for one moment throw stones at Peter. He that knows his own heart, as taught by the Holy Spirit, will ever be kept from that. Let us "be not highminded, but fear" (Rom. 11:20). "Let him that thinketh he standeth take heed lest he fall" (1 Cor. 10:12). But we might say, what has Peter done? Is it not covered by the principles I was bringing before you a fortnight ago? Was not what Peter did a matter of indifference? Had he not a liberty in those things? What is the problem?

Ah, it was not that eating with the Jews exclusively, this Jewish custom, was in itself necessarily wrong. As Paul points out to him, the problem with Peter was that when he came to Antioch he willingly mingled with the Gentiles. He ate with them, making no distinction either of meat or custom, and he plainly showed by his conduct in Antioch that there was no difference between Jew and Gentile. Why then did he change his behaviour? When some Jews came from the elders and apostles at Jerusalem, why did Peter behave differently, withdrawing himself from the Gentile believers in Antioch and confining himself to association with the Jews? What was behind this? As Paul shows here, it was "the fear of man [that] bringeth a snare" (Prov. 29:25). Paul shows him that by such behaviour he was compromising the very truth that he had preached and which the Lord the Holy Spirit had made so plain to him. Out of the fear of man, Peter withdraws himself from the Gentiles. He seemed to give credence to the belief held by some that Jewish regulations over those things were of real importance and vital to the truth as it is in Jesus. Yet he himself had been shown and had preached that those things were indifferent matters. Thus Paul says here, "But when Peter was come to Antioch, I withstood him to the face, because he was to be blamed."

Notice that Paul rebukes Peter, but he does it to his face. He deals with him in an honest and straightforward way. He does not report this behind Peter's back, complaining to others in the church at Antioch about what Peter is doing. No, he faces him openly and honestly according to the principles that the Lord Jesus himself had laid down. Is not this the right way? As Jesus himself tells us, if there is a matter of dispute between brethren then they are to speak to one another face to face, openly and honestly, but not in a spirit of confrontation. We are to handle matters of reproof and dissension as Paul did here with Peter. They are to be dealt with in an open, honest and a straightforward way.

How so much of the trouble among brethren in the church has often arisen because people are not open, honest and straightforward in their dealings. They will not say what they mean nor mean what they say. Friends, such behaviour only leads to further trouble and a widening of the gap, giving a road for Satan to enter and cause havoc unless the Lord prevent. Ah, let us be like Paul here, open and honest in all our dealings one with another. We are not to be afraid, even if there is need to reprove, so long as it is done in the spirit of love and with real concern for the glory of the Lord and the good of one another.

He says, "But when Peter was come to Antioch, I withstood him to the face, because he was to be blamed. For before that certain came from James, he did eat with the Gentiles: but when they were come, he withdrew and separated himself, *fearing them which were of the circumcision.*" And see, this is a matter in which not only Peter was involved, but he drew others along with him as well, so that "the other Jews dissembled likewise with him; insomuch that Barnabas also was carried away with their dissimulation." As I say, this was no small matter, for it infringed the vital truths of the gospel. True, those matters of themselves were indifferent. But when they come in this form, Peter acting as if there was some real value in this separation, as if it was almost a necessity, then Paul withstands these things. He will not have the true liberty of the gospel infringed by them at all. He says, "But when I saw that they walked not uprightly according to the truth of the gospel, I said unto Peter before them all, If thou, being a Jew, livest after the manner of the Gentiles, and not as do the Jews, why compellest thou the Gentiles to live as do the Jews?" He is saying that Peter was a Jew, and yet up to this point he had lived as the Gentiles, showing, as he had himself been shown by the Lord, that there was no distinction before God in these matters. These things were matters of total indifference. Ah, he says then, "Why compellest thou the Gentiles to live as do the Jews?" Paul points out that by his dissembling in this matter, Peter was in effect saying to the Gentiles that they must live as do the Jews and observe these Jewish practices.

Paul could see the real danger of bringing the church into bondage to the very things the false teachers at Galatia were advocating—not only was faith in Jesus Christ necessary but the keeping of the law was also necessary if they were to be saved. For he says, "We who are Jews by nature, and not sinners of the Gentiles." What he means there is, 'we are Jews naturally, we are born Jews, we are not of these Gentile nations.' He goes on, "knowing that a man is not justified by the works of the law, but by the faith of Jesus Christ, even we have believed in Jesus Christ, that we might be justified by the faith of Christ, and not by the works of the law: for by the works of the law shall no flesh be justified." Paul is reminding Peter here of the very truths that they had received, the gospel that had been delivered to them, and which they had believed through grace. 'Do we not well know, have we not been taught these things, that a man is not justified by the works of the law, but by the faith of Jesus Christ? Even we have believed in Jesus Christ. Is not this our profession and what we have in possession through grace?' See that Paul reproves Peter concerning this matter in the spirit of love, positively setting forth the truth as it is in Jesus.

Oh, what a statement does Paul give here, not only of his personal profession of faith, but of the gracious possession of those things that he knew in his own soul through grace. I have not time to enter into them this evening. We will leave this for another week. But what a truth is in that nineteenth verse, "For I through the law am dead to the law, that I might live unto God. I am crucified with Christ: nevertheless I live; yet not I, but Christ liveth in me: and the life which I now live in the flesh I live by the faith of the Son of God, who loved me, and gave himself for me."

But I will leave the remarks there. May the Lord add his blessing. Amen.

9

GALATIANS 2:15-21

We who are Jews by nature, and not sinners of the Gentiles, knowing that a man is not justified by the works of the law, but by the faith of Jesus Christ, even we have believed in Jesus Christ, that we might be justified by the faith of Christ, and not by the works of the law: for by the works of the law shall no flesh be justified. But if, while we seek to be justified by Christ, we ourselves also are found sinners, is therefore Christ the minister of sin? God forbid. For if I build again the things which I destroyed, I make myself a transgressor. For I through the law am dead to the law, that I might live unto God. I am crucified with Christ: neverthless I live; yet not I, but Christ liveth in me: and the life which I now live in the flesh I live by the faith of the Son of God, who loved me, and gave himself for me. I do not frustrate the grace of God: for if righteousness come by the law, then Christ is dead in vain.

Last Friday evening we considered in some measure these verses I have read again this evening. I want, as helped, to make further comments upon the important and glorious truths here brought before us. For surely we cannot have them set before us too much. Not only do we need them to be set before us again and again, but we need the Lord the Holy Spirit, to lead us into these things and establish us in them. For here is the very sum and substance of gospel truth. In this, real peace and joy is to be experienced, not just in knowing about these things, but being found in possession of them through the Holy Spirit's gracious teaching.

I remarked last week on Paul's reproving even the apostle Peter because he did not act uprightly in matters at Antioch, through the fear of man, the fear of those that had come from James. Though Peter had been associating and eating with the Gentile believers he withdrew himself and confined his association to Jewish believers only. He thereby gave the impression that there was some real importance in observing Jewish ceremonies and customs, even the law of Moses. Yet one of the essential things revealed in the truth as it is in Jesus, is that "Christ is the end of the law for righteousness to everyone that believeth" (Rom. 10:4). Though these Jewish customs of the law of Moses had served an important purpose, they were done away in the person and finished work of the Lord Jesus Christ. Indeed, Peter himself had preached this glorious truth as he had received it by the Spirit's teaching. He had testified that God put no difference between Jew and Gentile. There was no value now whatsoever in the Jewish ceremonies of the law of Moses. Those things could not justify men and women as they were sinners before God. By them, there could be no way of access to God, no ground of acceptance before him, for sinful men and women. Peter had preached as powerfully and effectually as any of the other apostles that salvation is by grace, through faith alone. "For by grace are ye saved through faith; and that not of yourselves: it is the gift of God: not of works, lest any man should boast" (Eph. 2:8-9). Yet by his actions at Antioch he seems to be going back upon all that he had formerly preached. Paul rightly rebukes him, as he says to him in verse 16, "Knowing that a man is not justified by the works of the law, but by the faith of Jesus Christ." How essential, how vital a truth is that which the gospel gloriously and wonderfully makes known, "that a man is not justified by the works of the law."

What is the religion that is rooted in human nature? Man cannot get away from the concept of one supreme being who has been offended and who needs to be placated. You see that illustrated in all the various religions that man has turned to since the time of Adam's fall in Eden. These things are rooted in human nature. The reaction of men and women in matters of religion is always to go about to produce a righteousness of their own, as the scripture puts it. They have the idea that something must be done, some atonement must be made, certain things must be attained to, for God to be reconciled to men. Now it is true that men and women are transgressors. Yes, they have offended against the holy and righteous law of God. Yes, God is the supreme being, the supreme good, the Creator of all things and the upholder of all things by the word of his power. Yes, there is alienation between this holy God and sinners. The great question indeed is, how shall men and women that are sinners and transgressors be just with God? That is, how shall they be found acceptable before him, be pleasing in his sight, and come to dwell with him, the supreme good? As I said, the natural reaction of the human heart is always to go about to attain these ends by its own doings. We see how sinners of themselves ever seek to obtain the favour of God by what they suppose is obedience to the holy law he gave to Moses on Sinai, with all the attendant revelation there made known to Israel.

Now Paul is saying here, not only to Peter, but also to us, "knowing that a man is not justified by the works of the law." That is, we *do* know this. It is clearly taught in God's word. By the teaching of the Holy Spirit, it is solemnly brought home to the heart of each and every one that is called by divine grace. I say again, this is the teaching of God in his word and it is the experience of each one taught by the Holy Spirit. We are not dealing with mere theoretical points. These things are painfully known and experienced in the hearts and lives of each of the Lord's people. Let me just open the point up in this way. "Knowing that a man is not justified by the works of the law." How do we know this? How is the child of God taught these things? As I have said, he is taught by most painful experience. They themselves have sought to be justified by the deeds of the law, as the solemn consciousness of their sin and guilt has been brought home to their soul. Their conscience has been awakened to the claims and demands of divine justice as given in the holy law of God. What is our reaction under this teaching? And oh, have we not known what it is to be found here? Sadly, do we not even have to say, that this lesson has to be learnt over and over again? "Knowing that a man is not justified by the works of the law."

Ah, when our conscience is alarmed with a sense of sin, when its guilt and defilement is known and felt, what is the reaction? Oh, do we not turn to endeavouring to be more circumspect in our lives? We will seek to stop doing this. We will put more efforts and endeavours into doing that. We know what the holy law of God requires. We will endeavour to live more by its clear and plain commands. And so we have set to work. But what is it when all is said and done? Friends, it is no different to what the Jews did in the blindness and ignorance of their hearts, as Paul speaks of them. "They being ignorant of God's righteousness, and going about to establish their own righteousness, have not submitted themselves unto the righteousness of God" (Rom.10:3). Were they not to attend to what the law of Moses required? Were they not to attend to the ceremonies of the Levitical law? True, they were to attend, but those things were never designed, they were never given, that sinners might be justified before God thereby.

To bring this point out further. Paul says here, "for by the works of the law shall no flesh be justified." What does he mean there by *no flesh*? The word *flesh* there means and includes the whole man, in his thoughts, words and deeds. No *flesh* shall be justified in God's sight. So often *flesh* is understood to be sinful, fallen human nature, manifest in those sinful acts of man which are more particularly recognised as being evil. But let us not overlook this as well. *Flesh* includes those things which can be esteemed good. It is *all* flesh. It is not only men and women that are seen to be notorious sinners. But even those who might think themselves as good, are not justified by the deeds of the law. No, to put it simply and plainly in this way, not all my religious exercises, not all my praying, preaching, or hearing the word of God, not even all my seeking to walk and abide by what God has revealed in his word, none of these things can justify me before God. We are not saying that they are not profitable in their right place, but what we are saying is that they do not justify us before God. "Knowing that a man is not justified by the works of the law." Ah, friends, how the Lord, in teaching his people, brings them to painfully realise this truth, as they have so often striven to be justified by the deeds of the law and sought to deal with the

working of sin in themselves by their own strength and efforts.
One well says:

> "The more I strove against sin's power,
> I sinned and stumbled but the more:
> Till late I heard my Saviour say,
> Come hither, soul, I AM THE WAY."

And this truth is well illustrated in that well known hymn we
sometimes sing:

> "Not the labour of my hands,
> Can fulfil thy law's demands;
> Could my zeal no respite know,
> Could my tears for ever flow,
> All for sin could not atone;
> Thou must save, and thou alone."

"Knowing that a man is not justified by the works of the law,
but by the faith of Jesus Christ." Ah, it is a blessed and glorious
truth to be justified by the faith which embraces the Lord Jesus
Christ in all the reality of his person and finished work. I also
believe the emphasis here is on faith being essentially the gift of
God. How so many look on faith as that which the sinner
produces in response to what God has done. They thereby make
faith a work, and salvation dependent on that work of faith. That
is no different from sending the sinner back to the law to be
justified, saying he must produce this faith to be right with God.
But faith is the gift of God.

This came to me so powerfully and sweetly in meditating
recently upon what the Lord said to the woman in the house of
Simon the leper. He said, "Thy faith hath saved thee. Go in
peace" (Luke 7:50). Her faith was genuine for you see its blessed
fruits in what took place in the house of Simon the leper. She was
found at the feet of the Lord Jesus Christ. From whence did she
receive that faith? Was it the product of fallen human nature? No
indeed it was not. It was the work of grace, the fruit of the blessed
unction and life-giving power of God the Holy Spirit. It was the
evidence of the reality of faith which is the gift of God.

"By the faith of Jesus Christ." Faith which is the gift of God,
living faith in exercise, always centres in its object—Jesus Christ.
He says, "Even we have believed in Jesus Christ, that we might

be justified by the faith of Christ." Look at that in the cases of Paul and Peter. "Even we have believed in Jesus Christ." True, but from whence came their believing in Christ? It was the fruit of the sovereign, gracious dealings of God with them. Paul did not have that faith of himself. He did not believe in Jesus Christ of himself. No, until God called him by grace he was in complete opposition to Jesus Christ, as he tells these brethren at Galatia. He had no time for him. "Even we have believed." Oh, Paul is emphasising that it was through the sovereign grace of God that he and Peter believed. "And not by the works of the law: for by the works of the law shall no flesh be justified."

He goes on in his rebuke of Peter here. "But if, while we seek to be justified by Christ, we ourselves also are found sinners, is therefore Christ the minister of sin? God forbid." He is saying, 'If we are professing in our preaching to be justified by faith and yet are now (as was Peter) giving credence to these Judaizers, who are teaching that faith in Christ is not enough but a man must keep the law to be justified, are we not then found to be sinners? If, on the one hand, we are professing to be justified by faith alone, and yet, on the other hand, are giving credence to those who are saying that justification is not by faith alone, are we not then found sinners?' See the solemn reality of what is being brought out here. To give any credence, in whatever way, to the idea that salvation is upon any ground or basis other than by grace through faith alone in Jesus Christ, where are we left? Friends, this leaves us as sinners under the curse and condemnation of the law. That is the solemn reality of these errors. That is why Paul so stood out against the judaizing teachers at Galatia and wherever else they made their appearance.

What they said seemed so plausible to human nature. It met with ready acceptance among men. It seemed so true, so good. What could be wrong with it? They were advocating things that God had revealed in the former dispensation. They appeared to be giving great glory to what God had made known to Moses. But Paul is saying, 'If we teach these things, sinners are not justified. No. It leaves us, whatever they say, under the curse and condemnation of the law.' We, the professed ministers of Christ teach that a man is not justified by the works of the law but by the faith of Jesus Christ, If we give credibility to the error being advocated, we are implying that Jesus Christ is "the minister of sin." We are saying Jesus Christ came to assert that sinners' obedience to the law of Moses is needful to salvation. Paul is saying that if this was the solemn implication of Peter's action at Antioch, how much more is this so with the judaizing teachers at Galatia.

He goes on: "If I build again the things which I destroyed, I make myself a transgressor." What were the things he had destroyed? He is referring to his former life as he had been a very strict devout and zealous Pharisee who had rested the whole hope of his salvation and acceptance before God on his obedience to the law. How vividly he brings this out in other epistles. For instance, in his epistle to the Philippians, he speaks of those things which at one time were gain to him, but which he now counted loss for Christ. He says, "Yea, doubtless, I count all thing but loss for the excellency of the knowledge of Christ Jesus my Lord: for whom I have suffered the loss of all things, and do count them but dung, that I may win Christ, and be found in him, not having mine own righteousness which is of the law, but that which is through the faith of Christ, the righteousness which is of God by faith" (Phil. 3:8-9). He had been brought to see the utter folly of resting and boasting in the supposed righteousness of his former life and conversation. In those things there was no ground of acceptance for him, a sinner, before a holy, heart-searching God. But now he says, 'If I build again those things which I have destroyed, where does it leave me? It leaves me still a transgressor, under the curse and condemnation of a holy God, and without hope in the world.' That is the solemn implication of these things.

In the nineteenth verse he makes this glorious claim: "For I through the law am dead to the law that I might live under God." Friends, what a powerful and profound statement is this which Paul makes! How amazing and surprising it was in the ears of all Judaizers. Why, what is Paul saying? Is not this plain contrary to all that the Jews had been taught? And has not the emphasis always been the very opposite of what Paul is saying here? It still is, sadly and solemnly, in many places where the gospel is

supposedly preached today? Do not many say, 'If we do not live
to the law, then we are dead to God'? Paul is here saying the plain
opposite. He says, 'Unless you are dead to the law you cannot
and do not live unto God.' 'Why Paul, this seems plain contrary
to natural reasoning, and to what many think the word of God
teaches? Are you not here setting at nought the holy law of God?
Are you saying that man is delivered from that law and that it has
no more dominion over him?' Yes, that is what Paul is saying.
Unless we are dead to the law we cannot and do not live unto
God. Being dead to the law means being brought out from under
its curse and its whole dominion, so that it has nothing more to
do with me. Unless we are brought here, says Paul, then we do
not live to God.

But oh, how alarming is such teaching to many in a profession
of religion. Ah, this is a most profound statement of Paul's. I
repeat, it goes plain contrary to what is commonly taught, that
unless you live unto the law then you are dead to God. But no.
Paul says we must be dead to the law. That is, we must be brought
from under its dominion and into a position where it has nothing
to say to us and cannot condemn us because its demands are no
longer required of us. Otherwise we cannot and do not live to
God. Now that is a strong statement indeed, but I believe it is the
teaching of the word of God and the glorious substance of the
gospel. I do not want us to be in any doubt as to what being dead
to the law really means.

"I through the law am dead to the law." How can that be? How
have I died to the law and the law to me, so as to be brought from
under all its curse, condemnation and its every demand? He says:
"I am crucified with Christ: nevertheless I live; yet not I, but
Christ liveth in me: and the life which I now live in the flesh I
live by the faith of the Son of God, who loved me, and gave
himself for me." Paul is saying, 'I through the law am dead to the
law, through the body of Christ, through what the Lord Jesus is
and has done for me, when he suffered on the cross at Calvery,
for I was crucified there with him.' This is true of each and every
believer, the whole elect of God. Why, they were not only
identified with Jesus Christ, they were one with him, so that in
his sufferings and death are *their* sufferings and death. Therein

all the demands of the holy law of God were fully met for them by him who is their glorious surety.

If through grace I am a believer in Jesus Christ, what has the law to say to me? True, in myself I am a sinner, I am a transgressor. Yet Paul reminds us in his epistle to the Romans of what David writes, "Blessed is he whose transgression is forgiven, whose sin is covered. Blessed is the man unto whom the Lord imputeth not iniquity, and in whose spirit there is no guile" (Ps. 32:1-2). What does that speak of? It speaks of a full free forgiveness of every sin. What has the law left to say to me, a believer in Jesus Christ? Friends, it has nothing to say, for he who is my surety has met all that divine justice requires of me on account of all my manifold transgressions. In his sufferings and death upon the cross he has paid the price that divine justice required, and thereby I am delivered from the law. And what's more, as Paul goes on gloriously to set forth, I am not only delivered from the law! I, a sinner, also have imputed to me a righteousness which meets with full acceptance before God, a righteousness which is in essence the very obedience of the Lord Jesus Christ. Oh, the perfection of that righteousness which is mine by grace through faith in Jesus Christ! That righteousness can never be sullied by sin, for it is the perfect righteousness of Jesus Christ. "I through the law am dead to the law, that I might live unto God." The point here then is that it is only when we are dead to the law through the body of Christ that we live unto God. And the fruits of that new spiritual life in Christ Jesus are truly seen in the hearts and lives of the living family of God.

He says, "I am crucified with Christ: nevertheless I live; yet not I, but Christ liveth in me: and the life which I now live in the flesh I live by the faith of the Son of God, who loved me, and gave himself for me." We see here the vital union of the believer with the Lord Jesus Christ. He and they are one. What a blessed union to be one with him! Oh, the wonder of his love and grace revealed here! May the blessedness of this be truly yours and mine, so that we are enabled to say with Paul, "Who loved me, and gave himself for me." What a wonderful truth is this. Oh, to know its power and the gracious sanctifying influence of it. How this will lay us low at the Saviour's feet. This will bring us to the position of the hymnwriter:

"Self-renouncing, grace admiring,
   Made unto salvation wise."

"I do not frustrate the grace of God," says Paul, "for if righteousness come by the law, then Christ is dead in vain."

But I will leave the remarks there this evening. May the Lord add his blessing. Amen.

10

GALATIANS 3:1-2

O foolish Galatians, who hath bewitched you, that ye should not obey the truth, before whose eyes Jesus Christ hath been evidently set forth, crucified among you? This only would I learn of you, Received ye the Spirit by the works of the law, or by the hearing of faith?

Over the past weeks on Friday evenings we have been considering this epistle to the Galatians. I would just remind you of its main theme for which the apostle so faithfully and zealously contends. As I have said on previous occasions it is not some secondary matter that is here in view. These things are essential for the glory of God and for the salvation of his people. The apostle contends for the vitally important foundation truths of the Christian religion. The apostle was only too well aware of the plausible ministry of those who had come among the churches at Galatia, teaching things that were undermining the truth as it is in Jesus. Sadly and solemnly, this teaching had tended to draw the believers away from salvation alone by faith in the Lord and Saviour Jesus Christ.

I would just make this point in leading up to the words before us this evening. How active in the early church was Satan, the enemy of souls. Not only did he often oppose the true church by outward persecution, as the apostle himself experienced many times, but he was active also in seeking to sow the seeds of error where the truth had been preached. He was active in promoting those things that were detrimental to the honour and glory of the Lord Jesus Christ and the true spiritual welfare of the living family of God. Let us not forget that the character of Satan, the great enemy of souls, has not changed. His opposition to the truth is no less than it has ever been. And remember that he is most dangerous to the church and people of Jesus Christ when he comes as an angel of light, promoting things which, though so close to the truth, are deadly errors and plain contrary to the truth as it is in Jesus. If we pay attention to what the new testament scriptures bring before us in Paul's epistles and in the Acts of the Apostles, we find that Satan was not active in this way among the churches of Galatia only. In other places where the gospel had been preached and made effectual in the hearts and lives of men and women, Satan was not far behind in sowing the seeds of error. He is always the same. Does not the child of God prove in his own life and experience that as surely as God works graciously the devil seeks to work maliciously? But oh, what a mercy it is that he can never overturn the foundation of God. He can never frustrate the work of God's grace in the hearts and lives of his people. The encouragement of the people of God is in what Paul himself testifies in his epistle to Timothy: "Nevertheless the foundation of God standeth sure, having this seal, The Lord knoweth them that are his" (2 Tim. 2:19).

We find throughout the epistle that the apostle is not only contending against the grievous errors being promoted among the churches in Galatia but he is setting forth the truth. And is not this the most effectual way to contend against error? Friends, we are not just to protest against error. The essence of right contention against error is the promotion of the truths of our most holy faith, even the wonders of redeeming love and grace centred in the person and work of the Lord Jesus Christ.

I would just remind you again what the error was that the apostle so contends against in this epistle. They were saying that faith in Jesus Christ was necessary for salvation but so also was the keeping of the law of Moses. To be saved, men and women must not only believe in Jesus Christ but also keep the law. These things were very plausible. Many were drawn aside by them. We see the subtle influences of this teaching in many aspects of the Christian world today. Paul however is setting forth that these two things must never be joined together in the matter of salvation for the sinner. Salvation is by grace through faith and that not of ourselves, "it is the gift of God: not of works lest any man should boast" (Eph. 2:8-9). Paul is saying that to teach it is necessary for the sinner to keep the law of Moses to be justified before God, is to deny the necessity of the sufferings, death and resurrection of the Lord Jesus Christ.

Look at what is brought out in the last verse of the second chapter. He says, "I do not frustrate the grace of God: for if righteousness come by the law, then Christ is dead in vain." What a solemn point is set forth in that statement of Paul. Was this being promoted by those false teachers in Galatia? Were they in effect denying the necessity of the person and offering of the Lord Jesus Christ? I am sure they would have vigorously denied such an accusation. But that was the solemn implication of their teaching. What does he mean by that statement, "if righteousness come by the law?" The righteousness of which Paul speaks justifies the sinner before God, so that he finds acceptance with God. Now he says, if that righteousness is obtained by the works of the law, then "Christ is dead in vain." If the sinner is able to render to the holy law of God that which it rightly and justly demands, where is the need of the sufferings, death and offering of the Lord and Saviour Jesus Christ? We see how incompatible these two things are. Yet in effect these false teachers at Galatia were saying that what Christ had done was not of itself sufficient to save the soul. If we are to be saved then we must keep the law of Moses. True, they would not advocate that the law could be kept perfectly, but the best endeavours must be made to keep it. Was not this to mingle things that should never be mingled? Do not these things cancel one another out? The great point is this: we are either saved by grace alone or we are not saved at all. It is either Jesus Christ, of God "made unto us, wisdom, and righteousness, and sanctification and redemption" (1 Cor. 1:30) or else we "sink in ruin, guilt, and thrall."

This teaching in Galatia neither gave honour and glory to God, nor met the deep needs of a guilty sinner. It did not honour God. Why? Because they were in effect saying that a holy God would be satisfied with a partial obedience to his law. Now that can never be so. How can a holy God be satisfied with that which only partially meets his holy and just demands, as set forth in the law of Moses? That law demands perfection. Paul says here, "Cursed is every one that continueth not in *all* things which are written in the book of the law to do them." I say their teaching did not honour God. It neither gave him the glory nor met the deep needs of the sinner.

Is there anything more unkind than to direct the sinner to do those things for life which are utterly impossible for him to do? Oh what is more cruel than to say that certain things are to be done by him if he is to obtain the favour of God? He himself knows, as taught by the Holy Spirit, that he is utterly incapable of rendering such obedience. It is like telling an utterly bankrupt man that he must pay his debts before his bankruptcy can be discharged. He well knows that! But he cannot pay that debt. It is utterly impossible for him to do so. What good news is such teaching to the debtor? Likewise, it is no good news to tell the sinner that he must keep the law of Moses if he is to be saved and obtain the favour of God. How plain contrary was such teaching to what is contained in the glorious gospel of God's grace. *That* is truly good news from heaven. It is the proclamation of saving grace and mercy. It does not make known what men and women have to do to be saved, but what God in Christ has done, the fulness and freeness of the salvation that is found in Jesus Christ.

Is not one of the most precious notes the gospel trumpet sounds found in the words we read in the Revelation? "Whosoever will, let him take the water of life freely" (Rev. 22:17). Ah, I say no sweeter or more precious note does the gospel trumpet sound. Oh, the blessedness of it to the guilty, the needy, the bankrupt sinner. How blessed is this to the men and women who have nothing of their own to bring, who are conscious of the demands of the holy law of God, and who hunger and thirst after righteousness. Oh, the wonders of grace. "Whosoever will, let him take the water of life freely." Friends, look through the gospel record at the manifestation of divine truth as it centres in the person and work of the Lord Jesus Christ. Take every invitation of the gospel. How the fulness and freeness of grace is set forth. It is not according to man's deserts. It is the word of God addressed to the guilty, needy and burdened soul, and it sets forth the wonders of divine grace in meeting the sinner's deepest need. The hymn writer well illustrates the point:

"The vilest sinner out of hell,
Who lives to feel his need,
Is welcome to a Throne of Grace,
The Saviour's blood to plead."

Paul says, "If righteousness come by the law, then Christ is dead in vain." What a solemn thing it is to imply that there was no necessity for the death of the Lord Jesus Christ. We might say, is not the denial of the necessity of the death of the Lord Jesus Christ one of the highest forms of blasphemy? I say, this teaching in the churches of Galatia neither honoured God, nor met the needs of a sinner. And solemnly, it came under the condemnation of a holy God. Paul sets forth this fact in the opening chapter when he says, "But though we, or an angel from heaven, preach any other gospel unto you than that which we have preached unto you, let him be accursed. As we said before, so say I now again, If any man preach any other gospel unto you than that ye have received, let him be accursed."

He turns here then to these Galatians and says, "O foolish Galatians, who hath bewitched you, that ye should not obey the truth, before whose eyes Jesus Christ hath been evidently set forth, crucified among you?" Well may he call them *foolish Galatians*, they having been drawn aside by the teaching of these who are described as false apostles. After the truth had been so evidently set before them in faithfulness and love, and after they had been brought to hear and receive that truth, they had now been drawn aside from it. Oh, what folly is here. Well may the apostle address them as foolish Galatians.

Let us pause here a moment in consideration of this. Indeed, the Galatians were foolish to give ear to these false apostles. They were foolish to be drawn aside from the truth as it is in Christ Jesus. But have we ourselves anything to glory in over them? Left to ourselves have we less tendency to be drawn aside from the truth as it is in Jesus? May these things be laid well to heart. As Paul wrote in his epistle to the Corinthians, "Let him that thinketh he standeth take heed lest he fall" (1 Cor. 10:12). Let not one of us glory in our own supposed superior knowledge or in any supposed ability of ourselves to cleave to the truth and never be moved away from it. You know, there is one thing that the Lord teaches his people. It is their complete dependence on himself. Oh, that we may realise this truth day by day. Let us "be not high-minded, but fear" (Rom. 11:20). May we be kept in the filial fear of his great and holy name.

Remember the language of the psalmist. Was not his cry, "Hold thou me up and I shall be safe" (Ps. 119:117). What were the words of the Lord Jesus to his own disciples in the garden of Gethsemane? He said, "Watch and pray, that ye enter not into temptation" (Matt. 26:41). May we have the grace which keeps us in all humbleness of mind at the feet of the Lord Jesus Christ, spoiled of our own wisdom. May our concern and desire be that he would lead us in his truth and teach us, and that he would uphold and keep us by his power. Did not the Lord Jesus also teach his disciples to pray, "lead us not into temptation, but deliver us from evil" (Matt. 6:13). May that be our prayer. Yes, in what Paul says here, "O foolish Galatians," there is warning and exhortation still for the church and people of God. Let us "be not high-minded, but fear."

"O foolish Galatians, who hath bewitched you?" Yes indeed, they had been bewitched by the subtle workings of the enemy of souls, who so plausibly presented deadly error among them under the semblance of truth. "Who hath bewitched you?" Truly the apostle was well aware that it was the subtle workings and deceptions of the enemy that had so affected them. Not only may *we* heed the warning not to be high-minded, but may we daily seek grace to have more of the spirit of the Bereans of whom we read in the Acts of the Apostles. We are told that they searched the scriptures to ascertain whether the preaching of *even the apostles* was truth. Friends, we are not directed here to be of a critical spirit but we are directed to take heed that we do not receive everything we hear merely on its surface appearance. May we be men and women of prayer who truly search the scriptures, not relying on our own natural wisdom and understanding, but seeking to be guided and enlightened by God the Holy Spirit.

He says, "Who hath bewitched you, that ye should not obey

the truth, before whose eyes Jesus Christ hath been evidently set forth, crucified among you?" We are reminded here of how great had been the privileges of these Galatian churches. The truth had been preached among them, even by the apostle himself, in all the glory and fulness of the gospel. They were without excuse in being drawn aside by the false teachers. The truth had been clearly set forth in such a way that Paul could say, "before whose eyes Jesus Christ hath been evidently set forth, crucified among you." What was the great theme on which he dwelt in his preaching and ministry? He emphasises it here as he did in his epistle to the Corinthians when he said, "I, brethren, when I came to you, came not with excellency of speech or of wisdom, declaring unto you the testimony of God. For I determined not to know any thing among you, save Jesus Christ, and him crucified" (1 Cor. 2:1-2)). The great theme of the cross of Jesus Christ was central to the preaching and teaching of the apostle. What did he mean by the cross of Jesus Christ, and Jesus Christ being crucified among them? What was the essential doctrine which was so central to the gospel that he preached? It was the great atonement that the Lord Jesus Christ had made. Should not this ever be the central theme of the gospel *we* preach, as it was with Paul? Herein is the glory of God's grace revealed and is there anything other than the gospel of Jesus Christ and him crucified to meet the deep needs of the sinner.

This is wonderfully opened up in those words of Isaiah. You remember Philip meeting the Ethiopian eunuch as directed by the Spirit of God. Philip found him reading out of the fifty-third chapter of the prophecy of Isaiah. The eunuch asks him, "Of whom speaketh the prophet this? Of himself, or of some other man? Then Philip opened his mouth, and began at the same scripture, and preached unto him Jesus" (Acts 8:34-35). That scripture sets forth Jesus as "he was wounded for our transgressions, he was bruised for our iniquities: the chastisement of our peace was upon him; and with his stripes we are healed" (Isa. 53:5). The prophet goes on to say, "All we like sheep have gone astray; we have turned every one to his own way; and the Lord hath laid on him the iniquity of us all." The central theme of the gospel is Jesus Christ and him crucified. It is the glorious reality of his atoning work. It is that "Christ is the end of the law for righteousness to every one that believeth" (Rom. 10:4), and that all the guilty, needy sinner requires is richly treasured up in Jesus Christ. For, as John writes in his epistle, "The blood of Jesus Christ his Son cleanseth us from all sin" (1 John 1:7).

Now these things had been evidently set forth among them. They had been clearly shown that as they were sinners, there was no acceptance for them before God but by grace through faith in Jesus Christ. This faith was the very gift of God by which they were brought to trust in Jesus alone for salvation. And in this third chapter, Paul also brings out the important truth that this faith is bound up with the promise of God. God had revealed this salvation from the time of man's fall. Throughout the entire old testament period these things were manifest, but they were fully revealed in the new testament in the person and work of the Lord Jesus Christ.

Paul puts to them the question in this second verse. "This only would I learn of you, Received ye the Spirit by the works of the law, or by the hearing of faith?" Now when he speaks of the Spirit here, he is speaking of the Holy Spirit. We need to look at this in the context of the Acts of the Apostles. On the day of Pentecost, the Holy Spirit was poured out upon the disciples. Also afterwards when Peter first preached to the Gentiles in the house of Cornelius, the Holy Spirit fell on them as he had on the disciples at the beginning. There is reference in these words of Paul to those first manifestations of the gift of the Holy Spirit to the Gentile church.

But he does not only refer to the gift of the Holy Spirit in the working of miracles. He refers to their receiving the Spirit as the power of the Holy Spirit accompanied the gospel preached, opening their blind eyes, bringing them from death in sins, to spiritual life. And this was evidenced in their repentance and faith in the Lord Jesus. Now, Paul says, was this "by the works of the law, or by the hearing of faith?" Were these great and precious blessings of gospel grace, of pardoning love and redeeming mercy, made known by the works of the law or by the hearing of faith?

The point is this. Did they receive these things because they deserved them, because they had attempted to keep what the holy law of God required? Surely friends, this question could be plainly answered from the experience of the Galatians and can be answered out of the experience of each one of the Lord's people. Does the blessing of gospel grace come to us because we deserve it, because we have earned and merited it, because we have striven after it in our own strength, because we have endeavoured to keep the holy law of God? No, the wonder of gospel grace is that it comes wholly undeserved, wholly unlooked for, by those who receive it. Gospel grace is the manifestation of the free and undeserved love and favour of God towards poor sinners.

It was so with these Galatians. What had they had to do with the law of Moses? They had never been under that law in the same way as the Jews. Yet truly the demands of that holy law of God were binding on them. They were found under its curse and condemnation. But they could never trace any of the manifestations of saving grace and mercy experienced by them, to any supposed keeping of the law. Paul says, "This only would I learn of you, Received ye the spirit by the works of the law, or by the hearing of faith?" This is an important question he asks. The answer is plain. That which they had received was entirely the work of the Spirit in regenerating grace, in pardoning love, and in the manifestation of the mercy of God to their souls. This was all of grace from beginning to end. And as it was with them, so it is with his people still. All that they have, they have as a result of God's grace. All the blessings they receive are not according to their deserts, but according to the manifestation of his sovereign purposes of love and mercy towards them. Therefore all the praise for these things belongs to God and not the creature. "Are ye so foolish? having begun in the Spirit, are ye now made perfect by the flesh?" But we will leave that verse to the next occasion, subject to the Lord's will.

May he add his blessing. Amen.

11

MATTHEW 5:20

For I say unto you, That except your righteousness shall exceed the righteousness of the scribes and Pharisees, ye shall in no case enter into the kingdom of heaven.

On recent Friday evenings we have been considering Paul's epistle to the Galatians, and last week we looked at the opening verses of chapter three. In the fifth, sixth and seventh chapters of Matthew, we find that the Lord Jesus deals with the very things that Paul sets forth in his epistle to the Galatians. I believe that the approach of many to this sermon of our Lord does not do justice to what he is actually setting forth. It is so with this verse that I have read by way of a text. But I want to make some general remarks on this fifth chapter of Matthew this evening. It may be, if the Lord will, that I shall continue with certain aspects of this passage on the coming Lord's day.

Let us look then at what we have read in this fifth chapter in particular. This discourse of the Lord Jesus is commonly called the sermon on the mount. Obviously, this is because we read, "And seeing the multitudes, he went up into a mountain: and when he was set, his disciples came unto him: and he opened his mouth and taught them." We may well say, oh what words of truth and grace proceeded from his lips! It could well be said, "Never man spake like this man" (John 7:46). What an opening up of the truth did the Lord Jesus give here in the presence of his disciples! We find him discoursing on the holy law that God had given to Israel by his servant Moses. We find him setting the law in its right and proper place and opening up its solemn implications. For the most part, the Jews had lost the right understanding of the law. The scribes and Pharisees professed, not only to know the law that God had given to Israel by his servant Moses, but to be experts in the interpretation of that law. Yet it had become only too obvious that they had completely lost sight of the essential meaning of the law. Interpretations that the Jews had put on the law down the generations to the very days of the Lord Jesus meant that they were mainly teaching for doctrine the traditions of men. The spiritual truths set forth in God's law had been almost wholly lost sight of. Now it is with those things that the Lord Jesus deals in this sermon on the mount.

Let us just glance at the opening of the Lord's sermon here. It begins with that word, *Blessed*. We find that word repeated throughout the next few verses. Oh let us not overlook this important truth. Is not *blessing* the very essence of the ministry of our Lord Jesus Christ? He brings blessings to sinful men and women, the revelation of God's grace and mercy. As John records, "The law was given by Moses, but grace and truth came by Jesus Christ" (John 1:17). It is not insignificant that even at the very beginning of the Lord's public ministry there is the essential note of blessing. Likewise, the last recorded act of our Lord Jesus Christ on the day when he ascended into heaven was the same. "He led them out as far as to Bethany, and he lifted up his hands, and blessed them. And it came to pass, while he blessed them, he was parted from them, and carried up into heaven" (Luke 24:50-51). Oh the significance of that act of our Lord Jesus. It was the blessing of sinners, and has he not been blessing sinners ever since?

Let us look a little closer at these opening verses called the beatitudes. "Blessed are the poor in spirit: for theirs is the kingdom of heaven. Blessed are they that mourn... Blessed are the meek... Blessed are they which do hunger and thirst after righteousness... Blessed are the merciful... Blessed are the pure in heart... Blessed are the peacemakers... Blessed are they which are persecuted for righteousness' sake." To whom do these blessings refer? Where are these people that are so blessed? Can we say that the things set forth in these verses are the essential traits of human nature? Are these things found in men and women, boys and girls, of themselves? This is an important point to notice. Do not we have to sadly and solemnly conclude that such characters as described by the Lord Jesus here, are never found among men and women of themselves? The traits brought out here are certainly not the characteristics of sinful, fallen human nature. Do men produce these things of themselves? Men may at times have a resemblance to what the Lord Jesus is saying here. But I state categorically that what the Lord describes here is not true of men and women as they are in an unregenerate condition. These characteristics are never brought forth by men and women of themselves. No, because as a result of the fall we are all sinners, not only by original sin, but by our own actual transgressions. The native tendency of our hearts and minds is the very opposite of what is set forth in these verses.

It is essential to recognise that the Lord is speaking here of those that are born again. And blessed indeed are they, for they know the great blessing of regeneration. Through his almighty grace they are made alive to God, partakers of the new birth, partakers of the divine nature. I say, the characteristics set before us here are the effect of grace. They are not evidenced in man by nature but in men and women as born again and taught of the Spirit of God.

It is not insignificant what the Lord Jesus said to Nicodemus who was a ruler of the Jews, one of the masters in Israel and one who professed to understand the old testament scriptures. He came to the Lord Jesus on that occasion when it was night. He sought a secret interview with him, not willing that his coming to Jesus should be publicly known. Yet no doubt he came there with a sincere desire to find out more concerning this one, Jesus of Nazareth, whose words he had heard and whose works he had seen. He acknowledges as he comes to the Lord Jesus, "Rabbi, we know that thou art a teacher come from God: for no man can do these miracles that thou doest, except God be with him" (John 3:2). How utterly beyond anything he could have thought or imagined was the answer the Lord Jesus gave to him, "Except a man be born again, he cannot see the kingdom of God." Ah, there is no entering into or even understanding what the Lord Jesus had to say, apart from the sovereign grace of God in the new birth. I do not want to go into that subject so much this evening. How utterly inconceivable to Nicodemus were the things the Lord spoke there, but how true, how vital and essential!

I say then that the characteristics the Lord brings out in the beatitudes, are the fruit of the new birth, by the sovereign working, leading and teaching of God the Holy Spirit. How much harm and damage is done when men advocate the characteristics and principles here as if they are within the reach of men and women of themselves. If they only strive to live according to the pattern the Lord Jesus gives here, things would be much better for them and for mankind. I say, how much harm is done when the beatitudes and the other things the Lord has to say in this sermon, are advocated in such a way! It is advocating that which is impossible to be realised by men and women of themselves. We might just as well expect a dead body to rise up at our word and do acts which only a living person can do, as to expect those who are dead in trespasses and sins to act in accordance with the spiritual principles of God's word. No, the Lord here sets out the wonders of sovereign, distinguishing grace, the blessed work of God the Holy Spirit in the hearts and lives of sinful men and women. Blessed indeed are they that know these things through sovereign grace!

Let me come closer to this verse that I have read as a text. The Lord here, particularly in verse 17, makes an essential statement. He says, "Think not that I am come to destroy the law, or the prophets: I am not come to destroy, but to fulfil. For verily I say unto you, Till heaven and earth pass, one jot or one tittle shall in no wise pass from the law, till all be fulfilled." The Lord Jesus did not come to deny what Moses had taught as it had been revealed to Moses by God. The Lord Jesus did not come to overturn what the prophets had preached and advocated. No, indeed not. He did not come to set aside the holy law of God. He did not come to say that the law had no longer anything to speak to sinful men and women. Far from it. In this sermon the Lord clearly and distinctly upholds the veracity of the holy law of God and gives it its due place in the lives of men and women. He emphatically shows our accountability to the holy law that God has given. Oh there is no question here of the claims of the law being set aside as no longer binding on sinful men and women.

But the Lord frees the law from the false interpretations the Jews had given and which the scribes and Pharisees taught. We do not deny that the holy law of God features prominently in the ministry of the Lord Jesus Christ. Paul advocated the same. In his epistle to Timothy he says, "The law is good, if a man use it lawfully" (1 Tim. 1:8). He was contending there against the wrong use of the law. As he says elsewhere, "The law is holy, and the commandment holy, and just, and good" (Rom. 7:12). Nowhere are its holy and righteous claims on mankind denied in the word of God. The ministry of the Lord Jesus Christ was not intended to overturn that law or to set it aside. He says, "I am not come to destroy, *but to fulfil.*" That is the keynote the Lord Jesus has to sound in this sermon. He upholds the law. He rightly advocates its just claims. Oh, what honour he put on the law. How he vindicates that law! In what way? By denying it, by setting it aside? No indeed not, but *by fulfilling it himself*. That, I say, is the keynote.

Remember that the Lord Jesus was "holy, harmless, undefiled, separate from sinners" (Heb. 7:26). Paul tells us, "the law is not made for a righteous man, but for the lawless and disobedient, for the ungodly and for sinners" (1 Tim 1:9). As one who was holy, righteous and true, he was not in that sense under the law. But the wonders of divine grace in the person and work of the Lord Jesus are seen in that he himself, as he came into this world, voluntarily came into that place of being under the law. He was "made of a woman, made under the law" (Gal. 4:4). To what end? That he might fulfil that law, vindicate it wholly, and meet all its just and due demands. For whom? For himself? No, for he was no sinner. He was the holy, harmless, undefiled, beloved Son of God. No, he came to fulfil that law, to vindicate it and meet all its just demands, as the surety of his people, the great mediator between God and man. Never lose sight of the fact that the Lord Jesus Christ is not only the head of the church but he is the representative of his people. As the scriptures speak of it, he is the surety of his people. This is central to the new testament revelation, indeed to all that God has revealed. What they could not do, being sinners, Christ himself has done for them in their stead as their representative and surety.

Ah, see how this is shown to us in the holy scriptures. A very real illustration of this is given in the book of Ruth. You are all familiar with the account of Ruth and Boaz. We see that Boaz acts the part of what is termed a *near kinsman* to Ruth. God had made provision in the administration of the affairs of Israel that the land of Canaan was divided to the tribes by lot. But also, within the tribes, every family had its portion of the land that was to be their inheritance for ever. It was not to pass out of the family. The inheritance was not to be sold but it could be mortgaged if the family fell on hard times. In the year of jubilee it had to be returned freely to its original owners. There was also the provision that one who was a near relative might redeem the land for them. In the case of Ruth and Naomi, their husbands had died. They were widows. In a situation such as that, there was provision for a near kinsman to take the widow and marry her himself and raise up children unto his brother. In doing so, he took on the whole responsibility for that widow. He took on all the debts that had accrued and gave satisfaction for those things. He redeemed the inheritance in that way.

Oh what an illustration is that of the glorious reality of what God has provided in the person and work of the Lord Jesus! Yes, all that God had chosen and given to the Lord Jesus in the covenant ordered in all things and sure from before the foundation of the world, have forfeited every right through the ruin of the fall. They come under the curse and condemnation of God's holy law. There is no exception to this. Therefore the law holds them liable. As they are transgressors and cannot meet the law's demands, they are under its curse. But in the manifestation of God's saving grace and mercy, Jesus Christ is revealed as their great kinsman redeemer. He is the one who, as Paul tells us in his epistle to the Hebrews, "took not on him the nature of angels; but he took on him the seed of Abraham" (Heb. 2:16). He is truly bone of our bones, flesh of our flesh (Eph 5:30), God manifest in the flesh (1 Tim. 3:16), that he might redeem his people "from the curse of the law, being [himself] made a curse for us" (Gal. 3:13).

Jesus says, "Think not that I am come to destroy the law, or the prophets; I am not come to destroy, but to fulfil." For, he says, "Till heaven and earth pass, one jot or one tittle," that is, the least particle, "shall in no wise pass from the law, till all be fulfilled." And the glory of God's grace revealed in the gospel is that "Christ is the end of the law for righteousness to everyone that believeth" (Rom. 10:4). He has fulfilled the law for his people and satisfied its just demands. He has brought in a perfect obedience to the law. It is described as the very "righteousness of God" (Rom. 1:17) which is fully and freely made over to each one that is truly brought through grace to repentance and saving faith in the Lord Jesus Christ. So then, though each one of his people is a sinner, yet what do they find through grace, as brought to repentance and faith? Not only are they made alive to God, but they receive a righteousness that is a perfect obedience to the holy law of God, in which alone they are accepted before him. The penalty that was due for their sin has been paid by the Lord Jesus Christ. Truly, of themselves they are debtors, but Christ has set them free from the debt. He has paid it all, and his obedience is that which avails for them.

So then, what has the holy law of God to say to the believer in Jesus Christ? It has nothing to say to him. Why? Because though it is true that they are sinners in themselves, yet the claims of that law are met in Jesus Christ. The apostle, under the inspiration of the Holy Spirit, puts it so clearly and wonderfully in his epistle to the Romans when he says, "Who shall lay anything to the charge of God's elect?" (Rom. 8:33)." What a statement is that! What a challenge is that! That is, who shall bring accusations against them which can be proved true and they be thereby condemned? Ah friends, are there not many things that are charged against them, and this often known in the conscience of a child of God? But there is an answer to those things, which fully meets every accusation that might be made,

"My Saviour's obedience and blood
Hide all my transgressions from view."

I believe the words of that hymn do not put it strongly enough. It is not that they are hidden from view. They are so totally covered and atoned for that they can never again be raised in condemnation of the believer as found in Christ Jesus.

Christ said he came not to destroy the law, not even the least particle of the law, but he came to fulfil it. He further says, "Whosoever therefore shall break one of these least commandments, and shall teach men so, he shall be called the least in the kingdom of heaven: but whosoever shall do and teach them, the same shall be called great in the kingdom of heaven." Friends, I believe the essential truth brought out in these words is what I have already said. Jesus nowhere advocates that the law of God is set aside or that its just claims must not be duly met. Those that teach such things do not teach according to the revelation that is given us in God's word.

The Lord then makes this profound statement, "For I say unto you, That except your righteousness shall exceed the righteousness of the scribes and Pharisees, ye shall in no case enter into the kingdom of heaven." Now this verse raises an important question with respect to what follows in this fifth chapter of Matthew. Is the Lord Jesus Christ, in opening up the holiness and the spirituality of the law of God, saying that here is the pattern to which people's lives must be wholly conformed if they are to be found righteous in God's sight? This is the way in which many take them. And in one sense that is true. He is showing that our righteousness must exceed the righteousness of the scribes and Pharisees. Now bear in mind that the righteousness of the scribes and Pharisees appeared to be real sanctity. They appeared to be holy people. They conformed in many respects, certainly outwardly, to what seemed to be the requirements of the law. Appearing as very religious people with all this outward conformity, surely such as these would be accepted before God? But Jesus is saying in effect that the righteousness of the scribes and Pharisees is no righteousness at all. It is of no avail before a holy righteous God. Something far better, far more than that is required. Friends, may we never be left to rest short of the righteousness the Lord Jesus Christ advocates here. "Except your righteousness shall exceed the righteousness of the scribes and Pharisees." It is not outward conformity, not even the most sincere attempt to obtain a right-eousness, that is here advocated.

Notice what the holy law of God requires, and Jesus in no way contradicts it. It requires perfection. It will be satisfied with nothing else. In heart, in lip, and in life, it requires perfection, a perfect conformity to the holy law of God. Now is not that a solemn truth? Indeed it is. What is the emphasis of the Lord Jesus here? Is he advocating that sinful men and women can of themselves reach that degree of perfection? Is he setting forth here the way in which men and women are to go to obtain the perfection that the law of God requires? This is the essential point. So many in expounding this sermon on the mount, say that here is the way that the Lord Jesus tells us to go. Here is the pattern he sets forth. We must strive for this perfect conformity in heart, in lip and in life, to God's holy law. True, we must have that perfect conformity, but is the Lord Jesus advocating that this can be obtained by men of themselves or even obtained by his help in these things? I do not believe he is doing so. The Lord Jesus sets before us here the holiness and spirituality of the law.

See that it is not merely outward conformity that is required, as the scribes and Pharisees believed. It extends to the innermost thoughts. Transgression of the law is not only in the outward act but in the very thoughts and intents of the heart also. Is there one of us that has not sinned in thought as well as in word and deed? Not one. Oh we may well tremble before the perfection of that law as the Lord Jesus brings it out here in its spiritual nature, showing how binding it is upon us. Can we ourselves find a way of life and deliverance in these things. Did Jesus advocate the law as such? I believe he sets forth the holiness and spirituality of the law to show that "by the works of the law shall no flesh be justified" (Gal. 2:16). These things brought home to the heart by the Holy Spirit, bring us into real conviction of sin and to see the hopelessness and helplessness of our condition. They show us the solemn reality that we are in a lost and utterly ruined state. But as our ruin is set forth by the law, showing us the impossibility of this being a way of life for the sinner and convincing us of our sin, Jesus sets forth the wonders of redeeming love and grace. Yes, Jesus Christ is set forth as the Saviour and the friend of lost, ruined sinners.

He says, "Think not that I am come to destroy the law I am not come to destroy, but *to fulfil.*" "For the son of man is come to seek and to save that which was lost" (Luke 19:10). Oh there were those among the scribes and Pharisees that were greatly offended at the Lord Jesus. They said, "This man receiveth sinners, and eateth with them" (Luke 15:2). What offended them is what still offends scribes and Pharisees, for the very leaven or, as the Lord meant, the doctrine of the scribes and Pharisees is no different today than it was in the days of the Lord Jesus. The truth of God's grace and the sovereign freeness of that grace is still offensive to men, particularly to those dead in a profession of religion. But he said that he came, "to seek and to save that which was lost" (Luke 19:10). He certainly never denied that he dined with publicans and sinners but rather goes on to wonderfully illustrate the reality of the grace, mercy and love of God, as revealed in his person and finished work.

But I'll leave the remarks there this evening. May the Lord add his blessing. Amen.

12

GALATIANS 3:6-9

Even as Abraham believed God, and it was accounted to him for righteousness. Know ye therefore that they which are of faith, the same are the children of Abraham. And the scripture, foreseeing that God would justify the heathen through faith, preached before the gospel unto Abraham, saying, In thee shall all nations be blessed. So then they which be of faith are blessed with faithful Abraham.

Last Friday evening I directed your attention to Matthew chapter 5 and particularly verse 20. There we read the words of the Lord Jesus, "Except your righteousness shall exceed the righteousness of the scribes and Pharisees, ye shall in no case enter into the kingdom of heaven." In his epistle to the Galatians the apostle opens up this teaching of the Lord Jesus. We find here that the apostle is contending for the righteousness which exceeds the righteousness of the scribes and Pharisees. And he shows that this righteousness is not by works but by faith. It is the gift of God. It is the imputation of the righteousness of Jesus Christ to the believer.

Now let us just notice this point in passing. What are we to understand by righteousness? We often use these terms. They are scriptural terms without question. But I think it is necessary for us to pause at times and consider and remind ourselves again what is meant by terms such as righteousness and the imputation of righteousness. Well, essentially righteousness is the state of acceptance in the sight of God. It is a condition that expresses one being right with God, being free from all the guilt and defilement of sin. It is not only a condition of deliverance from sin but it is the possession of a positive obedience to all that a holy and righteous God requires. That in essence is righteousness. Being righteous, we are not only acceptable before God but he dwells with us in deed and in truth.

Now the great point has always been, how can men and women that are sinners be just with God and righteous in his sight? The holy scriptures which deal with this point declare that nothing unclean, nothing sinful, can ever stand in his presence with acceptance. How then are sinful men and women to be made righteous? Is it by works or is it by faith? This is the great question. Is it by what we can do in striving to attain to a state of righteousness or is it freely and fully given? Now, as Paul contends in this epistle, it is not by works that we have done that we ever attain to a position of acceptance in God's sight or come into possession of a perfect obedience to what a holy God requires.

It is upon this very matter that he here introduces the case of Abraham who in holy scripture holds a very prominent place, always being considered as the father of the faithful. Paul shows that Abraham was not justified by works. He was not accounted righteous before God on the ground of doing, but upon the ground of believing. This righteousness which alone justifies the sinner before God is the righteousness of faith. It is that which we receive, which we do not earn. It is the righteousness of Jesus Christ, *his* positive obedience to the law, *his* holy life, that which *he* has done. This is received by faith and graciously imputed to us. Imputation means that what Jesus Christ has done is accounted ours by God, and that our sins are accounted to Jesus. When brought by grace to saving faith in the Lord Jesus Christ, what justifies me as a sinner before God, the whole ground of my acceptance, is not what I have done, nor what I can ever strive to attain. It is what God in Christ has done and in the riches of his grace imputes to me. My sins are charged upon Jesus Christ who has borne the curse and the punishment for those sins himself, redeeming his people from the curse, being made a curse for them.

Now I want to open up these things a little further in the light

of these verses before us. Let us not overlook the main matter
being dealt with in this epistle to the Galatians. Paul emphatically
states that these false teachers, these false apostles who had come
among them, were preaching things wholly contrary to the gospel
he had preached to them, wholly contrary to the truth as it is in
Christ Jesus. They were advocating salvation by works, not by
grace through faith in the Lord Jesus Christ. They were telling
these Gentiles in the churches of Galatia that not only had they
to believe on Jesus Christ but they must also keep the law to be
saved. If they were to be counted as the children of Abraham they
must submit to circumcision like the Jews, and to all the
requirements of the Levitical law.

The great boast and confidence of the Jews was that they were
the children of Abraham and therefore they surely had a claim on
God. Had not God taken Abraham, called him out of Ur of the
Chaldees, brought him into that favoured position and revealed
himself to him as his God? Was not Abraham described as the
friend of God? Had not God blessed him? Had not God spoken
to him concerning his seed, his descendants, that God would not
only give them the land of Canaan but that in his seed should "all
families of the earth be blessed"? (Gen. 12:3). The Jews rightly
claimed, 'We are the lawful descendants of Abraham.' True,
Abraham had descendants other than the Jews through his son
Ishmael but they were not included in this promise. It referred to
those that were descended from Abraham through Isaac and then
Jacob and then the twelve sons of Jacob. Their great boast and
claim was this, 'We are the children of Abraham. Therefore, if
there are any people in the world who are to be owned and
blessed of God, then surely it is us.' And these who had come
into the churches of Galatia and were causing so much trouble,
were saying in effect to these Gentiles, 'Yes, and if you want to
be children of Abraham, there is only one way you can be so.
You must become like the Jews and submit to the ordinance of
circumcision which God gave to Abraham.' And again, 'Only if
you obey the law that was given by God to Moses and thus walk
as children of Abraham should do, can you become pleasing to
God, and expect his blessing upon you.'

Now Paul, in the gospel that he preached and which was

preached by all the apostles, and for which he contends in this epistle, is saying the very opposite to those teachers. That was the greatness of the difference. It was not just different shades of opinion, not a matter of slight divergence. It was as fundamental as this: If what the troublers the church were saying was true, then what Paul preached was wrong. But if what Paul preached was true, then what they said was wrong. Paul was saying the very opposite to what they were preaching. He shows that salvation is not by works but by grace through faith alone. He shows that the true children of Abraham are not those that rely on natural descent from him. They are not those who submit to Jewish ordinances, however great and glorious those ordinances were which God had made known to the Jews through Moses. We do not become the children of Abraham, and thus in essence the children of God, by submitting to Jewish ordinances and practices. No. Paul shows that to do so is to be in bondage to the law and under its curse. It is contrary to the grace by which sinners are alone saved. Only by the gospel for which he is contending can sinners be truly blessed.

As we noticed over previous weeks, Paul asks the question, "He therefore that ministereth to you the spirit, and worketh miracles among you, doeth he it by the works of the law, or by the hearing of faith?" In answering that question, he refers to the case of Abraham. He says, "Even as Abraham believed God, and it was accounted to him for righteousness." Here is the righteousness that exceeds the righteousness of the scribes and Pharisees. Here is the only righteousness which justifies the sinner before God. It is the righteousness which is received by faith, even as it was by Abraham. Do the Jews account Abraham a child of God, one that was truly accepted in God's sight, one whom God loved and who loved God in return, and walked by grace in the ways the Lord made known to him? Indeed they do. But Paul says here, 'Whence did Abraham obtain that righteousness which justified him before a holy God?' For let us not forget, Abraham also was a sinner. Before God called him he was no different to other men. Abraham was a sinner, he was an idolater. God called him out of Ur of the Chaldees, not because of any worth in Abraham, but out of his sovereign will and good

pleasure. The Lord, through his servant Isaiah, says to his people
of those days, "Look unto the rock whence ye are hewn, and to
the hole of the pit whence ye are digged. Look unto Abraham
your father, and unto Sarah that bare you for I called him alone"
(Isa. 51:1-2). The emphasis there is that God's calling of
Abraham was wholly of grace. God's call to Abraham came
when he was a sinner, dead in trespasses and sins, an idolater in
Ur of the Chaldees. It was sovereign grace that called Abraham,
separated him from those things, brought him out and revealed
the truth to him.

As Paul shows here, the righteousness of Abraham in which
he was accounted righteous before God and accepted by God, is
the righteousness which comes through faith. He shows that it
was not of works. Oh, there was no question of that! Abraham
did not attain to righteousness by what he did but by believing,
as stated in the fifteenth chapter of the book of Genesis. See how
simply it is put, but what profound truth is opened up to us. Paul
quotes the same scripture in this verse before us.

The circumstances were after Abraham had returned from the
slaughter of the kings. You remember how God had given him a
notable victory, and he had brought again Lot and those who had
been carried away captive. God comes to him after those events
and says to him, "Fear not, Abram: I am thy shield, and thy
exceeding great reward" (Gen. 15:1). See how the Lord
addresses, not only the situation that Abraham was in, but the
very things that were in Abraham's heart at that time. "Fear not,
Abram." God had given him a notable victory but it was evident
that there were fears arising in Abraham. Would it not be possible
for those kings, whose armies he had defeated, to regain their
strength and come to seek revenge on him? He had only a small
company comparatively. True, he had over 300 armed or trained
servants but what were they against what those kings or their
successors might bring against him? See the fears that arose in
Abraham. What troubled him as well was that as yet he had no
heir. He had no child born to him to whom all that he possessed
could be left. As things were in those days, his heir was one that
was born in his house, a servant named Eliezer of Damascus.
True, that man obviously had an honoured and responsible

position in Abraham's house, and unless Abraham had a child, then all his possessions would pass to him. He would be Abraham's heir. Abraham was now 75 years old, and Sarah herself was old. There was no sign of any child being born to them. And yet God says to him, "Fear not, Abram: I am thy shield, and thy exceeding great reward." Ah! note the promise of the Lord to be his protector and deliverer. Remember that was not only true for Abraham but for every believer through grace. The Lord their God is their shield, that is, their protector and deliverer. He is also their "exceeding great reward." That is the very essence of the promise that the Lord would surely bless Abraham.

He says, as recorded in chapter 15 of Genesis, "Behold, to me thou hast given no seed: and, lo, one born in my house is mine heir." "And, behold, the word of the Lord came unto him, saying, This shall not be thine heir; but he that shall come forth out of thine own bowels shall be thine heir." God says he would give Abraham a son in his own appointed time. He would have a genuine heir to all his possessions. Not only that, but the Lord says, "I am thy exceeding great reward."

Oh, how this opens up to us the truth that in blessing, the Lord does indeed bless his people. How great is our God and how bountiful is he as well! He does not just tell Abraham he will have an heir. He brings him outside and bids him look up to the night sky. You know, if you have ever seen the sky on a clear night— oh, the myriad of the stars! We do not always see the full extent and beauty of the night sky in our environment, because of the artificial light in the towns in which we dwell. But here, as Abraham beholds the myriad of the stars, oh the vastness of their number! Who can number the stars of heaven? Yet remember, God knows them all, he created them all. "He calleth them all by names by the greatness of his might" (Isa. 40:26). He says to Abraham, "Look now toward heaven, and tell the stars, if thou be able to number them: and he said unto him, So shall thy seed be."

Is it not true what God says, "In blessing I will bless thee, and in multiplying I will multiply thy seed"? (Gen. 22:17). Such is the God and Father of our Lord Jesus Christ and of his believing people through grace. I brought before you on Sunday evening those words of the Lord Jesus to his disciples in the gospel of Matthew chapter 6. "Your heavenly Father knoweth that ye have need of all these things." See the greatness and glory of him who is our heavenly Father, he who spoke here to Abraham, and said to him, "So shall thy seed be." What a promise! What a word! Almost incomprehensible by men, and not only unlooked for but, as viewed by reason, how impossible! Surely this is an exaggeration! How can these things be? Abraham getting an old man, and Sarah old as well, and not having any children, how can these things be? Such is the questioning by fallen human nature to the words that God speaks. "So shall thy seed be."

But what do we read here? "And he believed in the Lord." Oh the vital importance of what is set forth there! See what blessings came, not by Abraham's doing, but by Abraham's believing. Not by God setting Abraham certain tasks to perform and promising him that if he performs those tasks faithfully he will grant him a reward. No, nothing of that. You know, if that was so, where would there be hope for any of us? Where would there be salvation for sinners? No, the things that God speaks to Abraham, and the blessings that are set forth here are not for Abraham's doings or God's setting him certain tasks to fulfil. They centre in the promise that God has spoken, "So shall thy seed be."

Let us not forget that he who promises is the "God that cannot lie" (Titus 1:2). He that promises is the very God who is able to perform what he has promised. As the foundation of the faith of his believing people, as encouragement to them to put their trust and confidence in him, Paul says that God has given us a "strong consolation, who have fled for refuge to lay hold upon the hope set before us" (Heb. 6:18). What is the strong consolation that God has given? It is the very promise and oath of God, of which Paul speaks as "two immutable things, in which it was impossible for God to lie." God cannot say more than what he has said. He said to Abraham, "So shall thy seed be." Here is the immutability of the promise, for God is faithful to that promise. Sooner shall God cease to be God than his promise fail. As if that was not enough, God also bound himself by an oath that he would fulfil his promise to Abraham. "Because he could swear by no greater, he sware by himself, saying, surely blessing I will bless thee, and multiplying I will multiply thee." And is not that the essence of the covenant that God made with Abraham as recorded in Genesis 15, when he entered into those solemn obligations to fulfil what he had promised to him. Ah, these are immutable things. And it is said, "Abraham believed God." These blessings to Abraham were not received by his doing but by his believing.

And as it was with Abraham, so it is with every one whom God calls by his grace. Abraham received this blessed justifying righteousness, not through doing, but by believing. And let us not forget that this believing is the gift of God himself. Faith, as this believing is known, consists not only in giving credit to what God has said, but in trusting and confiding in him alone. This believing is not natural to fallen men and women. It is of the grace of God. It is his own precious gift which he will not only own, but will honour, as he did here in the case of Abraham.

Some might think, 'Well, this is easy—not doing but believing.' But friends, to believe is not the work of men but the very work of God. Remember what Jesus said, as recorded in John chapter 6, when the Jews asked him, "What shall we do, that we might work the works of God? Jesus answered and said unto them, This is the work of God, that ye believe on him whom he hath sent" (vs. 28-29). Yes, it is the work of God, not the work of men. It is the work of God's Spirit within the heart and life of a poor sinner. It consists in quickening into life and blessing them with grace whereby they not only hear but receive the word that God has spoken. It is God's work to bring them to rest and trust in him whom that word reveals, even the Lord Jesus Christ.

"Abraham believed God, and it was accounted to him for righteousness." Ah, it is upon this ground that Abraham is accepted and righteous before God. As Paul says, "Even as Abraham believed God, and it was accounted to him for righteousness. Know ye therefore that they which are of faith, the same are the children of Abraham." This is the very opposite to what the Jews said, the opposite to what these false teachers who were troubling the church in Galatia were saying. They said that to be children of Abraham, and therefore children of God, you must be circumcised and keep the law. No, says Paul, that does not constitute us children of Abraham. "Know ye therefore that they which are of faith, the same are the children of Abraham."

This was always true, right from the very beginning. For as Paul shows here, from whence did Abraham receive the blessing? Was it by works or by faith? Was it by keeping the law or by believing and receiving the promise, through grace? Without question it was the latter. He shows that the promise was spoken to Abraham long before the law was given, and that the law never did countermand the promise God had spoken to Abraham. Indeed, circumcision came after Abraham's being justified by faith, not before it. He was not counted righteous before God on account of his submitting to the ordinance of circumcision which God had appointed. Rather he received the sign of circumcision as a seal of the faith which he already possessed even when he was uncircumcised.

The children of Abraham are not those that claim descent by natural generation from Abraham. They are not those that submit to Jewish ordinances and think that by keeping the law they attain to righteousness. They are those who are of faith. This is the portion of each true believer through grace. What does the expression, "children of Abraham," essentially set forth? Children of Abraham are the dear children of God, by grace through faith. This is the blessing that is received by all whom God calls by his grace. As he says, "And the scripture, foreseeing that God would justify the heathen through faith." Think of that for a moment! "The scripture foreseeing." We are told that, "Known unto God are all his works from the beginning of the world" (Acts 15:18). God's dealings with Abraham spoke of future things. What was in view in the mind and purposes of God? He told Abraham that he would justify the heathen.

There is great depth of truth in Paul's words in Romans 4 concerning Abraham, that God *"justifieth the ungodly."* Oh, the wonder of that grace still made known to men and women as they are sinners! That is wholly contrary to the thinking of so many. They think that a sinner must have something of worth or merit for God to justify him. Surely sinners cannot expect the blessing of God unless they attain to a certain degree of acceptability? We would not claim that they must be perfect before they can expect the blessing of God, but they must be along the way there, surely? Friends, that is not what the scriptures say. But how hard it is for us to get away from the idea that we must first of all attain to something before we can expect the blessing of God. The lie of Satan is still perpetuated in this way, even in religious circles. Men consider that they cannot expect any blessing from God unless they can show some evidence that they are worthy of that blessing. But oh, what does the gospel, the very word of God, say? See where it comes and meets the deepest need of the sinner. It tells us that God justifies the heathen, God justifies the ungodly. Grace, finding us in all the ruin and guilt of our sins, does not tell us what we must do to be saved, but reveals to us what God in Christ has done to save us. As he says here, "And the scripture, foreseeing that God would justify the heathen through faith, preached before the gospel unto Abraham, saying, In thee shall all nations be blessed."

See in what the preaching of the gospel to Abraham centred. "Now to Abraham and his seed were the promises made." Notice what is added. "He saith not, And to seeds, as of many." It is not in the plural but in the singular. "But as of one, And to thy seed, which is Christ." The gospel was there preached to Abraham. Jesus Christ was the seed promised to Abraham. Did not Jesus say, "Your father Abraham rejoiced to see my day and he saw it, and was glad"? (John 8:56). Truly he saw it. He saw it by faith in the gospel that was preached to him. Sinners are blessed in the Lord Jesus Christ, the seed of Abraham, of whom Paul writes, "But when the fulness of time was come, God sent forth his Son, made of a woman, made under the law, to redeem them that were under the law, that we might receive the adoption of sons." Therefore, the scripture declares that "In thee shall all nations be blessed. So then they which be of faith are blessed with faithful Abraham."

And what are their blessings who are blessed with faithful Abraham? What blessings did he receive? He "believed God, and it was accounted to him for righteousness." What does that mean? The blessings of those that are of faith are what David tells us and Paul confirms, "Blessed is he whose transgression is forgiven, whose sin is covered. Blessed is the man unto whom the Lord imputeth not iniquity, and in whose spirit there is no guile" (Ps. 32:1-2). The blessings of faith are the blessings of a full and free forgiveness of all our sins, past, present and to come. All are atoned for through the sacrificial death of Jesus Christ. The blessings of faith are the pardon of sin, peace with God, and the imputation to us of that perfect obedience of Jesus Christ, wherein we are truly justified and accepted before God. And these blessings are full and free. Ah, is not that the most glorious note that the gospel trumpet sounds, as we read in the Revelation, "Whosoever will, let him take the water of life freely"? (Rev. 22:17).

But I'll leave the remarks there. May the Lord add his blessing. Amen.

13

For as many as are of the works of the law are under the curse: for it is written, Cursed is every one that continueth not in all things which are written in the book of the law to do them. But that no man is justified by the law in the sight of God, it is evident: for, The just shall live by faith. And the law is not of faith: but, The man that doeth them shall live in them. Christ hath redeemed us from the curse of the law, being made a curse for us: for it is written, Cursed is every one that hangeth on a tree: That the blessing of Abraham might come on the Gentiles through Jesus Christ; that we might receive the promise of the Spirit through faith.

How glorious and important are the things the apostle deals with in this epistle to the Galatians. Surely in what he sets forth we have the sum and substance of the truth of the gospel of the grace of God, which in all its fulness is revealed in the person and work of the Lord and Saviour Jesus Christ. I do not want to spend much time this evening reminding you again of the main purpose for which Paul writes to the churches in Galatia. They were so troubled and disrupted by those who had come teaching things contrary to the gospel of the grace of God. In this third chapter, the apostle addresses them in a very personal way. In the opening verse he says, "Oh foolish Galatians, who hath bewitched you, that ye should not obey the truth, before whose eyes Jesus Christ hath been evidently set forth, crucified among you?" The gospel had been preached among them in demonstration of the Spirit and of power. They had professed to receive the sovereign grace and love of God made known in the gospel. Oh, to think that they should have been drawn aside and even be in danger of leaving this gospel and turning to ways which would bring them again under the curse of the holy law of God! In mentioning that, I would just add that the true believer can never be brought back under the curse and condemnation of the law. "Grace once received can ne'er be lost," as the hymnwriter well puts it.

What Paul was emphasising was the danger they were in of being robbed of their gospel peace and comfort and of Satan making havoc among them. How dishonouring it was to their Lord and Saviour that they should give ear to such error and be drawn aside by plausible words that were inconsistent with the gospel that had been preached to them. How important this is for the real peace and well-being of the people of God. Our Lord Jesus himself not only said "Take heed therefore *how* ye hear" but "Take heed *what* ye hear" (Luke 8:18 & Mark 4:24). Paul warns us in the fourth chapter of his epistle to the Ephesians about being "tossed to and fro, and carried about with every wind of doctrine." Satan is still active in seeking to undermine the truth by promoting error. And remember, those errors that make the most progress and havoc among the Lord's people, robbing them of their peace and comfort, often have a very close resemblance to the truth. Yet they are wholly contrary to the truth. How we always need to be seeking grace to be kept close to the Lord Jesus Christ and to his word. It is as the prophet Isaiah said in his day, "To the law and to the testimony: if they speak not according to this word, it is because there is no light in them" (Isa. 8:20). Let all be judged in the light of the teaching of God's word, comparing spiritual things with spiritual.

You remember how the Bereans are commended in Acts chapter 17 because they "searched the scriptures daily, whether those things" that were spoken by the apostles, "were so or not." This is not to be drawn away with a critical spirit, but to have the gracious concern that what is set forth is according to the word of God and the gracious teaching of the Holy Spirit. I verily believe that where a person possesses the grace of God they have a spiritual instinct. They may not always be able to fully explain it but if things set forth are not according to the truth, there will be warning signs, things that trouble them. They will not always at first be able to explain why, and yet they will feel a real uneasiness in receiving those things. Let me also just add this. You know, there are those that come professing to bring some new thing, claiming to have some fresh light on the word of God. Let us always be careful of such claims. True, we do want the word of God to be opened up to us in the freshness and the power of it but let us beware of those that profess to bring some new thing. That was so with these who troubled the church in Galatia. What they were bringing was plausible, but it was some new thing, different to what the apostle had taught, and therefore contained the most grievous pernicious error.

But we now come to this part of the third chapter of Galatians. Last week we considered the Lord's dealings with Abraham as set forth in verses 6 to 9. The apostle shows that those who are of faith are blessed with faithful Abraham. He underlines the important and glorious truth that salvation is "by grace, through faith; and that not of yourselves: it is the gift of God: not of works lest any man should boast" (Eph. 2:8-9). He shows that the way of salvation which he preached was known even throughout the old testament period by the riches of God's grace. It was so with Abraham himself. He was justified, not by doing but by believing, and even his believing was the work of God's grace in him. He says, "Even as Abraham believed God, and it was accounted to him for righteousness. Know ye therefore that they which are of faith, the same are the children of Abraham. So then they which be of faith are blessed with faithful Abraham."

Let me just briefly touch on that point again for it is a matter of great importance. It says, "Abraham believed God, and it was accounted to him for righteousness." A few weeks ago I brought before you the case of the woman in the house of Simon the Pharisee, to whom Jesus said, "Thy faith hath saved thee; go in peace" (Luke 7:50). The Lord Jesus spoke similar words to several other persons who were brought to seek him in their need. He speaks of the centurion who sent to him because his servant was sick, "I have not found so great faith, no, not in Israel" (Matt. 8:10). The question I just want to emphasise is, from whence came the faith they evidently possessed? Jesus said to that woman in the house of Simon the Pharisee, "Thy faith hath saved thee." We see the reality of her faith. In what? In that she, a woman known in the city as a sinner, came into a Pharisee's house and was found at the feet of Jesus. She washes his feet with her tears and wipes them with the hairs of her head and anoints them with ointment. The Lord says to Simon the Pharisee, "Seest thou this woman." What love she evidences, what devotion to the Lord Jesus Christ! He says of her, "Her sins which are many, are forgiven; for she loved much: but to whom little is forgiven, the same loveth little." From whence came this faith which was so evident in that woman, as it was in Abraham of whom it is said that *he believed God?* As I mentioned last week, the Lord bid him go outside his tent and look toward heaven, to behold the night sky, the myriad of the stars, and he said to him, "So shall thy seed be" (Gen. 15:5). Ah, 'those that come of thee shall be such a multitude even as the stars of heaven which are viewed by men as innumerable.' We read, "Abraham believed God." He received and rested on the word of God and the faithfulness of him who had spoken it. And it says, "It was accounted to him for righteousness" (Gal. 3:6).

I say, from whence did Abraham's faith come? This is not an unimportant matter. Far from it. So many set forth faith as being that which we produce in response to what God has done. But that is not how the scriptures speak of faith. To speak of faith in that way makes faith a work for which God is indebted to us. It is saying God will do what he has promised to do as long as we believe him and trust him. But friends, the scriptures speak of faith as the gift of God, that which is the fruit of the Holy Spirit's work in the soul of a sinner. As it was with Abraham, the gift of faith is wholly of grace. For he was no different to other men. He was a sinner dead in trespasses and sins. He was involved in the idolatry of Ur of the Chaldees, as all the others of his generation. What made the difference? How was Abraham brought out of that? Who was it who worked in his leaving Ur? It was God, who is rich in grace and mercy. As the apostle writes to the Ephesians, "But God, who is rich in mercy, for his great love wherewith he loved us, even when we were dead in sins, hath quickened us together with Christ, (by grace ye are saved)" (Eph. 2:4-5). He speaks there of the mighty operation of God's grace in the work of the Holy Spirit in regeneration. Faith is the gift of God. It is the fruit of the work of the Holy Spirit. Where the Holy Spirit quickens into spiritual life, calling a sinner by his grace, there also does he impart the precious gift of faith. Thereby, under the Spirit's teaching, we are convinced of our sin. We are brought to see ourselves as completely undone in the light of the holy law of God. Yet through that same almighty grace we are also brought to hear and receive the testimony that God has given of his only begotten Son.

It is these things that Paul further deals with in these verses before us. He says, "They which be of faith are blessed with faithful Abraham. For as many as are of the works of the law are under the curse: for it is written, Cursed is everyone that continueth not in all things which are written in the book of the law to do them." Now the false teachers who were troubling the church of Galatia were insisting that believers obey the holy law of God. They were saying believers must keep it, if they were to expect to receive the favour of God. Believing in Jesus Christ was not enough unless joined with their obedience to the law. Now that was very plausible as men view it. But Paul states the real position of those that think they can obtain the favour of God by the works of the law. He says, "For as many as are of the works of the law are under the curse."

Friends, that is the situation of all that are without faith in Jesus Christ and who look to their supposed obedience to the law. This is a solemn consideration. It has its application to every one of us. "As many as are of the works of the law are under the curse." Let me emphasise again that the law of which Paul is speaking here is the holy law of God summed up in the ten commandments given to Moses on mount Sinai. Therein God sets forth the holiness of his divine nature and what he requires of all his rational creatures. Let us never forget that the law is holy, just and good. There is no fault, no failing in the law. Therein is the holiness and justice of God made known. The solemn fact is that men are sinners. We are transgressors of this law. How can we as transgressors ever satisfy that which demands perfect obedience to all that it sets forth? That is what

Paul is saying here. For he says, "It is written." This is the word of God. The holy scriptures testify to this and there is no going back on it. "It is written, Cursed is every one that continueth not in all things which are written in the book of the law to do them."

As I have said many times, the holy law of God will be satisfied with nothing less than perfect conformity to all its requirements. Oh, if we think we can do that which can please God, let us remember what is required by the holy law of God. It requires *perfection*. Every part of the law must be perfectly kept by us, in thought, word and deed, every moment of our lives, and even then we are still under the curse. Why is that? Because we are the descendants of Adam it is utterly impossible that any person should ever keep the law of God perfectly. Therefore we are under the curse. "For as many as are of the works of the law are under the curse: for it is written, Cursed is every one that continueth not in all things which are written in the book of the law to do them. But that no man is justified by the law in the sight of God, it is evident: for, The just shall live by faith."

Now what is Paul opening up and emphasising here again? It is the wonder of God's grace and mercy as revealed in Jesus Christ. Does the law of God demand perfection? True it does. I cannot render it. Therefore I am under its curse. Does the divine justice of God demand that the penalty of the law which I have incurred be paid before I can be justified? Does it demand that the great debt we owe as the result of our sin and transgression be met before God can justify the sinner? *Indeed it does!* But he says, "That no man is justified by the law in the sight of God, it is evident: for, The just shall live by faith." Paul is saying that what was being taught among the Galatians brought men and women back under the broken law and left them under its curse. Nothing in that was pleasing to God. Just the very reverse. But he opens up here this glorious truth, "The just shall live by faith."

Who are these *just*? Ah, the wonder is that everyone of them is a sinner. There is no exception to this among them. They are all sinners. They are lost and ruined in the fall. They are sinners who in themselves are under the curse of the broken law. Yet they are sinners for whom a complete recompense has been rendered to what a holy God requires. They are sinners for whom the demands of the law have been met by the performance of the obedience it requires and by the suffering of the penalty that has been incurred. "The just shall live by faith." It is these who are pleasing in God's sight. Here he sets before us the way of salvation. Herein the blessings of pardon of sin, peace with God and eternal life are gloriously made known and realised. The *just man* is a man to whom spiritual life has been imparted by the Spirit and who has been brought by gracious teaching, to true repentance and saving faith in the Lord and Saviour Jesus Christ. These blessings are *freely given*. They come without money and without price.

He says, "The just shall live by faith." We meet this expression in both the old and new testaments. What does it mean? As I have said, it is to be taught by the Holy Spirit, not only our ruin and need by sin, but the salvation that centres alone in Jesus Christ. *The essence of it is in the daily living upon the fulness of the grace that is in Christ Jesus*. The "just" are those who daily realise their spiritual poverty and need and are ever brought to look out of themselves to the fulness of the grace that is Christ Jesus. As Paul says in the closing part of chapter two, "The life which I now live in the flesh I live by the faith of the Son of God, who loved me, and gave himself for me." I believe we can sum it up in those words of the Lord Jesus which I have often mentioned to you. He says, "All that the Father giveth me shall come to me; and him that cometh to me I will in no wise cast out" (John 6:37). That is the gracious mark and evidence of the just who live by faith. *They shall come,* says the Lord, and they do come to Jesus Christ. That is what characterises the very life of these described here as *just*, who live by faith. It was so with Abraham. He not only believed on the occasion we have mentioned, but the emphasis with Abraham is his continual believing, his looking alone to the Lord, his depending on his God, his trusting in him. This was the distinguishing feature of Abraham's life. He was one that truly knew his need as a sinner and yet as a sinner was brought to live upon the fulness of grace that is revealed in Jesus Christ our Lord. *They shall come,* says the Lord, and they do come.

He says, "And the law is not of faith: but, The man that doeth them shall live in them. Christ hath redeemed us from the curse of the law, being made a curse for us: for it is written, Cursed is every one that hangeth on a tree." What depths of divine truth, what wonders of love and grace, are manifest here! Here is the whole ground of the sinner's justification before God. Here is that which delivers us from all the curse and condemnation of the law. Here is the price that has been paid for the redemption of his people. He says, "Christ hath redeemed us from the curse of the law." Yes, he has paid the price. He has met the law's demands. Oh, what this involved for him, he "being made a curse for us"! Pause friends and consider. He "being made a curse for us." I say what wonders are revealed here, that he who is the Holy One of God, he who is without sin, he who is God manifest in the flesh, was made a curse for us. Yes, all the awful debt of sin which was owed by his people, was there made to meet upon him. The wrath of God was poured upon him as he was set forth as the surety of his people. He was *made a curse for us*. May the Holy Spirit seal this blessed truth upon our hearts. Is there not true divinity in this statement? "Made a curse for us: for it is written, Cursed is every one that hangeth on a tree." How real was that which our Lord Jesus endured. The curse of God was solemnly made to meet on him when, as the surety of his people, he paid the debt for sin that was owed by them.

"That the blessing of Abraham might come on the Gentiles through Jesus Christ; that we might receive the promise of the Spirit through faith," even all the blessings revealed in the gospel. The blessing of Abraham is the "being justified freely by his grace through the redemption that is in Christ Jesus" (Rom. 3:24). What a wonderful truth this is to the burdened, guilty, needy and distressed soul. See here how Jesus Christ is set forth. Behold here the Holy One of God bearing away the sins of the guilty, needy and burdened sinner who is quickened and awakened by the Holy Spirit to know his need. One has well summed it up:

> "Payment God cannot twice demand,
> First at my bleeding Surety's hand,
> And then again at mine."

Is not this "the blessing of Abraham" as revealed in the fulness of the grace of God in the gospel? I believe I said this the other week: the uniqueness of the gospel revelation is that it testifies of the actual full and free forgiveness of sin. I say this is unique to the gospel revelation. This is "the blessing of Abraham." It is not just the showing us a way in which, if we do what we can and are sincere in our endeavours, then we can hope that God will overlook our sins. No. The gospel makes known the actual reality of our sins being wholly forgiven—the blessings of pardon and peace with God. As the psalmist said and as Paul quotes, "Blessed is he whose transgression is forgiven, whose sin is covered. Blessed is the man unto whom the Lord imputeth not iniquity, and in whose spirit there is no guile" (Ps. 32:2). Only the gospel makes known such a blessing as that, and only the Holy Spirit seals this gospel upon the hearts of guilty, needy sinners. How full and free is this blessing of Abraham. It can never be taken away. As one well says:

> "If sin be pardoned, I'm secure,
> Death has no sting beside."

The curse of a broken law is completely removed. It has nothing more to say to the believer in Jesus. It is perfect righteousness and sin atoning blood which speaks for them. As one says:

> "What voice is that which speaks for me
> In heavens high court for good,
> And from the curse has set me free?
> 'Tis Jesus' precious blood."

But I will leave the remarks there. May the Lord add his blessing. Amen.

14

GALATIANS 3:15-18

Brethren, I speak after the manner of men; Though it be but a man's covenant, yet if it be confirmed, no man disannulleth, or addeth thereto. Now to Abraham and his seed were the promises made. He saith not, And to seeds, as of many; but as of one, And to thy seed, which is Christ. And this I say, that the covenant, that was confirmed before of God in Christ, the law, which was four hundred and thirty years after, cannot disannul, that it should make the promise of none effect. For if the inheritance be of the law, it is no more of promise: but God gave it to Abraham by promise.

As we look at these verses I want us to bear in mind the main theme of the epistle. The apostle emphatically sets forth the glorious truths of the gospel, over against those whose teaching in the Galatian churches was contrary to the gospel he preached. This false teaching was detrimental to the spiritual welfare of the churches and dishonouring to the Lord Jesus Christ. One fruit of grace that ever shone forth in the ministry of Paul was his deep love for the Lord Jesus Christ. His concern was for the honour of the Lord who had so loved him, called him and saved him by his grace. And surely if we know that same great love and mercy in our own souls, then the one whom the apostle loved, the name he reverenced above every name, the preciousness of the glorious person of the Lord Jesus Christ, will also be precious to us.

Now we need to briefly consider verse 14 again. He says, "That the blessing of Abraham might come on the Gentiles through Jesus Christ; that we might receive the promise of the

Spirit through faith." "The blessing of Abraham" comes on the Gentiles through what the Lord Jesus is and has done. As he says in verse 13, "Christ hath redeemed us from the curse of the law, being made a curse for us: for it is written, Cursed is everyone that hangeth on a tree." Well may we say, "Great is the mystery of godliness" (1 Tim. 3:16). Oh, the depth of divine grace and truth in this statement of verse 13. "Christ hath redeemed us from the curse of the law, being made a curse for us." It is very similar to what we read in the epistle to the Corinthians. "He hath made him to be sin for us, who knew no sin; that we might be made the righteousness of God in him" (2 Cor. 5:21). What a redemption that sets before us! What an offering, what a sacrifice has been rendered unto God! Not the offerings and sacrifices of the Levitical law but "the offering of the body of Jesus Christ once for all" (Heb. 10:10). There is no greater offering, no other sacrifice than this. We are reminded of the great and glorious truth again and again, that "Christ hath redeemed us from the curse of the law, being made a curse for us." He who is the Holy One of God, God manifest in the flesh, did himself bear the sins of his people. He himself has borne the curse of the holy law of God that they had broken, that they might be set free from that curse. Oh, may we know the blessedness of this truth in personal experience, not only in the scripture testimony that Jesus Christ is the Saviour of sinners, but knowing him by the Spirit's teaching as our Saviour, our all. Do not forget what the apostle returns to again and again. We have noticed it already at the close of chapter 2. He could speak of "the Son of God, who loved *me, and gave himself for me."*

"That the blessing of Abraham might come on the Gentiles through Jesus Christ." What is this "blessing of Abraham?" Is it not summed up in those words, "Being justified by faith, we have peace with God through our Lord Jesus Christ"? (Rom. 5:1). We read that Abraham "believed in the Lord: and he counted it to him for righteousness" (Gen. 15:6). Yes, this blessing of Abraham is the free and full justification "from all things, from which ye could not be justified by the law of Moses" (Acts 13:39). This blessing of Abraham is the receiving of a full salvation, a free forgiveness, the blessing of peace with God and the glorious inheritance of eternal life. I say this blessing of Abraham is the receiving of those things, not by having merited or earned them. It is the receiving of them as Abraham received them and as every sinner born again is brought to receive them, even as the free and sovereign gift of God. I say, it is the receiving of those blessings that come to sinners, in all the fulness and freeness of them, through Jesus Christ our Lord.

Now we come to this important point in verse 15. Here we see how this "blessing of Abraham" is most sure and certain to the promised seed, to the whole church of Jesus Christ, to every sinner called by divine grace. Let us not overlook this important and comforting truth. There is *certainty* in all that the apostle writes. All for whom Christ died must surely be saved. Without exception all of them are found dead in trespasses and sins, but such are the purposes and appointments of God that they shall surely be called by grace in his own appointed time. They shall surely be brought out of darkness into light and to repentance and saving faith in the Lord Jesus Christ. It is impossible that they should ever miss these things, should ever come short of them or ever come short of the eternal inheritance which is found in this "blessing of Abraham." Paul brings out the certainty of these things in this way. He says, "Brethren, I speak after the manner of men; Though it be but a man's covenant, yet if it be confirmed, no man disannulleth, or addeth thereto. Now to Abraham and his seed were the promises made."

Now brought before us here are the covenant and promise of God. This "blessing of Abraham" that comes on the Gentiles through Jesus Christ is bound up in the covenant that God has made and is made known through the promise. Let us look at these things in more detail. He says, "I speak after the manner of men." That is, look at this as it is among men. If they enter into a covenant and that covenant is signed and sealed, then no man can add to it or disannul it. We see this in the last will and testament of a person. We make a will. It is signed and sealed. Upon the death of the person, that will or testament comes into operation and nothing can be added to it or taken away from it. This stands among men in their dealings in these things. Paul says that if that is so among men, how much more is it true in that which God has revealed and made known. Not only are we reminded here of the faithfulness of God but of the important truth that he who is the God and Father of our Lord Jesus Christ, he who is the God of salvation, is a *God that cannot lie*. Now is that not a matter of importance and real consolation to the living family of God? He who is our God, the God of salvation, is a God that cannot lie. We can implicitly trust his word. He will be faithful to those engagements he has entered into. He shall fulfil them. "Though it be but a man's covenant, yet if it be confirmed, no man disannulleth, or addeth thereto. Now to Abraham and his seed were the promises made."

Let us look then at the important point spoken by Paul. Does he not refer to covenant engagements and promises? We are reminded how ancient are these things. They not only date back to the time when God first spoke to Abraham the promises to which Paul refers here. They are of more ancient date than that. This covenant was made from before the foundation of the world. These gracious transactions were made in eternity, not between God and men, but between the three persons of the holy Trinity, Father, Son and Holy Spirit. In those eternal engagements the Father chose a people in sovereign grace and mercy. They were given in that covenant to Jesus Christ, who undertook to be their surety and their one mediator between God and men. He undertook to redeem them from the curse of the law, being himself made a curse for them, and to procure for them the blessings of pardon, peace and eternal life. And those whom the Father chose in love and gave to his beloved Son, and whom the Lord Jesus undertook to redeem, the Holy Spirit also covenanted to call by grace. He covenanted to bring them into the saving knowledge of these things, and to cause them to persevere and enter into the fulness of these blessings. Let us never forget how full of gracious truth and comfort are the covenant mercies of God set before us in the scriptures. In all their fulness they centre in the person of Jesus Christ.

What blessings are contained in this covenant of grace that God has made! It comes to sinners, not as something to be attained by them, not as something to be earned by their doings. It comes as the blessing came to Abraham. In what way? In sovereign grace and mercy! It comes to them in all the fulness and freeness of a gracious, sovereign gift of God to them, contained as it is in the promises that he has spoken. Look at it in the concept of a testament. Paul deals with it in this light in his epistle to the Hebrews. I mentioned that when a man dies his last will and testament comes into operation. Nothing can be added to it, nothing can be taken away from it. Now what do the beneficiaries under that testament perform to receive its benefits? They can never be said to have earned them. No, the inheritance comes to them freely as a gift. The person that made the will had the right to dispose of his possessions just as he saw fit. The beneficiaries under the testament receive those things as a gift. Now that is so among men. And how gloriously is that so as it concerns the covenant God has made and the blessings that flow from it. Yes, they are sure. They can never be more sure. Why? Because this covenant is signed and sealed with blood.

Paul reminds us of this. He says that the covenant or testament that God gave to Moses was ratified with the sprinkling of the blood of the sacrifices that were appointed. So the blessed new testament covenant of sovereign grace and mercy is sure for elect sinners through the sufferings, death and resurrection of our Lord Jesus Christ, to the praise of the glory of God's grace. Yes, that covenant is signed and sealed with blood, and that blood is the precious blood of our Lord and Saviour Jesus Christ. It is sure through the fact that he has "suffered for sins, the just for the unjust, that he might bring us to God" (1 Pet. 3:18).

Now we see the blessings of this covenant set forth in the promises God has made. As he says here, "Now to Abraham and his seed were the promises made. He saith not, And to seeds, as of many; but as of one, And to thy seed, which is Christ." Abraham had a number of children. Isaac was the promised seed but he also had Ishmael. He had a number of children as well by Keturah after the death of Sarah. But he was told, "In Isaac shall thy seed be called" (Gen. 21:12). The promise God made that, "In thee and in thy seed shall all the families of the earth be blessed" (Gen. 28:14) indicated that through the line of Abraham, Isaac and Jacob and later David, should come he who is God's salvation to the ends of the earth. In this one, even the Lord and

Saviour Jesus Christ, all the promises centred,. Every grace, every favour, every blessing to the church, comes to us through him as a sovereign gift both full and free.

I would emphasise not only the sovereignty but the fulness and freeness of the grace of God and of his pardoning love and mercy and the way of access to him. For this is what Paul emphasises against those who were teaching very contrary things in Galatia. They were saying the blessing of God depended on the obedience of the Galatians to the law. Without that, no blessing could come to them. They must not only believe in Jesus Christ but must keep the law to be accepted before God. Paul teaches a very different thing. He speaks of the blessings coming through covenant promises and engagements, not with any respect to the worthiness of those who are the recipients of the blessings. They are blessed solely through what Jesus is and has done. Oh, how the blessings come so fully and freely through Jesus Christ to those undeserving of the least of them! Friends, is not this a glorious truth? If salvation required even the very least effort on our part we should never attain to that salvation. If salvation depends on my obedience, even my obedience in receiving it, some saying, 'Well it is free, you only need to stretch out your hand and take it,' then I will come short of it. Paul is saying that the salvation in Jesus Christ is not hedged about with conditions that must be met by the sinner. It speaks of a salvation that is eternally secured and comes in all its fulness and freeness through Jesus Christ to those who are wholly undeserving.

Paul brings the great contrast before us in his epistle to the Romans. He says, "The wages of sin is death" (Rom. 6:23). Yes, that is what we have earned, that is what we deserve. One says:

> "My sins deserve eternal death,
>
> But Jesus died for me."

Yes, what we earn and what will always be the result of our doings, is death, eternal death. Even the best of our doings deserves eternal death. Isaiah says, "All our righteousnesses are as filthy rags" (Isa. 64:6). He does not say '*all our sins, all our failings.*' We could well understand that. He says, "All our *righteousnesses,*" that is, what we consider our best things, what we might prize the most highly of our doings. Surely if anything is the ground of our acceptance before God these things must be? The prophet says that even all our best religious observances are filthy rags in the sight of God. Oh, what do we deserve, what do we earn by them? "The wages of sin is death," says the apostle. My sins deserve eternal death, and my righteousnesses deserve no less. "But the gift of God is eternal life through Jesus Christ our Lord."

Oh, the blessedness of the salvation that comes to such a sinner as I am. Friends, this salvation is for sinners, make no mistake about it. It is for sinners and how the blessedness of that is realised as they are taught by the Holy Spirit their ruin, guilt and need, and as the righteousness of Jesus Christ is made known to them. How they realise the blessedness of the free gift of salvation by grace coming to them, not when they have sought it, not when they themselves have even asked for it, but coming to them in all their ruin and need. Friends, that is how salvation comes. That is how it is made known. It is by the gracious sovereign work of God the Holy Spirit. He says, "I am sought of them that asked not for me; I am found of them that sought me not" (Isa. 65:1). Ah, precious truth!

See this brought out in the case of the apostle himself. When the grace of God came to him in all its fulness and freeness, was it when he sought it? Was it when he was making a determined effort to obtain it? No, it was when he was in rebellion against God, when in all the pride of his own religion and self-righteousness he thought he was doing the will of God by persecuting the church. He was blaspheming the very name of Jesus, rejecting everything concerning the Lord Jesus Christ, despising his truth and his ways. That was when salvation came to him. Sovereign grace met with him on the road to Damascus when his heart was filled with rage and enmity against the word and work of Jesus Christ. What a mighty operation of grace was there, that such a rebel sinner should be brought to the feet of the Lord Jesus Christ and brought to preach the very gospel he once sought to destroy.

But you say Paul was a remarkable case. True he was. But is it any different with any manifestation of sovereign grace? Surely if we know anything of this same grace and the gift of grace upon ourselves, we have to answer it was no different in principle with us. When was it this grace came to us? When was it made known to us? When we sought it? When we made a determined effort to obtain it? When we were aware of our need of it? No. Friends, I believe that as we are truly taught by the Holy Spirit we shall have to acknowledge it came to us when we never sought it and had no desire after it. True, we may have been in the way of religion. Many of us here tonight have been brought up from our earliest days under the sound of the truth and were taken to chapel from the time we were babies. We grew up under the sound of the truth and were familiar with these things. But were we any more ready for it? Did we any more desire it and seek it? No. I believe when the grace of God comes, it comes to us in the fulness and freeness of a gift, it comes to us in all our undeserving, and it comes just where we are. It is the mighty work of God.

It was so with Abraham. "To Abraham and his seed were the promises made." God reminds his people again and again that as it was with Abraham, so it is still in his sovereign dealings with the true children of Abraham. He reminds them to "Look unto Abraham your father, and unto Sarah that bare you: for I called him alone, and blessed him" (Isa. 51:2). It was sovereign grace that sought out and found Abraham, not Abraham's seeking out and finding God. Sovereign grace sought Abraham in Ur of the Chaldees when he was a sinner dead in sins and involved in all the idolatry of the place. As sovereign grace sought him and found him, so also it brought him out and made him willing in the day of the Lord's power. So it is with the Lord's dealings with each one of his own.

"He saith not, And to seeds, as of many; but as of one, And to thy seed which is Christ." As I mentioned a few moments ago, see how all these things centre in Jesus Christ. "To thy seed which is Christ. And this I say, that the covenant, that was confirmed before of God in Christ, the law which was four hundred and thirty years after, cannot disannul, that it should make the promise of none effect." Now true, at that time there was the manifestation and sealing of that covenant and all the promises of God to Abraham. Yet the covenant that was

confirmed before of God in Christ, is a covenant that existed and
was confirmed of God in Christ before the foundation of the
world. It was not first *made* when those promises were spoken to
Abraham. There was the *unfolding* of those things to him, the
showing to him the wonder and blessedness of sovereign grace
and divine mercy and the confirming of his interest in the
promise. He says that nothing can disannul this covenant that was
confirmed before of God in Christ, so as to make the promise of
none effect. "The law, which was four hundred and thirty years
after" cannot disannul it. The law came four hundred and thirty
years after the event of which we read in Genesis 15. God there
confirmed to Abraham the covenant which was made of God in
Christ before the foundation of the world. He revealed to him the
wonders of his grace and mercy. God spoke to Abraham at that
time of events which were to take place four hundred and thirty
years later. He said that his posterity after him should dwell in a
land that was not theirs. They would be afflicted in that land. At
the appointed time God would bring them out. When he brought
them out by the hand of Moses he gave to them his holy law on
mount Sinai. Yet even the giving of that law did not disannul or
make the promise of none effect. As Paul says here, "If the
inheritance be of the law, it is no more of promise: but God gave
it to Abraham by promise."

The point I am just wanting to make, which I believe is
wonderfully brought out here, is that the blessings of grace
always come to sinners through the covenant that was made
between the eternal Three and confirmed by God in Christ Jesus.
The blessings of grace and salvation for those who are wretched,
ruined, lost and undone, flow not from what the sinner has done.
They flow from what God has unfolded in the promises that
centre in the person and work of the Lord Jesus Christ. He says,
"For if the inheritance be of the law." That is what those false
teachers in Galatia were advocating. They were saying that the
entering into the blessings of this inheritance was upon the
ground of the obedience of men to the law. Without this
obedience men and women could not obtain the blessing. But
Paul is saying, 'No, if that be so, it is no more of promise: but
God gave it to Abraham by promise.' Yes, all the blessings of it

were given to Abraham *in the promise, and not according to his obedience to the law*. And the blessings of Abraham still come to the Lord's people through the redemption that is in Christ Jesus. True, it *is* upon the law being *fulfilled,* upon the ground of sin *atoned for,* but not by them but by him who is their great surety, the mediator of the everlasting covenant, even the Lord Jesus Christ. As one says:

> "Upon a life I did not live,
> Upon a death I did not die,
> Another's life, another's death,
> I stake my whole eternity."

He says that God gave the inheritance to Abraham by promise. This is a precious truth. May the Lord the Holy Spirit open it up to us more and more. You remember that well known precious stanza which has been used more than once in the revealing of the saving mercy and grace of God to sinners. May we know the truths contained in it. It is but a little stanza but oh, what truth it sets forth!

> "My sins deserve eternal death,
> But Jesus died for me."

But I will leave the remarks there this evening. May the Lord add his blessing. Amen.

15

GALATIANS 3:19-26

Wherefore then serveth the law? It was added because of transgressions, till the seed should come to whom the promise was made; and it was ordained by angels in the hand of a mediator. Now a mediator is not a mediator of one, but God is one. Is the law then against the promises of God? God forbid: for if there had been a law given which could have given life, verily righteousness should have been by the law. But the scripture hath concluded all under sin, that the promise by faith of Jesus Christ might be given to them that believe. But before faith came, we were kept under the law, shut up unto the faith which should afterwards be revealed. Wherefore the law was our schoolmaster to bring us unto Christ, that we might be justified by faith. But after that faith is come, we are no longer under a schoolmaster. For ye are all the children of God by faith in Christ Jesus.

Paul is here dealing with the place of the holy law of God in the light of what he had already set forth concerning the promises of God and salvation by grace for sinful men and women. I surely do not need to remind you that he is contending against those in the churches of Galatia who were saying that sinners not only had to believe in Jesus Christ, but also had to keep the law of Moses to be justified before God. Paul's purpose in this epistle is to show that such teaching was wholly contrary to the glorious gospel of God's grace to which the Holy Spirit had borne powerful witness in the hearts and lives of many of them. And, as he brings out in this epistle, for them to give heed to such teaching was to bring themselves into bondage again. He shows the utter foolishness of such a course. Would they turn aside from the true liberty of the gospel and come under the bondage of the law again? Would they turn from that wherein alone is justification for the sinner, peace with God, the full pardon of their sins and a glorious eternal inheritance, to that which brought them into bondage and condemnation under the curse of a broken law? Paul shows here the foolishness of the fanciful idea that their supposed keeping of the law could satisfy a holy heart-searching God. He emphatically sets forth the glory of God's grace revealed in the gospel, that salvation is by the grace of God alone, "through faith; and that not of ourselves: it is the gift of God, not of works lest any man should boast" (Eph. 2:8-9).

Last week we noticed that Paul was setting before them the covenant of grace, showing them that their salvation is rooted in the promises God has spoken and his faithfulness to fulfil those promises. He showed that the promise centres in the person and finished work of Jesus Christ. He says, "For if the inheritance be of the law, it is no more of promise: but God gave it to Abraham by promise." God gave to Abraham by promise, not just the inheritance of an earthly Canaan, but the inheritance of everlasting life and the full pardon of sin. "For if the inheritance be of the law, it is no more of promise." If it is to be obtained by our obedience to the law then it can be no more of promise. It is of works. It is what we have earned, what we have contributed to, what the holy God is obligated to give to us because of our obedience to what he requires. But he says that the inheritance is not received by obedience to the law, "but God gave it to Abraham by promise." His purpose is to show the utter impossibility of the inheritance ever being by the law. How false and perverse was the teaching of those who had come into the churches in Galatia. It had a certain plausibility viewed from a human standpoint and was very acceptable to fallen carnal nature but it was perverse erroneous teaching. No wonder Paul says so strongly, "Though we, or an angel from heaven, preach any other gospel unto you than that which we have preached unto you, let him be accursed" (Gal. 1:8). The vehemence of that statement of Paul emphasises how pernicious was this false teaching. It was so harmful to the souls of men and women and so dishonouring to a holy God. Professing to honour God by their emphasis on the keeping of the law, they were dishonouring God. For they were speaking contrary to the only way that God himself has revealed whereby a sinner can be saved, to the praise and glory of his great and holy name.

Paul then deals with the matter of the law. He says, "Wherefore then serveth the law?" Why did God give it to the children of Israel through Moses on mount Sinai? If the law cannot justify, if eternal life is not to be obtained by it, if the inheritance is only through the promise, why was the law given? What purpose does it serve? He deals very emphatically with this question in the verses that follow. How important it is that we do not merely receive this teaching of Paul in an intellectual way but have a clear understanding of these truths as taught by God the Holy Spirit. How important that we know how the holy law of God solemnly applies to ourselves. As Paul says in the verses that follow, "The law was our schoolmaster...unto Christ, that we might be justified by faith."

He says, "Wherefore then serveth the law?" I read Exodus chapter 20 this evening because it tells how God gave the law to Moses on mount Sinai in an awful solemn display of his divine majesty and holiness. We see the effect that it had on the people. They feared exceedingly. "They removed, and stood afar off. And they said unto Moses, Speak thou with us, and we will hear: but let not God speak with us, lest we die" (Exod. 20:18-19). As Paul says here, the law "was ordained by angels in the hand of a mediator." The mediator was Moses. Was he not the one raised up and appointed by God? Was he not the go-between, the mediator between God and the people? God spoke to Moses. Moses spoke to the people. And the people spoke to Moses. He conveyed what they said to God. Thus Moses was a mediator, and more than once when Israel sinned he stood in the breach between them and a holy God. But I want to come to this point, "Wherefore then serveth the law?" It was given with awful solemnity on mount Sinai. What a holy perfect law it was. There God declares what he righteously and justly requires. We see in it the solemn prohibitions of God. Let us never forget that God is holy righteous and just in giving the law. He has the supreme authority to do so. In the law of God there is nothing unrighteous or unjust. It is not just an arbitrary law given at the whim of a supreme all-powerful being. It is in perfect conformity with the holiness and righteousness of God. We must never lose sight of that. It laid down what a holy God justly demands of his creatures.

"Wherefore then serveth the law? It was added because of transgressions." Now this is an important point to notice. The law was given because of transgressions, because man was and is a sinner. This can have reference to the sin of Adam. Through his disobedience to God the curse he incurred came upon the whole of the human race. In his sin all have been ruined. "It was added because of transgressions," because of Adam's sin. God displays his righteousness, justice and truth in his holy law. The law exposes the grievousness of Adam's sin, his disobedience to God. In the light of the law, we see it was righteous and just that the curse came on Adam and all his posterity. And also, "it was added because of transgressions," because men and women are sinners, and sin is found in all they do, in thought, word and deed. Ah, how important! What does that holy righteous law of God, which was given to Moses on mount Sinai, bring to light? What was its application to Israel of old? What are its solemn implications for each of us as brought to see ourselves in the light of its just demands. I say, what does the law bring to light? It shows we have sinned and are disobedient to that law. Can any one of us claim otherwise? I believe even if our outward actions only were examined, it would be plainly seen that we are transgressors of the law, disobedient to it. But friends, if our whole lives, our inner thoughts and the workings of our hearts are exposed to the just and holy claims of the law, is it not surely evident that we are transgressors? Remember the word of God says, "For whosoever shall keep the whole law, and yet offend in one point, he is guilty of all" (Jas. 2:10). It is the law of a holy God and therefore our transgression of it is an affront to a holy God. Its divine sacredness and majesty is fully consistent with the holy God who has righteously and justly given that law.

"It was added because of transgressions." I want to emphasise what Paul shows us here, that the law was never given as a way of life for sinful fallen men. God never gave the law with the intention that if men would only keep its righteous demands they would then be justified before him. That was never why the law was given. Those to whom it was given were transgressors. How can they who are already transgressors meet the demands of the law? That is impossible. No, the law "was added because of transgressions," that sin might be manifested to be exceeding sinful. As Paul says in another place, "by the law is the knowledge of sin" (Rom.3:20). That is the purpose of the law. It curses righteously and justly. It condemns all that are under it because they are transgressors of it. "It was added because of transgressions," and all the law can do for you and me, as sinners, is condemn us. It exposes our sins and transgressions. Friends, is not this a very solemn thing? Yet such is the perverse foolishness of human nature, such the utter folly of those false preachers in Galatia, that they were saying it was essential for men to keep the law to be justified. What an utterly impossible task for them to set! How wholly inconsistent, on the one hand, with the purpose for which the law was given, and, on the other hand, with the only way God has revealed for the salvation of sinners!

He says, "It was added because of transgressions, till the seed should come to whom the promise was made." Who was this seed? Surely Paul is setting forth in this chapter that the seed was the Lord Jesus Christ. He was born under the law and was subject to all its holy requirements. He fulfilled the law, he satisfied its just and due demands, yet not for himself, for he was "holy, harmless, undefiled, separate from sinners" (Heb. 7:26). In him was no sin for he was the Holy One of God. For whom then did he fulfil that law? He did so for all that the Father had given him. It is the satisfaction he rendered to the law that alone justifies the sinner before God. This is the way of salvation that the gospel makes known. Oh, the glory and the blessedness of this truth! Salvation is not in my keeping the law, but in my being brought as a sinner to flee to the refuge the gospel makes known. It is not by my strivings to keep the law but as I am taught my sinnership by the Holy Spirit and brought to look to the person and finished work of the Lord Jesus Christ. At Gethsemane and Calvary, I am brought to behold the holy *Lamb* of God.

What saved the Israelites when they came up out of Egypt on the night when the Passover was instituted and when the destroying angel went through the land to destroy all the firstborn of the Egyptians? What prevented the destroying angel coming into their households? Was it their obedience to the law of God? Was it not rather the blood that was sprinkled on the door posts and lintel? Was not that the tremendous importance of the passover lamb? As the Lord said, "When I see the blood, I will pass over you" (Exod. 12:13). And so with poor sinners still. They are not saved by their strivings to keep the law. That only condemns them. It is the obedience of the Lamb and the satisfaction given by the precious blood that was shed on Calvary that saves them. As I, a sinner, am taught by the Holy Spirit, I find that all the law demands of me has been met by my surety, the Lord Jesus Christ. My Saviour has endured for me all the curse I have incurred. It is the blood of Jesus Christ his Son that cleanseth from all sin.

"It was ordained by angels in the hand of a mediator." As I have said, this mediator was Moses. "Now a mediator is not a mediator of one, but God is one." The point being brought out is that a mediator is one who acts between two parties, and here we have on the one hand an offended almighty God of whom it is written "I am the Lord; and there is none else" (Isa. 45:5).

Now does not the law solemnly manifest that God is offended and is justly angry with all transgressors of his law and therefore they are under its curse and condemnation? Paul says, "Is the law then against the promises of God? God forbid." The law of God is not against the promises. It did not nullify the promises God had given, far from it. He says, "God forbid: for if there had been a law given which could have given life, verily righteousness should have been by the law." How significant is that point. If God had given a law that was possible for men to keep, then "verily righteousness should have been by the law." The inheritance would have been obtained in that way. But no, he says that "the scripture hath concluded." That is, the teaching of God's word from beginning to end is that all men are under sin. There is no exception. "There is none that doeth good, no, not one...all have sinned, and come short of the glory of God."

(Rom. 3:12,23). Therefore to expect to obtain righteousness by the deeds of the law is an utterly foolish assumption. For people to teach that, is not only foolish but grievously erroneous and deceiving of men and women, make no mistake about it.

He says, "But the scripture hath concluded all under sin, that the promise by faith of Jesus Christ might be given to them that believe. But before faith came, we were kept under the law, shut up unto the faith which should afterwards be revealed." And he goes on to illustrate this point by saying, "Wherefore the law was our schoolmaster to bring us unto Christ, that we might be justified by faith." Now that was true of the Jews as they were under the law God gave them by Moses. They were not justified by the keeping of that law in any way whatsoever, but it was their schoolmaster to give them instruction. Here we see the right use of the law. It is a schoolmaster which imparts instruction. What instruction? It exposes and brings to light our sins and transgressions. Do we know what it is to be thus taught under the law as a schoolmaster? Do we know the law as brought home to our conscience by the Holy Spirit, pointing to every particle of our lives and revealing our transgression in the light of its holy requirements?

What does the law also do? It condemns us. It can do nothing else but that. It demands perfection and is ready to punish even the slightest deviation from the perfection of its requirements. The law condemns and is ready to punish. And it is righteous and just in doing so. If we know the law in our conscience as our schoolmaster by the effective teaching of the Holy Spirit, we not only see how just the law's requirements are. We shall also be brought to own that God is righteous in condemning us for our transgressions. And when the law as our schoolmaster condemns us it will kill us to any hope of life and acceptance before God by the law. He says, "The law was our schoolmaster…unto Christ." The law does not bring us unto Christ, for the gospel alone does that. The law condemns. It shows us what a holy God requires and it curses our transgressions. And this instruction lays us low in the dust before a holy heart-searching God as a justly condemned sinner. It is sovereign grace that brings us there, make no mistake about it. We are brought to know in our souls that we are a guilty, needy, hell-deserving sinner, our conscience witnessing to what the law righteously declares. And it is in this place of self-condemnation that the gospel in all its fulness and freeness is revealed, and we see that the wonder and blessedness of the gospel is that Jesus Christ is the Saviour of sinners.

He says, "That we might be justified by faith." You know, as taught our ruin through sin and our condemnation under the law, oh how readily will the gospel be heard and received. What great and good news the gospel speaks to the heart of a guilty needy sinner, not telling them what they have to do but revealing what God in Christ has done for them! What good news is this, of pardon, peace and an eternal inheritance, not coming to them on the ground of what they do but freely through what the Lord Jesus has done for them. And it is to such whose consciences are feelingly under the curse and condemnation of the law that the gracious invitations of the gospel are set forth. What words of truth and grace are found therein as Jesus himself declares "Come unto me, all ye that labour and are heavy laden, and I will give you rest" (Matt. 11:28). What a word is that as it comes to the guilty, burdened soul of a sinner! Oh, one says:

> "What sweet invitations the gospel contains,
> To men heavy laden with bondage and chains;
> It welcomes the weary to come and be blessed
> With ease from their burdens, in Jesus to rest."

Yes, as the prophet Isaiah declares, "Ho, every one that thirsteth, come ye to the waters, and he that hath no money; come ye, buy, and eat; yea, come, buy wine and milk without money and without price" (Isa. 55:1). And does not Paul show here a full and complete deliverance from the curse and condemnation of the law? He says, "But after that faith is come, we are no longer under a schoolmaster." As brought through grace to saving faith in Jesus Christ we are no longer under the law. Its curse and condemnation have no more to do with us because what the Lord Jesus has done answers its every demand. Therefore, as a sinner justified by faith through the rich and free grace of God, the law has no more to do with me. It has nothing more to speak to me.

Paul says, "But after that faith is come, we are no longer under a schoolmaster. For ye are all the children of God by faith in

Christ Jesus." That is a very significant statement. Ye are no longer under the law as the schoolmaster, no longer a servant or a slave but a dear child of God, a son, a daughter of God. The Spirit bears witness to this. Is he not set forth as "the Spirit of adoption, whereby we cry, Abba, Father"? (Rom. 8:15). "For ye are all the children of God by faith in Christ Jesus." See the reality and blessedness of that relationship. No longer a servant but a son with all the privileges, with all the true liberty of a son as well. Ah, I want to emphasise this. He says, "The law was our schoolmaster to bring us unto Christ," but faith being come, being justified by faith, we are no longer under that schoolmaster. It has no more to say and do with us, for "we are all the children of God by faith in Christ Jesus."

Who is the teacher of these children of God? Who is their guide and companion? Very significant words in the prophecies of Isaiah and Jeremiah express one of the real blessings of the new covenant of grace, a blessed privilege of the children of God by faith in Christ Jesus. Jeremiah proclaims, "Behold, the days come, saith the Lord, that…they shall teach no more every man his neighbour, and every man his brother, saying, Know the Lord: for they shall all know me, from the least of them unto the greatest of them, saith the Lord: for I will forgive their iniquity, and I will remember their sin no more" (Jer. 31:31,34). Isaiah proclaims this precious promise to the church, "All thy children shall be taught of the Lord; and great shall be the peace of thy children" (Isa. 54:13). Here is the blessed privilege of the children of God by faith in Christ Jesus. They are no longer under a schoolmaster. As brought into living union with Jesus Christ they are all taught of God. They have the blessing, not only of the promise of the Holy Spirit, but of his gracious indwelling as their guide and teacher, as the one who will lead them into all truth.

Oh, some will say, 'What, no longer under the law, delivered and freed from it, then that surely means they are under no restraint at all.' Paul answers that accusation which many were making against the truths of free and sovereign grace which he preached. He asks this question, "Shall we continue in sin, that grace may abound? God forbid" (Rom. 6:1-2). And he shows the impossibility of such a course, for though the Lord's people are delivered from the law, they are brought into a glorious union with Jesus Christ. As "the love of God is shed abroad in our hearts by the Holy Spirit that is given unto us" (Rom. 5:5), what is the joy and delight of a child of God? It is to know and do the will of his Father in heaven. And who is his guide and teacher with respect to the will of his heavenly Father and his Lord and Saviour? Is it not the Holy Spirit of whom Jesus says, He shall "abide with you for ever" (John 14:16). "He shall take of mine, and shall show it unto you"? (John 16:15).

"We are no longer under a schoolmaster. For ye are all the children of God by faith in Jesus." As I say, the promise runs, "All thy children shall be taught of the Lord; and great shall be the peace of thy children." But I must leave the remarks there this evening. May the Lord add his blessing. Amen.

16

GALATIANS 3:26-29

For ye are all the children of God by faith in Christ Jesus. For as many of you as have been baptized into Christ have put on Christ. There is neither Jew nor Greek, there is neither bond nor free, there is neither male nor female: for ye are all one in Christ Jesus. And if ye be Christ's, then are ye Abraham's seed, and heirs according to the promise.

It is surely not necessary for me to again go over the main point Paul is dealing with in this epistle to the Galatians. He is contending against those that were preaching things contrary to the gospel that he preached and which he had received from the Lord and Saviour Jesus Christ. But I would just add this point. As we consider this epistle one fact comes out very clearly. How serious a matter is error. How solemnly and vigorously does Paul testify against the false teaching in Galatia. He does not consider error a matter of indifference. He does not consider the mixing of faith and works an insignificant thing. He expresses his abhorrence of it. He shows clearly how it is contrary to the revealed will of the Lord Jesus Christ and dishonouring to his person and work. He emphatically shows how damaging it is to the souls of men and women—we might solemnly say even damning. We must not lose sight of the fact that Paul shows no compromise whatsoever with error, nor does he give any countenance to those who preach anything apart from Jesus Christ and him crucified. He does not consider those who were teaching error in Galatia to be brothers in Christ. Oh, some might say, 'Well, they were not far off. Did they not say that faith in

Christ was needful even though they laid great stress on circumcision and the keeping of the law of Moses? Surely these people were not so altogether astray from the truth that Paul should so vigorously condemn them as he does? Surely he could at least accept them as brothers in Christ though they are sadly astray on some things?' No, the apostle, as led of God the Holy Spirit, does not compromise with them or even receive them as brothers in Christ. Indeed, he says, "Though we, or an angel from heaven, preach any other gospel unto you than that which we have preached unto you, *let him be accursed*" (Gal. 1:8).

We have noticed in previous weeks how Paul brings out in this third chapter the glorious things the believer receives through faith in Christ Jesus. He shows that "Christ is the end of the law for righteousness to every one that believeth" (Rom. 10:4). And the true mark of God's living children is faith which is given by God out of the fulness and freeness of his grace.

Now without going into the things that we have dealt with previously, I will come to these words that I have read by way of a text. He says, "For ye are all the children of God by faith in Christ Jesus." And he further opens up this truth in the following verses. Bear in mind how the Jews laid great stress on the fact that they were the descendants of Abraham. Being his children they thought they could lay claim to the favour of God. To be the natural children of Abraham was in their estimation equivalent to being the children of God. But as the Lord Jesus showed and as the apostle here clearly brings out, it is not descent from Abraham that constitutes a man a child of God. What a great favour and inestimable blessing to be a child of God! We are born into this world as sinful and fallen creatures under the curse and condemnation of a holy God. How high a blessing and favour it is then, to be brought into the relationship of children of God. The scriptures go further. We read not only of believers being children of God, but "heirs of God, and joint-heirs with Christ" (Rom. 8:17).

"For ye are all the children of God by faith in Christ Jesus." How great is this blessing! How is it entered into? It is by grace through faith. The work of nature does not constitute us children of God. It is no outward thing that brings us into this relationship.

It is the outworking of God's sovereign grace and distinguishing mercy wherein he manifests his love to us in calling us by his grace and bringing us to true repentance and saving faith in the Lord Jesus Christ. This is why Paul can say, "For ye are all the children of God by faith in Christ Jesus." Repentance and living faith are the outward distinguishing evidences of the internal teaching and grace of God the Holy Spirit. The faith that Paul is setting forth here is that precious grace whereby we are brought as sinners to the feet of the Lord Jesus Christ, to believe in him, to receive him and to trust in him alone. Paul tells us that this is a "faith which worketh by love" (Gal. 5:6).

Now he goes on in verse 27, "For as many of you as have been baptized into Christ have put on Christ." What does the apostle mean by this statement? All in the church in Galatia had been baptized. All persons in the early church were baptized on a profession of their faith in the Lord and Saviour Jesus Christ. And here Paul makes distinct reference to baptism. "As many of you as have been baptized into Christ." Now he is not just alluding to the ordinance of believers' baptism though he does have that in view. It is not attendance on the outward ordinance of which it could be said, "As many of you as have been baptized into Christ have put on Christ." It is not by attendance on the ordinance that we come into the relationship of the children of God. Let us not forget that though the ordinance of believer's baptism is important, it is inward grace that is the vitally essential thing. Some in the early church professed to believe and were baptized, yet it was solemnly evident that they were destitute of the true grace of God in their heart. But what is brought before us here? What does this ordinance graciously set before us? "As many of you as have been baptized into Christ." It is a true identifying with the Lord Jesus Christ himself in his suffering, death and resurrection. What a vivid setting forth of those things is the very mode of believer's baptism, the being immersed in water. It is the profession that all their hope for time and eternity centres in Jesus Christ, in who he is and what he has done for them. For believer's baptism not only identifies the believer with Jesus Christ but signifies his vital union with him. Without that vital union by grace through faith what is the outward ordinance?

"As many of you as have been baptized into Christ have put on Christ." They have done so by the outward profession of the Lord's name, identifying with him and his people in believer's baptism. There they professed to be dead to their old ways and their old life and to be risen again in newness of life. There they professed to be followers of the Lord and Saviour Jesus Christ. What then is the significance of this statement in the context of this epistle in which Paul is dealing with the grievous error in the Galatian churches? Well, this relates to what he says in the opening part of this chapter, "O foolish Galatians, who hath bewitched you, that ye should not obey the truth, before whose eyes Jesus Christ hath been evidently set forth, crucified among you?...Are ye so foolish? having begun in the Spirit, are ye now made perfect by the flesh?" He would bid them bring to mind that their baptism signified not only their identity with Jesus Christ but their union with him. In their baptism they professed to put on the Lord Jesus Christ. Would they now turn back into ways in which there is the denying of what they have professed in their baptism. The point he is making is that they could not hold to both the keeping of the law of Moses for salvation *and* profession of faith in Jesus Christ for salvation. These two are mutually exclusive. Friends, how little is it realised that salvation is either by works or faith. It is either through what the sinner can do, albeit as some profess, with the help of the Lord Jesus, *or* it is wholly of grace through the Holy Spirit bringing the sinner into living vital union with Christ. It is one thing or the other. To turn back to circumcision and the keeping of the law is to deny what was professed in believer's baptism. And what profit is Jesus Christ to them who seek to be justified by the law? Paul shows how mutually exclusive these things are. In their turning away they were rejecting the Lord Jesus Christ who is the only way of salvation for sinners.

He says, "For as many of you as have been baptized into Christ have put on Christ." Oh, how precious and vital is that union with Jesus Christ and what blessings flow from it to the Lord's people! The Galatians, in turning again to circumcision, were turning away from the only source from whence true blessing flows. What could circumcision and the professed keeping of the law of Moses do for sinners? All it could do was condemn them and bring them into bondage. In it there was no way of peace or blessing, no comfort for a guilty needy sinner. True, as I have emphasised before, the law that was given to Moses was the holy law of God. It was "holy, and just, and good" (Rom. 7:12). But for sinful men and women it yields no real lasting good. All it can do is condemn them for their sins. But oh, the blessings that flow to the believer through Jesus Christ! They are the blessings of pardon, yes, the pardon of their sins righteously and justly through the redemption that is in him. They are the blessings of peace with God and the glorious hope of eternal life in eternal living union with Jesus Christ. Being "all the children of God by faith in Christ Jesus," what privileges and blessings are theirs. Is it not the gracious work of the Holy Spirit to graciously seal these glorious truths in the believer's heart? He witnesses that they are brought into the relationship of sons and daughters of the great God, their Father in heaven, with all that implies. "For as many of you as have been baptized into Christ have put on Christ." Oh do not lose sight of the greatness and blessedness of the believer's privileges by grace through faith in Jesus Christ.

He says, "There is neither Jew nor Greek, there is neither bond nor free, there is neither male nor female: for ye are all one in Christ Jesus." What a divisive thing was their turning again to circumcision. It divided the church. It did not promote the true unity of the brethren. Their preaching of circumcision was very divisive! Is it not true that where works are set up, as by these teachers in Galatia, such doctrine is ever divisive? It does not promote the union and fellowship of the people of God. By their contending for circumcision they kept open the breach which existed between Jew and Gentile. Or, to use Paul's expression in the second chapter of his epistle to the Ephesians which we read this evening, they built up again the middle wall of partition that separated Jew and Gentile. Now, says Paul, all those distinctions have been done away by grace through faith. He brings this out most beautifully in that chapter in Ephesians. He says, "Wherefore remember, that ye being in time past Gentiles in the flesh, who are called Uncircumcision by that which is called the

Circumcision in the flesh made by hands; that at that time ye were without Christ, being aliens from the commonwealth of Israel, and strangers from the covenants of promise, having no hope, and without God in the world: but now in Christ Jesus ye who sometimes were far off are made nigh by the blood of Christ. For he is our peace, who hath made both one [that is, Jew and Gentile], and hath broken down the middle wall of partition between us; having abolished in his flesh the enmity, even the law of commandments contained in ordinances; for to make in himself of twain one new man, so making peace; and that he might reconcile both unto God in one body by the cross, having slain the enmity thereby: and came and preached peace to you which were afar off, and to them that were nigh. For through him we both (that is, Jew and Gentile) have access by one Spirit unto the Father" (Eph. 2:11-18). Oh the teaching of circumcision and all that went with it was divisive. For, as Paul shows, those distinctions no longer exist between Jew and Gentile as they are brought into the blessings of the grace of God through Jesus Christ our Lord. As they are brought into the oneness and unity of the children of God, "there is neither Jew nor Greek, there is neither bond nor free, there is neither male nor female; for ye are all one in Christ Jesus."

Now let me just add one or two other points with respect to this verse 28. Paul is saying that all distinctions are done away between Jew and Gentile, bond and free, male and female, in the sense that as all are sinners they are all saved by free and sovereign grace. They are not saved because they are a Jew or rejected because they are a Gentile. They are not saved by distinctions of race or class or whatever position they may have in this world. No, the salvation of God through Jesus Christ our Lord is sovereign and free. Both Jew and Gentile, bond and free, male and female, are all saved by free and sovereign grace. All owe everything to Jesus Christ. All have nothing to glory in of themselves. All their glorying is in what Paul writes in his epistle to the Corinthians. He says, "But of him are ye in Christ Jesus, who of God is made unto us wisdom, righteousness, sanctification and redemption: that, according as it is written, He that glorieth, let him glory in the Lord" (1 Cor. 1:30-31). Ah, that is the place of glorying for every one of the Lord's people. It is in the Lord, in what he has done for them. What debtors they are to his free and sovereign grace! "There is neither Jew nor Greek, there is neither bond nor free, there is neither male nor female: for ye are all one in Christ Jesus." Let us not lose sight then of the oneness and unity of the church in Jesus Christ.

Now we know from the new testament scriptures that in the relationships of brethren to one another here on earth and in their positions in civil society there are distinctions to be observed— masters to servants and so on. But Paul in this verse is not dealing with those things. He is showing the oneness of the church, as "ye are all one in Christ Jesus," all dependent on the Lord and indebted to him for everything. Remember what he writes in his epistle to the Romans. "There is therefore now no condemnation to them which are in Christ Jesus, who walk not after the flesh, but after the Spirit" (Rom. 8:1). In that truth is all the blessedness of his people found. It is as they are all "in Christ Jesus" and one with him for time and eternity. Let us not lose sight of the essential identity of the believing people of God with Christ Jesus their Lord, the gracious truth that he and they are one. You know, Paul speaks of this as well in his epistle to the Ephesians where he refers to the marriage union. "For this cause shall a man leave his father and mother, and shall be joined unto his wife, and they two shall be one flesh. This is a great mystery: but I speak concerning Christ and the church" (Eph. 5:31-32). "All one in Christ Jesus."

"And if ye be Christ's, then are ye Abraham's seed, and heirs according to the promise." See the point being brought out. The Jews claimed, and these judaizing teachers who were crying up circumcision in Galatia were saying, that the important thing is to be the children of Abraham. If you were not a Jew by birth then you needed to become a proselyte to the Jewish religion by being circumcised. They were claiming that this made them the children of Abraham. But Paul says, No. He says, "If ye be Christ's, then are ye Abraham's seed, and heirs according to the promise." Oh he places the whole emphasis on the glorious reality of saving grace. We see here that all blessings flow not from what believers were or what they could claim of relationship to Abraham, but from what they were brought to possess in Christ Jesus their Lord through sovereign grace. "If ye be Christ's." How were they Christ's? They were his by grace alone through faith, through the sovereign choice of God, through the gracious work of the Holy Spirit in his calling them and bringing them into a living relationship with Christ Jesus their Lord. "And if ye be Christ's, then are ye Abraham's seed, and heirs according to the promise." Yes, John brings it out in his first epistle when he says, "Beloved, now are we the sons of God, and it doth not yet appear what we shall be: but we know that, when he shall appear, we shall be like him; for we shall see him as he is" (1 John 3:2).

But I will leave the remarks there this evening. May the Lord add his blessing. Amen.

17

GALATIANS 4:1-3

Now I say, That the heir, as long as he is a child, differeth nothing from a servant, though he be lord of all; but is under tutors and governors until the time appointed of the father. Even so we, when we were children, were in bondage under the elements of the world.

In the first verses of this chapter, Paul continues to open up what he had been setting forth in the closing verses of chapter 3. He further illustrates the important truth of verses 26 and 29, "For ye are all the children of God by faith in Christ Jesus...And if ye be Christ's, then are ye Abraham's seed, and heirs according to the promise."

We must still bear in mind that Paul's main purpose in writing this epistle was to contend against those who were troubling the churches in Galatia with grievous error. They were teaching that it was necessary for those who professed faith in Jesus Christ to keep the law that God had given to Moses and to submit to all its ordinances and appointments. Paul is emphasising that those things were good in their place and profitable for the purpose for which God gave them, yet it was a retrograde step for believers in the Lord Jesus to return to such observances. It did not give them liberty but brought them into bondage again. Paul states that if such teaching is true, then salvation is not of grace but of works, and the person and work of Jesus Christ availeth nothing, whatever these teachers may protest to the contrary.

As I have said on previous occasions, Paul is dealing with a very serious matter. This is not a secondary issue on which we may hold any view. This is vital to salvation, to the glory of God, and to the eternal welfare of the living family of God. So in this chapter Paul continues his teaching on this essential doctrine. He continues to confront and confute the errors that were being promulgated in Galatia. And he uses some very vivid illustrations to put over the points he is making. In the latter part of the chapter he even uses an allegory.

But in these opening verses we read, "Now I say, That the heir, as long as he is a child, differeth nothing from a servant, though he be lord of all; but is under tutors and governors until the time appointed of the father." What is meant by this illustration? I just want to read one or two extracts to you at this juncture: "The illustration that Paul is using here, that the heir, as long as he is a child, differeth nothing from a servant, though he be lord of all, is like unto the custom that prevailed in houses of the nobility and is used as an illustration. The heir to an estate so long as he is in infancy is placed under restraint just as the servants are. Tutors and governors hold him in what appears to him to be bondage. He has just to do as he is told. He knows not the reason why he cannot yet be given the full liberty of his father's house and estate, for his character and intelligence is not yet sufficiently formed. However his father knows when the time will arise, and the day is fixed when he will come of age and enter into the privileges and responsibilities of life." Paul is applying that illustration to the situation of the Jews under the Levitical dispensation.

There is also a vivid point brought out here respecting the Lord's people, before he calls them by his grace. I would just also read this. "It was thus with God's people in the former day under the law, which was as a schoolmaster to them. Children they might be, but they were treated as servants and rightly so. It was no question of their individual eminence as saints of God, but simply of the dispensation in which they lived. No greater man than John the Baptist was ever born, yet as the Lord told us, he that is least in the kingdom of heaven is greater then he. In their days God had not yet been fully revealed, redemption had not been accomplished, the Spirit had not been given. Until these three great events had come to pass, the conditions were not established which permitted the coming of age of the people of God. All three did come to pass when on the scene there arrived the Son of God."

As Paul says here, "Even so we, when we were children, were in bondage under the elements of the world." This refers to the Jews. They were the people of God but they were under the tutelage of the law and of that dispensation. True, without question there were very eminent saints of God under the old testament. Yet they did not enter into the fulness and blessedness of the grace and truth of God which is revealed since the coming of the Lord Jesus Christ. Paul brings this point out in the eleventh chapter of his epistle to the Hebrews. In the closing part he says of all that long catalogue of men and women of faith, "And these all, having obtained a good report through faith, received not the promise" (Heb. 11:39). What does he mean? All these men and women lived and walked by faith and died in faith, yet Paul says they "received not the promise." They did not live to see the full fruition of the coming of the Lord Jesus Christ. Even though the blessings and benefits of the only way of salvation were theirs by grace through faith in the coming One, yet they did not receive the promise. They did not enter into the fulness and liberty of the gospel as it is made known in the coming of the Lord Jesus, "God having provided some better thing for us, that they without us should not be made perfect" (v.40).

This point is very succinctly brought out in the case of John the Baptist as I have mentioned. The Lord Jesus said of John, "Among those that are born of women there hath not risen a greater prophet that John the Baptist" (Luke 7:28). He was the last, and in a real sense, the greatest of the old testament prophets. They had all prophesied of the coming of the Lord Jesus. John's privilege and office was to cry, "Behold the Lamb of God, which taketh away the sin of the world" (John 1:29). Yet, though John was the last and greatest of the prophets and though Jesus said, "Among those that are born of women there hath not risen a greater than John the Baptist," he also added, "Notwithstanding, he that is least in the kingdom of heaven is greater than he." How could that be? What are we to understand by that statement of the Lord Jesus? How can the least in the kingdom of heaven be greater than John the Baptist, that eminent servant of God, one faithful in the work to which he was called of God? It is because John came as part of the old testament dispensation which was bound up with the Levitical law. As I have said, those things were indeed of God. They were good and profitable for the purpose for which God gave them. But they had their fruition and end when the promise was fulfilled by the Lord Jesus Christ in his life, death, resurrection, ascension and his outpouring of the Holy Spirit on the day of Pentecost.

Paul's illustration in these verses contrasts law and gospel. Glorious was the revelation that was given by God under the law, but greater is the glory of the gospel revelation. What a holy God requires was distinctly set forth under the law. It made known the awful reality of the malady of sin and the guilt and condemnation that men and women are in as transgressors of that holy law. True, there were blessed glimpses given of the salvation that was to come. But oh, when we come to the gospel revelation in the manifestation of Jesus Christ, how vast is the difference! It is as John says, "The law was given by Moses, but grace and truth came by Jesus Christ" (John 1:17). Again, "As in Adam all die, even so in Christ shall all be made alive" (1 Cor. 15:22). Paul is saying that the Jews, including himself, in the time of the Levitical dispensation were truly children but children in their infancy under the tutelage of the law as their schoolmaster. They did not enjoy the full realisation of the blessed liberty and privileges of the children of God. But how all this had changed through the coming and finished work of the Lord Jesus Christ! Truly, through him is the coming of age of the church. The blessed fulfilment of the promise is ushered in through the grace that is in the Lord Jesus. Believers now need no human mediator between themselves and a holy God.

The Jews, God's people of old, approached him through the offerings of the sacrifices and the medium of an earthly priesthood. In that sense there was no direct access to God. Access was in the way he had appointed, and as Paul says to the Hebrews, as long as that appointment continued it witnessed "that the way into the holiest of all was not yet made manifest" (Heb. 9:8). For even Aaron, the high priest ordained of God for men in things pertaining to God, only had liberty to enter into the presence of God in the holiest place once a year. And that was "not without blood which he offered for himself, and for the errors of the people" (Heb. 9:7). But now, through the coming of Jesus Christ and through the glory and blessedness of the things made known in the gospel, poor sinners have the right of direct access to God in Christ. We may now "come boldly unto the throne of grace, that we may obtain mercy, and find grace to help in time of need" (Heb. 4:16).

Let me take this a step further. He says, "Now I say, That the heir, as long as he is a child, differeth nothing from a servant, though he be Lord of all; but is under tutors and governors until the time appointed of the father. Even so we, when we were children, were in bondage under the elements of the world." But when the Son of God came, God's people passed from under the schoolmaster of the law, whose control was exercised according to the elements or principles of the world, and they came under the control of the Spirit of God exercised according to the principles of grace. As I have said, Paul here distinctly refers to the Jews, God's chosen people under the Levitical law and dispensation. And is not each one whom God calls by divine grace brought to know in their measure, the tutelage of the law as a "school master...unto Christ"? As taught of the Holy Spirit they are convinced of their sin and know condemnation by the holy law of God in their conscience. If there is one thing a child of God is taught under the law, it is the deep sense of his ruin and need through sin.

Friends, is not one of the problems today that there is apparently so little understanding of this solemn truth. I am quite sure that was the case of these who were insisting even in the days of Paul that the law had to be kept for salvation, and that this was even more important than faith in Jesus Christ. I say that such advocates of the law do not know what the law is, and certainly do not know it in their own conscience. If we know what Paul is saying in this epistle about the tutelage of the law as a schoolmaster we shall not advocate the law as a way of life. We will know that it not only convinces us of our sin but it condemns us. It shows us our utter ruin through our sin. We will know it demands that we do perfectly what it requires and yet we solemnly realise our utter inability to meet those requirements. I say, if we truly know the law laid home to our conscience as a condemning and killing law, we shall never advocate the law in any respect as a way of access and acceptance before God. Why, as taught by the Holy Spirit under the solemn convictions of the law, we will be chased out of every hope and refuge but that which the gospel makes known. Outside of Christ is no salvation, though we may be deluded into fondly thinking there is hope and refuge for us in the keeping of the law. Toplady sums it up so well in his well-known hymn, Rock of Ages:

> "Could my zeal no respite know,
> Could my tears for ever flow,
> All for sin could not atone;
> Thou must save, and thou alone."

Friends, what a mercy to be brought there. As Toplady further expresses in that hymn:

> "Foul, I to the fountain fly;
> Wash me, Saviour, or I die."

Paul says, "Even so we, when we were children, were in bondage under the elements of the world." The point is this. What alone delivers us from bondage and guilt under a broken law? Paul says, "But when the fulness of the time was come, God sent forth his Son, made of a woman, made under the law, to redeem them that were under the law, that we might receive the adoption of sons." Such is the freedom and blessedness that is ours by grace through faith in the person of the Lord Jesus Christ. Such are the blessings of the gospel. Those who were advocating the law were bringing believers back under its bondage. It was a retrograde step. They were saying that a position of servitude was far greater and more glorious than the position of a free born son of God! Yet the son experiences right of access to God, fellowship with Jesus Christ, free and full pardon of sin, peace with God and the glorious hope of eternal life! See the comparison I am trying to make. One position is servitude and hard bondage. The other is the liberty of the free born son of God.

Let me illustrate the point in this way. You remember when Paul was apprehended in Jerusalem. When the chief captain rescued him from the Jewish mob, Paul was bound and was about to be examined by scourging to find out why he was accused of the Jews. Paul there claimed the right of Roman citizenship. One of the rights of Roman citizenship was that a Roman citizen was not to be bound or scourged without a fair trial and proper judgment. When Paul makes known the fact that he is a Roman citizen, the chief captain is greatly afraid that he had bound him being a Roman. He says to Paul, "With a great sum obtained I this freedom. And Paul said, "But I was free born" (Acts 22:28). That is a vivid illustration of the glorious truth that Paul is bringing out in our text. He is saying to these Galatians, 'Do you want to be under servitude and bondage? That is what the law brings. Would you despise the blessed privilege and glory of a free-born son, preferring the position of servitude and bondage under the law?' Ah friends, remember that in the kingdom of Jesus Christ there are no bond servants. All are free-born sons and daughters. This is the glorious privilege of the children of God. These are the blessings of the gospel, which come to us through the person and finished work of the Lord Jesus Christ.

He says, "God sent forth his Son, made of a woman, made under the law." Yes, Jesus Christ, as the great head and surety of his people took their position under the law. He, as "made of a woman," took a sinless human nature into union with his divine nature. As the great head and surety of the church he was made under the law, he was born under the law, he voluntarily subjected himself to it. Did he not declare, "I delight to do thy will, O my God: yea, thy law is within my heart" (Ps. 40:8). He was not only made under the law and subject to its just and righteous demands but as the God-man he fulfilled every part and particle of its requirements. What is more, he made atonement for all the transgressions of the law by his people, bearing its curse and condemnation to redeem them from its power.

Thus Paul shows that to be a believer through grace in Jesus Christ is to be brought from under the law. What more can it say to the believer? Can it justly condemn the believer in Jesus Christ? Oh, you say, they are sinners and have transgressed the law's commands. Indeed they have. But Jesus Christ has redeemed them, he has paid the penalty, he has fulfilled the law for them! Hear the language of holy scripture on this point. Paul sounds out a glorious note of victory. He says, "Who shall lay any thing to the charge of God's elect?" (Rom. 8:33). Is not that a most emphatic challenge? Surely there are many things that can be laid to their charge? Are they not sinners and transgressors of the law? Cannot Satan bring many charges against them?

See this illustrated in the prophecy of Zechariah. He is shown in vision, "Joshua, the high priest, standing before the angel of the Lord, clothed with filthy garments, and Satan standing at his right hand to resist him" (Zech. 3:1), that is, to accuse him. And Satan is ever the accuser of the brethren. All the marks of guilt and condemnation are upon Joshua. He is "clothed with filthy garments" which indicate his utter ruin and guilt by sin. What more does Satan need to accuse him. He only needs to point at him. Look at the condition God's people are found in by nature. It is clear that they are transgressors and have broken the law. But what is the word that comes from the angel of the Lord! Ah, his sentence is this: "The LORD rebuke thee, O Satan…is not this a brand plucked out of the fire."

Paul takes up that glorious theme. "Who shall lay anything to the charge of God's elect? It is God that justifieth" (Rom. 8:33). And who is going to countermand the judgment that God passes? It is God that justifies. Yes, he declares that the sinner who is a believer through grace in Jesus Christ is indeed accepted and righteous in his sight. And who is going to countermand the sentence passed by God the righteous Judge of all the earth? In effect, he says, 'In the believer, I see no sin. I see nothing to condemn. All I see is the righteousness of Jesus Christ and his atoning work. I see all his sin covered, fully atoned for, through the redeeming work of the Lord Jesus Christ.' All he beholds is his only begotten, dearly beloved Son in whom he is well pleased. As Paul goes on to say, "Who shall lay anything to the charge of God's elect? It is God that justifieth. Who is he that condemneth?" And we have the full glorious answer to all condemnation of the believer. "It is Christ that died, yea rather, that is risen again, who is even at the right hand of God, who also maketh intercession for us."

Continuing further in chapter 4 of Galatians, Paul says, "God sent forth his Son…to redeem them that were under the law, that we might receive the adoption of sons. And because ye are sons, God has sent forth the Spirit of his Son into your hearts, crying, Abba, Father." This witness of the Spirit in the hearts of his people is not that which constitutes them sons of God. They are the sons of God by his eternal choice and by the redeeming work of Jesus Christ. It is to the reality of this sonship that the Lord the Holy Spirit bears witness. Was this ever heard of under the law? Was this freedom, access and liberty known by the Levitical dispensation? But in the gospel dispensation, through the ministration of the new testament "that excelleth" (2 Cor. 3:10), sinful men and women are brought to repentance and faith in the Lord Jesus Christ and into the blessed privilege of the sons of God, "Whereby we cry, Abba, Father."

"Abba, Father." What blessings that relationship contains! As one well says:

> "My God, my Father, blissful name!
> Oh may I call thee mine?
> May I with sweet assurance claim
> A portion so divine?"

But I will leave the remarks there this evening. May the Lord add his blessing. Amen.

18

GALATIANS 4:4-7

But when the fulness of the time was come, God sent forth his Son, made of a woman, made under the law, to redeem them that were under the law, that we might receive the adoption of sons. And because ye are sons, God hath sent forth the Spirit of his Son into your hearts, crying, Abba, Father. Wherefore thou art no more a servant, but a son; and if a son, then an heir of God through Christ.

Last Friday in speaking from the opening part of the fourth chapter of this epistle, I touched upon what is brought before us in these verses I have read this evening. But I want to return to them again, for what a fulness of truth is here set before us! Oh the wonders of redeeming love we see here in the unfolding of God's sovereign purposes of grace and mercy, in the person and the work of the Lord Jesus Christ, for the salvation of his people.

Let us not overlook this important fact. It is something which is sadly neglected in the days in which we live. We find there is much emphasis placed on man and on man's salvation. In many respects, the gospel is often set forth with the main emphasis man-ward, in that it meets and solves the problems of men and women. There is indeed what we might term a man-ward aspect of the gospel, that which by free and sovereign grace meets the deep needs of guilty sinful men and women. But I say the glory of the gospel is that it is essentially God-ward. It is that which meets the requirements of a holy and righteous God. It is that which we might say solves the problem of how God can be just and yet justify the sinner. As one has well said, the gospel is that which solves God's problem, if we might term it in that way. The problem is, how can God be just and yet pardon sinners in a way consistent with the holiness of his nature and with the demands of his holy and righteous law. Oh the glory of the gospel is essentially in that it not only meets the need of guilty sinners but it reveals the glory of God as "just, and the justifier of him which believeth in Jesus" (Rom. 3:26).

We have touched upon this on other occasions, but is not this the great question? How can sinful, fallen, guilty men and women be just with God? How can the holy righteous God receive such and pardon their sins and bring them into a living relationship and fellowship with himself, in a way which is consistent with all the demands of divine justice? The answer is made known in the gospel. It is what Paul brings before us here, "But when the fulness of the time was come, God sent forth his Son, made of a woman, made under the law." Now surely all the old testament scriptures reveal the glorious promises of God concerning the one who was to come? He was made known to the patriarchs. Of him Moses witnessed and the old testament prophets testified. He was made known in the promise that God gave our first parents in the garden, that the seed of the woman, in the fulness of time, should bruise the serpent's head though it should bruise his heel.

Friends, let us not overlook this important fact. The word does declare that there is a time to every purpose under heaven. God does not work in a haphazard way. We express ourselves in respect to many occurrences as if they were accidental happenings or mere coincidences. People put down many of the events and circumstances of life to chance and fortune. But let us not forget that there is nothing haphazard. All is according to the sovereign council, purpose and foreknowledge of God. The time of the coming of the Lord Jesus Christ on earth was appointed and fixed of God. Let us not forget this either. Was not the *coming of the Lord Jesus*, the reality of his person and his work, his life, death and resurrection, the *greatest event* the world has ever witnessed? In the outworking of God's purposes, in the unfolding of his divine providence, we see a set time in the purposes of God for the coming of the Lord Jesus Christ. This is an instructive and profitable subject. We could trace in the history of the Jews and in God's ordering of the affairs of men and nations, how all was directed to the glorious event of the coming of the promised seed, Jesus Christ, the Son of God. He was sent forth of God in the fulness of time, made of a woman, made under the law. I say, surely this is central to the salvation of the church and people of God.

We were considering last Lord's day, godly Job's confession of his faith, "I know that my redeemer liveth, and that he shall stand at the latter day upon the earth" (Job 19:25). Was not that central to Job's faith and hope and the joy of his soul, that his redeemer "shall stand at the latter day upon the earth"? And is not that still central to the faith of the living family of God? Friends, have we not been brought I trust through grace to believe, rest, and rejoice in the truth that God was manifest in the flesh? Is not the truth that God was manifest in the flesh, central to all our preaching, and central to our worship as we come together, week by week, around the word of God?

See the testimony of the apostles in all their preaching and teaching. As Paul wrote in his epistle to the Corinthians, "I determined not to know any thing among you, save Jesus Christ, and him crucified" (1 Cor. 2:2). He determined only to know this great and glorious person, his work, life, death and resurrection! This was the whole substance of the preaching and teaching of the apostles. It was the same glorious truth to which Paul had borne witness among the churches in Galatia. Under the Spirit's blessing, it had been used to the calling of many of them by divine grace and bringing them to know the one of whom Paul preached, as their Lord and Saviour.

What I am just wanting to emphasise is this. He says here, "When the fulness of time was come, God sent forth his Son." As taught by the Holy Spirit, is not faith brought to rest in the incarnation of our Lord Jesus Christ and in what was accomplished by him in his holy life and in his great work of redemption on the cross? Is it not in these realities that the sinner, taught of the Holy Spirit, is brought to find that which is to the true joy and peace of his soul? Does he not behold in the sufferings, death and glorious resurrection of the Son of God as manifest in the flesh, that wherein all the demands of divine

justice have been fully met? I say again, central to the glorious
revelation God has given to us in his word is the *coming* of the
Lord Jesus Christ. Are we among those that "love his
appearing"? (2 Tim. 4:8). Are we, as taught by the Holy Spirit,
brought to say with the hymnwriter:

> "My soul looks back to see,
> The burdens thou didst bear,
> When hanging on the accursed tree,
> And knows her guilt was there."

"When the fulness of time was come, God sent forth his Son."
You know, what a profound statement is that: *"God sent forth his
Son."* This very one is none other than the only begotten and
eternal Son of God. Friends, we cannot stress this enough. Oh
that our eyes may be opened and our hearts truly prepared by the
Holy Spirit to receive this great and glorious truth. "God sent
forth his Son." Oh the wonder there of redeeming love and grace.
There are those words in the gospel of John which we often quote
but which are often sadly misused. What a depth is contained in
them! The Lord Jesus himself says, "God so loved the world, that
he gave his only begotten Son, that whosoever believeth in him
should not perish, but have everlasting life" (John 3:16). Is there
a greater gift that God could have given than his only begotten
Son? Is not this the evidence of the greatness of his love towards
those whom he had chosen and given to the Lord Jesus Christ in
that covenant made before the foundation of the world? I say, oh
the greatness of his love that he sent his Son. As Paul reminds us
as well, God "spared not his own Son, but delivered him up for
us all" (Rom. 8:32). Yes, upon what an errand did he send his
only begotten Son! What a great and glorious work did the Lord
Jesus come to perform for the salvation of his people, to the
praise and glory of the thrice holy God.

He said, "Made of a woman, made under the law." God sent
his Son clothed in human nature. John bore witness to this when
he said, "The Word was made flesh, and dwelt among us, (and
we beheld his glory, the glory as of the only begotten of the
Father), full of grace and truth" (John1:14). "Made of a woman."
What is the importance and significance of these things? We are
not to just pass these matters over lightly. We may say, 'Well, do

not we have an understanding of them?' I trust we do, but do we not need to be reminded again and again of these important and glorious facts? "Made of a woman." What was so significant in that? Paul reminds us in the epistle to the Hebrews that herein is manifest the greatness of God's grace and love towards his own. He says, "He took not on him the nature of angels; but he took on him the seed of Abraham. Wherefore in all things, it behoved him to be made like unto his brethren" (Heb. 2:16-17). Why? "That he might be a merciful and faithful high priest in things pertaining to God, to make reconciliation for the sins of the people." Yes, this was essential to the coming of the Lord Jesus Christ, and for the work and office he undertook, to be the mediator and Saviour of his people. He is manifest in the nature that sinned. He is the one mediator between God and men. He is the man Christ Jesus. "He was made of a woman."

Let us not forget either, the important fact that though he was made of a woman and though that holy thing was formed in the womb of the virgin Mary, it was not by human generation that Jesus Christ came. The scripture emphasises this important point. He was made of a woman, yet it was not by natural generation but by the overshadowing of the Holy Spirit. "Great is the mystery of godliness: God was manifest in the flesh" (1 Tim. 3:16). How vital is this to the salvation of the church and people of God that Jesus Christ is manifest in the very nature which sinned.

He was "made of a woman" but he was without sin. Oh the importance of that truth. He not only did no sin but he was without sin, and I would even go further than that and say that he was beyond the very possibility of sinning as well. He was "made of a woman," of true human nature, subject to all the infirmities that human nature is subject, sin excepted. Oh when we say he was subject to the infirmities of human nature we mean that he knew what it was to hunger, to thirst, to be weary with his journeying. He knew what it was to suffer pain and even deep anguish of soul. Ah, how he entered into such deep anguish of body and soul as the wrath of God was poured out upon him when he stood as the surety of his people, and as he satisfied divine justice for their sins imputed to him.

He was, "Made of a woman, made under the law." How important that the Lord Jesus was made under the law! As concerning his human nature our Lord Jesus was a Jew. He was under all that the Levitical law and dispensation required. He was subject to the law of God in every aspect of his life here on earth. He was not only subject to it but he also delighted in it, as the Psalmist reminds us. He says, "I delight to do thy will, O my God: yea, thy law is within my heart" (Ps. 40:8). Our Lord Jesus lived in perfect obedience, in thought, word and deed to all the requirements of that law. There has only been one truly holy righteous man, only one that has completely fulfilled the law, and that is our Lord Jesus Christ. "He was made under the law."

Let us just notice this. It came to me in speaking out of the third chapter of the book of Genesis the other evening. Take our first parent Adam there in Eden before the fall. Without question, Adam as he came from the hand of his Creator was upright. God could say of his handiwork in the creation of man, the crowning work of his creation, "It was very good" (Gen. 1:31). What wisdom did Adam possess before the fall! Oh we see how great were the privileges and advantages Adam had as he enjoyed fellowship with his Creator. Yet even there in his innocency, surrounded as he was with all those advantages and privileges in Eden, Adam sinned and fell. There he solemnly and sadly disobeyed what God had spoken to him. But our Lord Jesus Christ, "made under the law" and subject to the infirmities of human nature, gloriously fulfilled the law. Take the great comparison. Adam was in Eden in that state of innocency with all those advantages and privileges, yet he fell before the temptation of the evil one. See the great contrast. The Lord Jesus fasted in the wilderness forty days and forty nights and was tempted of the devil, yet there we see him triumphing in all those things. We see him "made under the law," subject to all its requirements and fulfilling it in every particle. Why is this so significant? What is the importance of these things? Friends, if our Lord Jesus Christ has not truly fulfilled the law, and that on the behalf of his people, what hope is there for them?

What I am saying here is not unrelated to what Paul is bringing out in this epistle to the Galatians. You know the grievous error that was being set forth in the churches of Galatia. In effect, false teachers were saying that the finished work of Jesus Christ, the obedience he had wrought to the law, the price that he had paid for the redemption of his people, was not sufficient. Something more was required by a holy God if sinners were to be saved. True, they were not saying it in as blatant a way as that, but that was the solemn implication of their teaching. They were saying, 'Yes, you must believe in Jesus, but also you must keep the law to be saved.' Now Paul shows that what they taught was not the gospel but a grievous perversion of the truth. How it dishonoured the Lord Jesus and his finished work. How it took away from his perfect obedience and that which he had obtained by his one and true sacrifice of himself on the cross. No wonder Paul so stands out against such grievous errors as these and condemns them in such an emphatic way. And friends, I believe we should not overlook the solemn fact that the teaching of things which are contrary to what God reveals in his holy word is not an insignificant thing. It is condemned by the word and is to be condemned by us as well if we are truly among the people of God.

See the warnings that are given us in the word of God, in the language of Paul in all his epistles and in the writings of the other apostles. See what John says on this point in writing concerning the doctrine of Jesus Christ. As he says, even in those early days the spirit of antichrist was abroad. And what was the spirit of antichrist? What is the present-day spirit of antichrist against which we are warned in the word of God? The spirit of antichrist is the denying that Jesus Christ has come in the flesh. John says that this is the spirit of antichrist which should come and which was even then manifest (1 John 4:3). All that would take away from the glory of our Lord Jesus Christ and the salvation of his people, anything that would in any way detract from his finished work, is the very spirit of antichrist. We are not only warned against it but we are also exhorted to contend *against* these things, and to "Earnestly contend *for* the faith which was once delivered unto the saints" (Jude 1:3).

He was "made under the law, to redeem them that were under the law that we might receive the adoption of sons." Just one final point to bring out this evening. Let us not overlook what is wonderfully set forth here of the blessings and benefits that flow to God's people through the person and the finished work of the Lord Jesus Christ. For through his redeeming atoning work he procured for his people the blessedness of the forgiveness of sins. When we are brought through grace to saving faith in the Lord Jesus Christ, we know the wonderful reality that our sins which are so many and grievous are forgiven. They are blotted out, never more to be raised against the believer in the Lord Jesus. We have this brought before us again and again in the scriptures. The Lord says, "I have blotted out, as a thick cloud, thy transgressions, and, as a cloud, thy sins" (Isa. 44:22). "As far as the east is from the west, so far hath he removed our transgressions from us" (Ps. 103:12).

But not only is there the blessing of the pardon of sins but see also what comes as the precious blessed gift of God's grace through the redeeming work of the Lord Jesus Christ. "That we might receive the adoption of sons." He brings us into the believing realisation of what Paul is setting forth in these verses, even the blessed portion and privilege of the sons and daughters of the one and only true God. Believers are not God's sons and daughters merely as he is their Creator. They are his children in a more glorious way than that, being adopted into the living family of God. They were chosen and predestinated to be "conformed to the image of his Son" (Rom. 8:29). He says, "That we might receive the adoption of sons," that this blessing might be made known by the witness of the Holy Spirit in the hearts and lives of his people. He says, "And because ye are sons, God hath sent forth the Spirit of his Son into your hearts, crying, Abba, Father." See the reality of this blessing that Paul is speaking of here. It comes to us, in all the blessedness of it, through the redeeming work of the Lord Jesus Christ. It is through his finished work that the Holy Spirit is given. And the Spirit witnesses in sinner's hearts to their sonship, to the blessed relationship they have through grace with God as their Father and their all.

"Because ye are sons, God hath sent forth the Spirit of his Son into your hearts, crying, Abba, Father." Do we know that witness of the Holy Spirit? Oh, the blessedness of the sonship that is here set forth, the relationship into which believers are brought through the redeeming work of our Lord Jesus Christ! And Paul adds, "Wherefore thou art no more a servant, but a son; and if a son, then an heir of God through Christ." May we know in our souls the Holy Spirit's witness to this sonship. By his grace, may we know what it is to walk in the light and comfort of this truth, realising more and more our high calling in Christ Jesus our Lord. "If a son, then an heir of God through Christ."

But I will leave the remarks there. May the Lord add his blessing. Amen.

19

GALATIANS 4:8-20

Howbeit then, when ye knew not God, ye did service unto them which by nature are no gods. But now, after that ye have known God, or rather are known of God, how turn ye again to the weak and beggarly elements, whereunto ye desire again to be in bondage? Ye observe days, and months, and times, and years. I am afraid of you, lest I have bestowed upon you labour in vain. Brethren, I beseech you, be as I am; for I am as ye are: ye have not injured me at all. Ye know how through infirmity of the flesh I preached the gospel unto you at the first. And my temptation which was in my flesh ye despised not, nor rejected; but received me as an angel of God, even as Christ Jesus. Where is then the blessedness ye spake of? for I bear you record, that, if it had been possible, ye would have plucked out your own eyes, and have given them to me. Am I therefore become your enemy, because I tell you the truth? They zealously affect you, but not well; yea, they would exclude you, that ye might affect them. But it is good to be zealously affected always in a good thing, and not only when I am present with you. My little children, of whom I travail in birth again until Christ be formed in you, I desire to be present with you now, and to change my voice; for I stand in doubt of you.

These verses evidence the increasing concern that the apostle had toward those churches of Galatia. Paul's soul was grieved that they should be brought again into bondage through those that taught a gospel so-called that was so contrary to the glorious grace of the gospel of our Lord Jesus Christ which he had preached to them. Paul here manifested the great concern he had for the honour and glory of the Lord Jesus Christ and his love of the souls to whom he writes under the inspiration of the Holy Spirit. His concern for them, as he writes with such faithfulness and straightforwardness, was not because these troublers of the churches in Galatia were drawing men away from his own influence. Such personal considerations did not enter into the matter. Paul's concern was that these things not only touched the honour and glory of the Lord Jesus Christ but were deadly dangerous to the souls of men and women.

Now I just want to touch again on the main thrust of this epistle though I know I have reiterated it several times now. Paul was contending against a grievous error. Some men had come into the churches of Galatia teaching that you must believe on Jesus Christ for salvation but that is not sufficient of itself. You must also keep the law if you are to be saved. Paul shows that such teaching does not bring sinners into liberty but into bondage again under the curse and condemnation of the holy law of God. They taught that the finished work of Jesus Christ was not sufficient to save sinners and to put away the sins of the Lord's people. They said that the justifying righteousness of Jesus Christ was not enough unless joined to the supposed obedience of the sinner. Now he plainly shows that if this is the case, then without question, no soul can be saved, no sinner can ever be justified before a holy and just God. For a holy God, whose holiness is revealed in his just and holy law, can be satisfied with nothing less than *perfect obedience* to the commands and demands of that holy law. And no sinner can ever render that, either fully or in part. So then, what was being taught in those churches of Galatia did not bring the souls of men and women into life, light and liberty, but into the curse and condemnation of the law. It left sinners on the ground of what they could supposedly do themselves to meet the claims of divine justice.

We might say, well, what has this to do with ourselves? What are the important practical implications for us in our generation? What is the relevance of this to the people of God today? Is not Paul dealing here with an ancient heresy, something very rife in the time when he wrote this epistle? But has it anything to do with us today? Friends, I believe the issues brought before us in this epistle are as alive today as they were when Paul first contended against those errors. Ah, we still see the subtle continual workings of the enemy to undermine if possible the truth as it is in Jesus and to leave sinners short of Jesus Christ. That is essentially what this false teaching in Galatia did. It leaves sinners short of Jesus Christ and therefore under the curse and condemnation of God's holy law, whatever may be said and done. So then, in looking at this passage from verse 8, I want as helped to bring this teaching before you in its practical implications for today.

He says, "Howbeit then, when ye knew not God, ye did service unto them which by nature are no gods." He is here referring to the condition they were in when he first preached the gospel among them as led by the Holy Spirit. What was their condition then? Where were they found? Well, this verse clearly indicates they were idolaters. Oh, they worshipped, but they worshipped gods of their own making. We know the nations of the ancient world worshipped various idol gods and the Galatians were no different. If you read the fourteenth chapter of the Acts of the Apostles, you will find that shortly before Paul visited the churches in Galatia he had been preaching in the districts of Lycaonia. At Lystra in particular, when they saw the miracle Paul had wrought upon that impotent man, they came out of the city bringing garlands of flowers. They would have done sacrifice to Paul and Barnabas. They called Barnabas, Jupiter, and Paul, Mercurius, because he was the chief speaker, and thereby thought they would do honour to the false idol gods they worshipped. Paul says, "Howbeit then, when ye knew not God, ye did service unto them which by nature are no gods?"

The point I want to bring out is this. What was the service they did to these that were no gods? What was the whole purpose of their sacrifices to them, and the various rituals they performed in the supposed worship of them? All the ritual, all the sacrifices, all the ceremonies associated with their idol worship was intended to placate those gods. It was to obtain their favour, to stand high in their esteem, so that they might have those gods, as they thought, on their side and not against them. You know, this is the object of all natural religion, all that can well be termed a religion of works, whether it be an idol god that is in view or even whether it be the one true God who is supposedly worshipped.

We find that this was the very thing these Galatians were going back to. True, it was not to the worship of idol gods. We might say, well, did they not now worship the one and only true God? Was not he in view even though they were reverting to Jewish ceremonies and customs and observances and to the rituals of the Levitical law and dispensation? What was wrong with this? Were not these things commanded of God? Surely the judaizing teachers had a point. They could say, 'Well, we bring you what God has revealed, what he made known by Moses. The ceremonies that we are advocating, that you are to attend to, the ritual to follow, have all been revealed from heaven. God made it known to Moses.' Paul never denied that truth. But he is saying, 'Howbeit then, when ye knew not God, ye did service unto them which by nature are no gods. The whole end of your ritual worship of those false gods was supposedly to obtain their favour. And your false teachers preach the error that Levitical ritual worship will obtain the favour of the true God."

What an important statement is that by Paul in the ninth verse. "Now after that ye have known God." True, through the preaching of Paul and the gracious working of God the Holy Spirit, they had been brought to know the one and only true God, and to wait for his Son from heaven, the Lord Jesus Christ. But he says, "Or rather are known of God." You see how Paul ever lays the emphasis on sovereign grace and divine mercy. Ah, they had come to know God, yes, but it was because God had made himself known to them. "Or rather," he says, "are known of God." I say that the emphasis is on the sovereign grace and free mercy of God! It is not as if their coming to know God had been anything of their own doing. No, it was by the sovereign gracious working of God himself. And is not that so in the case of each one who is brought to know God through sovereign grace? They do not come to that knowledge by themselves. It is not that we first seek the Lord. No. Rather it is that we *"are known of God."* The Lord manifests himself in sovereign grace, goodness and divine favour towards us.

He says, "How turn ye again to the weak and beggarly elements, whereunto ye desire again to be in bondage? Ye observe days and months and times, and years." As I said a little earlier, before the gospel came they were in bondage to all the rituals involved in the worship of their false idol gods. They had received the gospel Paul had preached in all its gracious fulness and freeness but were now turning from it to observance of days, months and years. For their false teachers were saying they must observe all the laws and ordinances of the old testament Levitical dispensation to be saved. We might ask again, what was wrong with that teaching? What is Paul's contention? He does not deny that those ordinances had been appointed by God. He does not charge them with going back to idol worship. Paul's concern is that their returning to old testament ritual was no different in essential principle to their former worship of idols. For in their observing of these Jewish ceremonies, even of what was advocated in the Levitical law, they were verily thinking that they placated God. He would be well pleased with them and would bless them accordingly. Thereby they thought they would obtain the favour of the Lord. Ah friends, see the subtle evil evident in this Galatian heresy.

Paul says, "I am afraid of you, lest I have bestowed upon you labour in vain. Brethren, I beseech you, be as I am; for I am as ye are: ye have not injured me at all." Let us look again at this Galatian error and learn the practical implications for ourselves. We might ask, was it wrong for them to observe circumcision? Had not that been appointed by God? Was it wrong for them to observe set times and seasons for the worship of God? In one sense those things were not wrong. The wrongness lay in their thinking that the doing of those things was the ground on which they obtained the favour of God. This was their sad solemn delusion.

Is that not the same solemn delusion of many today in matters of religious observance? Let me just put it in this way. We come to chapel regularly. We attend on the word of God. We seek the Lord in prayer. We thus endeavour to walk according to the principles set before us in the word of God. We might say, "What is wrong with these things? Is not this what must be done?" In a way, that is true. But friends, I am wanting to emphasise the point brought out in what Paul writes to the Galatians. Why do we do these things? What is our end and purpose? You say, 'Well, has not God commanded them? Is it not right to attend the chapel, to read the word, to come under the sound of the truth, to observe these things, to observe the Lord's day?' Indeed, those things in themselves are not wrong but what is our main purpose in them? Is it that by doing them we shall obtain God's favour, we will placate divine justice, we will merit some access to God and acceptance before him? Because if that is the object for which we do these things, we are no different than these Galatians. We are in the same error against which Paul contended in Galatia. This was what grieved Paul. They were observing things to thereby obtain, as they thought, the favour of God. They thought God would thus be pleased with them. They were resting the salvation of their souls on their observance of these matters. Friends, that is ever the very essence of the work of the flesh. It is not of the Spirit.

The great issue here surely is this. To think we can merit favour and acceptance with God by any of our religious observances is to ground salvation on works, not grace. Why was this so contrary to what Paul had preached among them and which they had professed to receive? Well, consider what he essentially advocates in this epistle as brought out in these first eleven verses of this chapter. He says, "Wherefore thou art no more a servant, but a son; and if a son, then an heir of God through Christ." I say that the great difference between Paul and the false apostles is in this. Paul teaches that, as brought through sovereign grace to saving faith in the Lord Jesus, *we do not have to do anything to obtain the favour of God.*

The wonderful truth of the gospel as made known under divine teaching is that it reveals to the sinner, not what they have to do to appease divine justice and obtain God's favour, but what God in Christ has done for them. It makes known the favour of God towards them in that he has loved them in his Son long before the world began and is well pleased with them in him. It communicates the wonder of his mercy, his favour and his love to them by providing for them such a Saviour as Christ Jesus the

Lord. And I say that the great difference that Paul shows here is that the Galatians were turning to things that brought them into bondage, fondly thinking that they would thereby obtain the favour of God. But the glorious truth of the gospel makes known, not what we have to do to obtain God's favour or placate divine justice, but God's great love towards us. It shows that he is well pleased for his righteousness' sake, that he has magnified the law and made it honourable (Isa. 42:21) in the person and finished work of the Lord Jesus Christ.

I just come back to this practical application. The Lord's people are sinners taught of the Holy Spirit and brought to saving faith in the Lord Jesus. God reveals to them that he is pleased with them, that he loves them, that he has fully and freely forgiven them their sins. By the riches of his grace he reveals to them their adoption, through Jesus Christ, into his one living family and that he is their Father. As Paul says here, "God hath sent forth the Spirit of his Son into your hearts, crying, Abba, Father."

Now true, such believers do desire to be found walking in the ways of the Lord. They do attend the means of grace, the preaching of the word. They seek to set forth the praises of God. They desire to walk in all the ways and ordinances that the Lord has commanded but not thereby thinking that by doing so they merit the favour of God. No. As recipients of God's great love and being brought to realise God's mercy and favour towards them, they desire to do those things. But not out of a sense of having to do them to obtain God's favour but as having tasted that the Lord is gracious. Knowing his mercy and love towards them, they desire to follow him. They seek in all things to do his will and to serve God as enabled "in newness of spirit, and not in the oldness of the letter" (Rom. 7:6). They do not serve him out of a sense of compulsion and duty but out of the realisation of his great love to them, desiring to do those things that are pleasing in his sight. As the hymnwriter puts it,

> "To see the law by Christ fulfilled,
> And hear his pardoning voice,
> Changes a slave into a child,
> And duty into choice."

As Paul showed them, going back to those Jewish observances was not bringing them into liberty but into bondage again under the curse and condemnation of the law. Could they thereby pacify a holy God? Could they thereby satisfy the claims of divine justice? Could they thereby do those things that are pleasing in God's sight? No, never. But what is it that pleases God? What is it that brings these blessings? Is it my seeking and striving to keep the law of God? No. It is what is received by grace through faith as I am brought as a sinner to saving faith in Jesus Christ. There I receive all these blessings fully and freely. What is pleasing in God's sight is not the doings of the sinner striving to keep the law. It is the sinner brought by grace to trust in Jesus Christ, to look to him, to cleave to him only, as all the hope and consolation of the soul for time and for eternity.

How little we consider as we ought what Paul says in that eleventh chapter of his epistle to the Hebrews. He says, "Without faith it is impossible to please him: for he that cometh to God must believe that he is, and that he is a rewarder of them that diligently seek him" (Heb. 11:6). Not all the workings and strivings of men can ever be pleasing in God's sight, however much they may try to keep his holy commands. Why, as we are sinners, all those things of themselves are stained and dyed with sin. How can that which has any taint of sin be acceptable in his sight? If I were from this moment forward to strive for the rest of my life (and how men have done so!) I could not thereby please God.

I remember some years ago how this was very clearly brought before me in reading two books. How greatly they differed. The first one was Thomas à Kempis' Imitation of Christ. Indeed, he had some good things to say in it in one sense but the whole emphasis is on striving to imitate the Lord Jesus Christ. The other book was Luther's Commentary on the Galatians. I believe we see there the great difference—the bondage of the one and the liberty of the other. Oh, Luther in his Galatians brings out the glorious truth that it is not the sinner striving to imitate Christ to obtain the favour of God. It is the sinner brought through almighty divine grace to the feet of Jesus Christ to believingly receive what he has done and to trust in him only. This is pleasing in God's sight. It is as we are brought to saving faith in Jesus Christ.

Let me just illustrate this further. You remember what Jesus spoke of those two who went up to the temple to pray, one a Pharisee, the other a publican. Who was pleasing in God's sight there? Who did Jesus say went down to his house justified? It was the man who was brought to smite upon his breast and cry, "God be merciful to me a sinner" (Luke 18:13). That is where grace brings us. There is the reality of faith manifested. It is as the sinner is laid low at the feet of Jesus Christ, knowing his own utter ruin through sin, yet through grace brought to receive what God freely and fully gives in Jesus Christ.

Paul goes on to say, "Ye know how through infirmity of the flesh I preached the gospel unto you at the first." He here brings out some things about himself. He says, "My temptation which was in my flesh ye despised not, nor rejected; but received me as an angel of God, even as Jesus Christ." He reminded them of what happened when he first preached among them and the word of God was made effectual to them. He says, 'Have you so soon forgotten those things? Oh now you seem to be offended with me and at the things I am saying to you. You are turning away from this ministry and are listening to these who have come to you from Judæa and who are bringing things contrary to what I taught you. Ah, it was different when I first came, even though I came with much weakness and infirmity.' He refers here to a temptation which was in his flesh. Now just what that was we do not know. It was some particular infirmity in his flesh from which Paul suffered. Yet he says, "And my temptation which was in my flesh ye despised not, nor rejected; but received me as an angel of God, even as Christ Jesus. Where is then the blessedness ye spake of? for I bear you record, that, if it had been possible, ye would have plucked out your own eyes, and have given them to me." Such was the joy with which they had received the word of the truth of the gospel—and Paul the preacher of that gospel. Such was the expression of their gratitude to God for the word of truth he had sent to them.

He said, "Am I therefore become your enemy, because I tell you the truth? They zealously affect you, but not well; yea, they would exclude you, that ye might affect them. But it is good to be zealously affected always in a good thing, and not only when I am present with you. My little children, for whom I travail in birth again until Christ be formed in you."

Ah friends, look at the importance of that statement of Paul. It is as he says in his epistle to the Corinthians, "I determined not to know any thing among you, save Jesus Christ, and him crucified" (1 Cor. 2:2). The whole glory of the gospel is what it testifies of Jesus Christ. And is that not wherein the whole essence of true religion is found? It is not whether we attend to a round of religious observances and services. It is, 'Do we know the Lord Jesus Christ?' Are we brought through divine grace to rest and trust only in him. Peter writes in his epistle, "Unto you therefore which believe he is precious" (1 Pet. 2:7). It brings us back to that vital question,

> "What think you of Christ? is the test,
> To try both your state and your scheme;
> You cannot be right in the rest,
> Unless you think rightly of him."

He says, "I desire to be present with you now, and to change my voice; for I stand in doubt of you." He then puts forward this question, "Tell me, ye that desire to be under the law, do ye not hear the law?"

But I will leave the word there this evening and will return to it on a future occasion, if the Lord will. May he add his blessing. Amen.

20

GALATIANS 4:21-31

Tell me, ye that desire to be under the law, do ye not hear the law? For it is written, that Abraham had two sons, the one by a bondmaid, the other by a freewoman. But he who was of the bondwoman was born after the flesh; but he of the freewoman was by promise. Which things are an allegory: for these are the two covenants; the one from the mount Sinai, which gendereth to bondage, which is Agar[1]. For this Agar is mount Sinai in Arabia, and answereth to Jerusalem which now is, and is in bondage with her children. But Jerusalem which is above is free, which is the mother of us all. For it is written, Rejoice, thou barren that bearest not; break forth and cry, thou that travailest not: for the desolate hath many more children than she which hath an husband. Now we, brethren, as Isaac was, are the children of promise. But as then he that was born after the flesh persecuted him that was born after the Spirit, even so it is now. Nevertheless what saith the scripture? Cast out the bondwoman and her son: for the son of the bondwoman shall not be heir with the son of the freewoman. So then, brethren, we are not children of the bondwoman, but of the free.

I do not want to go over the things that we have already considered from this epistle of Paul to the Galatians. As helped, I want to come directly to these verses in which Paul brings before us the cases of Abraham, Sarah, Isaac and Ishmael. I want to consider the use the Apostle makes of them for the instruction

[1] i.e. Hagar

of the people of God with respect to the essential truths he is proclaiming and the very grievous error against which he is contending. He uses this scripture against the error which was having such a devastating effect on the churches of Galatia in bringing them away from the truth that salvation is by grace alone through faith in Jesus Christ. To those in the churches of Galatia who were being drawn aside by the erroneous teachers from Judæa, Paul puts this question in verse 21. "Tell me, ye that desire to be under the law, do ye not hear the law?" Paul brings out a most important and solemn fact in this question. In effect he is saying, 'You are very concerned to be under the law. But do you really desire to be under the law? Do you really know and understand what that means?'

The Apostle is dealing here with things that vitally concern the glory of God and the salvation of the sinner. As he says in chapter 5, "Christ is become of no effect unto you, whosoever of you are justified by the law; ye are fallen from grace." To be under the law is to be under solemn condemnation. It is to be not only subject to its demands but to its curse as well. All who are under the law of God are condemned and cursed because they are sinners and transgressors of that holy law. It holds out no hope to the transgressor in that it shows no way of escape, no way of deliverance from its just and holy demands. But these in the churches of Galatia were saying they truly held that there must be the believing in Jesus Christ for salvation, yet they insisted on the keeping of the law of Moses as well. But Paul shows that the mixing of these two things will not do. It is either one thing or the other. We are either justified by the law or we are justified by faith alone in Jesus Christ. It must be one or the other. It cannot be a mixing of the two. And it is impossible that any sinner can come to justification and acceptance before God by the deeds of the law, for to be under the law is to be under its curse. That is what Paul is showing.

So is this such an attractive position as these that were troubling the church in Galatia were claiming? Remember that they professed to be concerned for the glory of God and for the spiritual welfare of the brethren in Galatia. Did they not seem very plausible as they came advocating faith in Jesus Christ and also keeping the law God commanded by Moses as absolutely necessary for salvation? But this is a most dangerous deadly heresy. It is the mixing of things which the word of God distinctly set forth as mutually exclusive. As Paul had shown, to be under the law is to be under its curse, for all have sinned and come short of the glory of God. There is no hope of salvation that way. "Tell me," he says, "ye that desire to be under the law, do ye not hear the law?" And I say that the sinner taught of the Holy Spirit to know the solemn reality of the holiness, righteousness and justice of God's law in his own conscience will never advocate the law as a way of acceptance by God. Neither will they advocate the law as the way of life and conduct for the believer. Having known and felt the holiness of that law in their conscience, they know it can do nothing but condemn.

Has it not always been so? You take the case of Moses and the children of Israel when that law was given. What was its effect on them? It brought a most solemn sense of dread. They feared and trembled before that display of divine holiness and righteousness in the giving of the law. Even Moses said, "I exceedingly fear and quake" (Heb. 12:21). And so those taught of the Holy Spirit to know the law do not desire to be kept under its demands because it justly condemns them for their sin. The very cry of the heart quickened by divine grace is, "God be merciful to me a sinner" (Luke 18:13). True, the sinner owns the sentence just. The sinner owns that God is righteous in the condemning sentence of the law. But oh, the cry of the sinner is for deliverance from the law, not by obeying its demands, but in the way that the Lord himself has provided in the person and work of the Lord Jesus Christ.

"Tell me," he says, "ye that desire to be under the law, do ye not hear the law?" Now Paul introduces what we might say is a very remarkable illustration of the truths he is setting forth. He says, "For it is written" (that is, in the book of Genesis), "that Abraham had two sons, the one by a bondmaid, the other by a freewoman. But he who was of the bondwoman was born after the flesh; but he of the freewoman was by promise. Which things are an allegory." We have read in the book of Genesis this evening the account of Abraham, Sarah and Hagar. We have read of Ishmael, the child born to Hagar, and Isaac, the child born to Sarah. Now who would have thought that all we read in that account sets forth the essential truths which Paul brings out in this epistle?

Let me just pause a moment in reference to those events in the lives of Abraham, Sarah and Hagar and what was done to bring about the birth of Ishmael. What an example is there given us of the truths I was endeavouring to bring before you last Sunday out of those words in Romans, "And we know that all things work together for good to them that love God, to them who are the called according to his purpose" (Rom. 8:28). We cannot for one moment suggest it was right for them to enter into the alliance proposed by Sarah and to which Abraham agreed. There were sad consequences. What grief it brought, what contention in Abraham's household. But we see even there the solemn gracious over-ruling of God. Even in the mistakes his people make and in their sad infirmities, God brings forth that which is for the glory of his great and holy name. Yet he is never the author of sin. Both Abraham and Sarah suffered as a result of those things they entered upon, and yet I say that the Lord brought forth praise and glory to his name from those events. Oh how in the outworking of such providences, and the working together of all things for good, there is that which ever humbles his people and manifests the greatness of his grace and glory!

Now we find that Paul uses those events as wonderfully setting forth the truth for which he here contends. He says that Abraham had two sons, one born of a bondmaid, the other of the freewoman. One was of the flesh. The other was the child of promise. Remember, Abraham not only had those two sons. Afterwards he had a number of other children. But it is in those two particularly that a great contrast is brought before us. One was born after the flesh, the other was by promise. "Which things are an allegory," an allegory being that which shows forth important glorious spiritual truths. Now we have to be very careful in using allegory. You go back to the times of the Middle Ages and before and you will find a great deal of the preaching in those days was in the form of allegory. The scriptures were taken entirely out of their context. They were spiritualised totally out of their true meaning. And we find that if men are not careful in the use of allegory they can fall into most foolish things in seeking to set forth what they think is the meaning of God's word. But here we have the lawful use of allegory as the apostle Paul writes this epistle under the inspiration of God the Holy Spirit.

He says, "Which things are an allegory: for these are the two covenants; the one from the mount Sinai which gendereth to bondage, which is Agar. For this Agar is mount Sinai in Arabia, and answereth to Jerusalem which now is, and is in bondage with her children. But Jerusalem which is above is free, which is the mother of us all." What are these two covenants? It is important that we have a clear understanding of what the scriptures teach. We know there are a number of covenants brought before us in the word of God but there are two vitally essential covenants. One is, as Paul says here, "from mount Sinai which gendereth to bondage." Now this is the covenant of works which Adam was under as he came forth from the hand of his Creator. As God created him upright in his own image and placed him in the garden he had prepared for him, Adam was under that covenant of works. His continuance in the state he enjoyed, depended on his obedience to what his God had commanded. "Of every tree of the garden thou mayest freely eat: but of the tree of the knowledge of good and evil, thou shalt not eat of it: for in the day that thou eatest thereof thou shalt surely die" (Gen. 2:16-17). We know how Adam failed, how he sinned against God, how he not only ruined himself but the whole of his posterity as well. What was the result? The curse of a broken covenant came on Adam and the whole of his posterity as a result. As the Lord had said, "In the day that thou eatest thereof thou shalt surely die."

At Sinai the Lord again set forth that covenant of works. What he there promised the children of Israel was dependent on their obedience. Their entrance into Canaan and their enjoyment of all the blessings and benefits of that promised land were dependent on their obedience to what God had commanded. The Lord summed up in the ten commandments the substance of what the covenant of works required. Obedience to God's commandments was solemnly required for the enjoyment of the benefits of which God had spoken to them.

Now let us not overlook this. As we come into this world we are all found under that covenant of works. The demands of that covenant as summed up in what God gave to Moses on mount Sinai are on each of us. All are to meet its requirements. But is it not a solemn truth that none ever meet those requirements? That is why Paul says here of the covenant from mount Sinai, which is Agar, that it "gendereth to bondage. For this Agar is mount Sinai in Arabia, and answereth to Jerusalem which now is, and is in bondage with her children." He there makes direct reference to the Jews, saying they and their children were in the same bondage to which these judaizing teachers were desiring to bring back the Galatian believers. They were desiring to bring them back under the demands of the holy law of God, back under the covenant of works. But under that covenant of works we are in condemnation for not being able to meet its demands and are solemnly under the curse as a result. Here he is saying, "Ye that desire to be under the law, do ye not hear the law?" All that are under it are in bondage. They are under the curse of a broken law and condemnation must ever be their lot, apart from sovereign distinguishing grace.

But Paul goes on to say, "But Jerusalem which is above is free, which is the mother of us all. For it is written, Rejoice thou barren that bearest not; break forth and cry, thou that travailest not: for the desolate hath many more children than she which hath an husband." This is what Paul gloried in. This was the whole substance of his preaching. It was what he was advocating as he contended against the grievous error sadly affecting the brethren in Galatia. I have mentioned the first covenant of which he speaks—the covenant of works. But here he speaks of another covenant, even the covenant of grace. In this, all blessings for guilty needy sinners are bound up. They are not secured by any attempted obedience of the sinner. They are secured by the Lord Jesus Christ whom God appointed from before the foundation of the world to be the great mediator of this new covenant.

As Paul says, "But Jerusalem which is above is free, which is the mother of us all." He directs our attention, not to the works of men, but to the glorious provision of God in the wonders of his sovereign grace and mercy. He speaks of this covenant of grace in which was secured the salvation of all whom God had chosen in his only begotten and dearly beloved Son and given to him from before the foundation of the world. Paul preached that all the salvation and blessings of the elect are secured in Jesus Christ upon the ground of his obedience and the great atonement he made for the sins of his people. In this covenant of grace there is no condition to be met by the sinner. Some put repentance and faith as conditions of the covenant. They say, yes, blessings are secured in Jesus Christ but they are ours through repentance and faith. But friends, even repentance and faith are not conditions of the covenant but are blessings that flow out of the covenant of grace. They are evidenced in all that are born from above. God freely gives them as the gracious outworking of his sovereign eternal purposes towards his people.

He says, "Now we, brethren, as Isaac was, are the children of promise." The emphasis here is on the fact that Isaac, as a child of promise, was graciously freely given by God to Abraham. There were no interventions of fleshly workings whatsoever in the procuring of the birth of Isaac to Abraham and Sarah. For do not forget that Isaac was born when humanly speaking it was impossible. This was one of the things that rejoiced the very hearts of Abraham and Sarah. Oh, how God had so graciously wonderfully dealt with them. How his promise had been fulfilled, not upon any ground of deserving in them, but out of the fulness of his mercy and goodness to them. Yes, Isaac was the child of promise and Paul says that "we brethren, as Isaac was, are the children of promise." And that is true of every one that is called by divine grace. The distinguishing mark of this is in the reality of the work of regeneration as evidenced in the hearts and lives of all called by God. We sometimes sing:

> "Free election, known by calling,
>   Is a privilege divine;
>   Saints are kept from final falling;
>   All the glory, Lord, be thine!"

The emphasis here is on God's sovereign operations. As the birth of Isaac came in the fulness of time according to God's promise, even when it was beyond possibility as men viewed it, so is the work of God's grace in all whom he calls. It is not what men can do but what God graciously manifests. Is not the work of regeneration, the very calling of his people, a miracle of divine grace? It is a manifestation of the sovereignty of God in his greatness, goodness and mercy.

He says, "We brethren, as Isaac was, are the children of promise. But as then he that was born after the flesh persecuted him that was born after the Spirit, even so it is now." Let us just pay a little attention to this statement. We have read in Genesis chapter 21 of Sarah's distress when Isaac was weaned, when she saw Ishmael the son of Hagar mocking and despising the child born to her. Notice this. From whence do we find some of the bitterest persecutions have arisen for the church and which so often distress the people of God still? It arises, not from a profane or even a pagan world, but from the religious world. It was so with Ishmael and Isaac. Ah, the one "that was born after the flesh persecuted him that was born after the Spirit." A real mark of false religion is always the persecuting nature of that religion. A true mark of the church of Jesus Christ is that she is persecuted. She is never encouraged to indulge in persecution in return but rather the reverse.

Hear the words of divine truth in this matter as Paul writes in his epistle to the Romans. He says, "Dearly beloved, avenge not yourselves, but rather give place unto wrath: for it is written, Vengeance is mine; I will repay, saith the Lord. Therefore if thine enemy hunger, feed him; if he thirst, give him drink: for in so doing thou shalt heap coals of fire on his head" (Rom. 12:19-20). See how it was with the Lord Jesus when he was here on earth. See it with the apostles and the early church. And so the people of God have proved down the generations. "But as then he that was born after the flesh persecuted him that was born after the Spirit, even so it is now. Nevertheless what saith the scripture?" Ah friends, what a mercy it is that the work of God can never be frustrated. As I have said a number of times recently, the work of God's grace in the hearts and lives of his people, with all that they may be subject to, can never be frustrated. It is as Paul writes to the Philippians, "Being confident of this very thing, that he which hath begun a good work in you will perform it unto the day of Jesus Christ" (Phil. 1:6).

"Nevertheless what saith the scripture? Cast out the bondwoman and her son: for the son of the bondwoman shall not be heir with the son of the free woman. So then, brethren, we are not children of the bondwoman, but of the free." See the solemn distinction that God makes here between those that are born of the bondwoman and those that are born of the freewoman. As I say, there is never any bringing together of the covenant of works and the covenant of grace. They are distinct things. We are either under one or the other. So see Paul's distinct question: "Tell me, ye that desire to be under the law, do ye not hear the law?" What is it to be under the law? It is to be under its curse and condemnation. To be the children of the bondwoman is to be cast out and rejected of God. That is the solemn implication of those things.

But oh the wonders of divine grace as the sinner is brought in all his need to the Lord Jesus Christ to receive the blessings of salvation that flow fully and freely through him. All is to the praise of the glory of God's grace. To be brought to saving faith in the Lord Jesus Christ is to be brought into true liberty. The law has nothing more to say to the sinner that through grace is brought to saving faith in the Lord Jesus Christ. There the believer is finished once and for all with the law. He is for ever brought from under the covenant of works. He is brought under the blessings of the covenant of grace. Why? "For Christ is the end of the law for righteousness to everyone that believeth" (Rom. 10:4). Jesus Christ has fulfilled that law. He has met its just demands and as one says,

> "Payment God cannot twice demand,
> First at my bleeding Surety's hand,
> And then again at mine."

But I will leave the remarks there. May the Lord add his blessing. Amen.

21

HEBREWS 10:38-39

Now the just shall live by faith: but if any man draw back, my soul shall have no pleasure in him. But we are not of them who draw back unto perdition; but of them that believe to the saving of the soul.

Though I have read these verses 38-39 by way of a text, I want as helped this evening to bring before you what the apostle writes from verse 26 to the end of this 10th chapter of his epistle to the Hebrews. I verily believe that the subject he deals with is not unrelated to what we have been considering in the epistle to the Galatians over some weeks now concerning the grievous error manifesting itself in those churches. I want to bring out yet again what I feel is so little considered of how the apostle under the gracious teaching of the Holy Spirit viewed the false teaching troubling the Galatian church. He emphasises the solemn condition of those false teachers and of those that were being sadly led astray.

Now we find that the error evidenced in the churches of Galatia was by no means confined to them. Paul has something to say about it in other epistles. As we have read recently in the Acts of the Apostles, we know how seriously the apostles considered this matter at the council at Jerusalem and how they confirmed the truth as it is in the Lord Jesus. It was no secondary matter against which Paul wrote so vehemently to the Galatians. It concerned essential fundamental truths, truths to which these words of Paul to the Hebrews relate. I believe in view in this 10th chapter of the epistle of the Hebrews is the same grievous error, the same soul-deceiving teaching he was dealing with in Galatia. From verse 26 we have these solemn words brought before us: "For if we sin wilfully after that we have received the knowledge of the truth, there remaineth no more sacrifice for sins." I know there has been much debate about the meaning of these verses. But, as helped, I want to bring before you what I feel is consistent with the Lord's teaching, not only in this chapter but in all the scriptures.

Now we must pay some attention to the whole of this epistle to the Hebrews. Paul was writing to those of the Jews that had been brought through divine grace to repentance and saving faith in the Lord Jesus Christ and had made an open profession of his name. They had been brought to receive the gospel and had endeavoured to walk consistently with it by grace. So it was to believers among the Jews that this epistle was addressed in the first instance. How Paul wonderfully opens up the truth of the Lord Jesus Christ as foreshadowed in the Levitical order of divine worship which God had commanded the Jews by his servant Moses. Paul establishes that though the Levitical order was of God and was indeed glorious, that which is contained in the gospel excels those things in glory. They were but a sign and shadow of the glorious substance possessed by the true church in the person and finished work of the Lord Jesus Christ.

Paul opens up the blessings of grace that the true church, the believing people of God, possess in Jesus Christ. Notice one of the essential blessings here set before us. Paul has much to say in the opening part of this chapter on the forgiveness of sin. Oh this is no insignificant thing. It is a gloriously vital matter. Is this not the essence of what the gospel makes known? Is there any comparable blessing for guilty, needy, hell-deserving sinners? The psalmist knew something of this forgiveness of sin. It filled his heart with joy and peace. As he could say, "If thou, Lord, shouldest mark iniquities, O Lord, who shall stand? But there is forgiveness with thee, that thou mayest be feared" (Ps. 130:3-4). By divine grace the truth of forgiveness was known to believers under the old testament dispensation and Paul expounds its fulness and blessedness. He shows that forgiveness of sins is found alone in what the Lord Jesus Christ has done in his finished work—his justifying righteousness, and the shedding of his own precious atoning blood at Calvary. He shows the way opened into the blessings of pardon of sin, peace with God, and the glorious hope of eternal life for the sinner born again of the Holy Spirit and brought to repentance and saving faith in Jesus Christ.

What a precious view of the Lord Jesus Christ he brings before us for the encouragement of the people of God. He says, "Seeing then that we have a great high priest" (Heb. 4:14). The Lord Jesus is set forth in this epistle as the ever-living one, the great high priest over the house of God, who ever lives to make intercession for all who come unto God by him. He says, "Having therefore, brethren, boldness to enter into the holiest by the blood of Jesus, by a new and living way, which he hath consecrated for us, through the veil, that is to say, his flesh; and having an high priest over the house of God; let us draw near with a true heart in full assurance of faith, having our hearts sprinkled from an evil conscience, and our bodies washed with pure water. Let us hold fast the profession of our faith without wavering; (for he is faithful that promised;) and let us consider one another to provoke unto love and to good works; not forsaking the assembling of ourselves together, as the manner of some is; but exhorting one another: and so much the more, as ye see the day approaching."

Paul thus opens up to these believers among the Jews and to us the blessings of sovereign grace and divine mercy in the fulfilment of the old testament patterns in the person and work of the Lord Jesus Christ. Remember he is writing to them as those who had professed faith in Jesus. And an important fact to bear in mind is that they were those also that suffered much for their profession of his name. They had endured "a great fight of afflictions" from the very beginning. They suffered much from their own brethren after the flesh. You are well aware of the deep enmity that the Jews had in general and which devout orthodox Jews still have today to the very name and truth of the Lord and Saviour Jesus Christ. As a result these believers suffered much and there was little alleviation of their distresses from the opposition they experienced. And was it not at such times that there were real pressures on them, tempting them to compromise their faith in the Lord Jesus?

The Judaizers who had come to Galatia professed faith in Jesus Christ but taught that not only is faith in Jesus Christ necessary for salvation but the law of Moses must also be kept for you to be saved. This was the doctrine against which Paul contended. It was very plausible to the natural mind. It began to find favour among Gentiles and Jews in the churches of Galatia. Could there not be a compromise here? If they still accepted the necessity of circumcision and the keeping of the law would not this help to alleviate the troubles arising from their standing for faith alone in Jesus Christ as the only way of salvation for sinners? There were some Jewish believers that were being taken up with this. They were being drawn aside to it. As I have said, Paul wrote to the Galatians concerning the grievousness of this error. And I believe that he is dealing with the same error in these verses to the Hebrews, for he says, "If we sin wilfully after that we have received the knowledge of the truth, there remaineth no more sacrifice for sins."

Now let us look at this a little closer. What can this mean—sinning wilfully after we have received the knowledge of the truth? How often has this verse and similar statements in the new testament scriptures deeply exercised and troubled the living family of God, the consciences made tender in the fear of the Lord. For the child of God is conscious of what he is in himself. He daily realises the workings of a body of sin and death and that "that which is born of the flesh is flesh; and that which is born of the Spirit is spirit" (John 3:6). He finds that his fallen carnal nature is no different even after the Lord has called him by grace. Even after the implanting of divine life and brought to living faith in Jesus, the believer finds his old nature is no different. It still desires and seeks after the very things that it once did. True, having spiritual life there will be conflict against the things of the flesh. But what so often troubles the child of God is what troubled Paul when he says, "In me (that is, in my flesh,) dwelleth no good thing" (Rom. 7:18).

And oh when we come to a verse such as this, "If we sin wilfully after that we have received the knowledge of the truth, there remaineth no more sacrifice for sins," what exercise does it occasion! Ah, the child of God finds there is sin in him. He dare not say that he does not sin every day of his life and in so many things has come short. How true what John writes in his epistle, "If we say we have no sin, we deceive ourselves, and the truth is not in us…If we say that we have not sinned, we make him a liar" (1John 1:8,10). Solemn truth! I repeat, the child of God, having a conscience made tender in the fear of the Lord, cannot say that they have not sinned nor, sadly, that they do not sin every day of their lives. This is not to excuse sin—far from it. But let us face the reality of sin which is ever the source of grief and sorrow for a believer.

Furthermore, he cannot say that all those sins are always involuntary, that they take him by surprise, that there is not something of a deliberate nature in them. No, the deepest grief of a child of God is that they sin against light and knowledge, love and blood, against the very goodness and the mercy of the Lord. This is very humbling. Also at times the child of God can get into a very cold, careless and indifferent frame of heart and mind. Ah when the Lord himself again draws near and such a word as this is brought before them and their conscience is made tender in the fear of God, oh what fear and trembling they have!

Now does this verse apply to the case I have described? "If we sin wilfully after that we have received the knowledge of the truth, there remaineth no more sacrifice for sins." Friends, I believe we can categorically say that what the apostle is dealing with here does not apply to the situation that I have just described. The word of God is clear that "a just man falleth seven times, and riseth up again" (Prov. 24:16). I emphasise, we make no excuse for sin nor for the failings of the child of God. Neither do they excuse themselves. The experience of Romans 7 is ever the experience of the living family of God. I refer again to those words in 1 John chapters 1 and 2. He says, "If we confess our sins, he is faithful and just to forgive us our sins, and to cleanse us from all unrighteousness ... My little children, these things I write unto you, that ye sin not. And if any man sin, we have an advocate with the Father, Jesus Christ the righteous." Blessed precious truth!

What then is meant in this statement of Paul's, for it surely does have an application? We cannot just pass it by. He says,

"For if we sin wilfully after that we have received the knowledge of the truth, there remaineth no more sacrifice for sins." I believe that what is specifically dealt with here is the turning away from Jesus Christ. It is apostasy from the truth. This was at the very root of what Paul was dealing with in his epistle to the Galatians. See how he warned them of this evil. He says to those turning again to the yoke of the law, "Christ shall profit you nothing...Christ is become of no effect unto you, whosoever of you are justified by the law; ye are fallen from grace" (Gal. 5:4). Solemn are those statements of Paul. He warns the Galatians of the sin described in the verses here before us this evening. It is the turning away from Jesus Christ. It is the being brought off and away from the one foundation "that is laid, which is Jesus Christ" (1 Cor. 3:11). Solemnly, it is being removed from faith alone in Jesus Christ and turning again to what Paul calls "weak and beggarly elements," things which can never profit.

But sadly, some in the churches of Galatia were being drawn aside to that erroneous doctrine. Paul says they were bringing themselves again under condemnation. Solemn truth. "If we sin wilfully after that we have received the knowledge of the truth." Paul is warning them against the real temptation to turn away from faith alone in Jesus Christ. He warns them of being drawn into the error so prevalent in the churches, of resting part on faith in Christ and part on justification by works in obedience to the law of Moses. That is no way. No salvation is there. That is to bring us again under condemnation.

Now I want to make this plain as well. If we turn from Christ, what do we turn to? Friends, we turn to utter condemnation and black despair. For is there any other sacrifice for sin apart from that found in the person of Jesus Christ? If we turned to them again could all the sacrifices of the Levitical dispensation put away sin? They never put away sin in the past and they will never do so now. Their purpose was never to put away sin but to direct the guilty, needy sinner in faith to God's promise of him who was to come. One says:

"Depart from thee? - 'tis death - 'tis more;
'Tis endless ruin, deep despair!"

"If we sin wilfully," that is, if we turn away from faith in Jesus

Christ as the ground of justification before God, to what do we turn? "There remaineth no more sacrifice for sins" but the inevitable consequence of such apostasy is "a certain fearful looking for of judgment and fiery indignation, which shall devour the adversaries." That was not what the judaizing teachers were promising those in the churches of Galatia, was it! That was not what was being held out as they sought to spread their pernicious errors in other churches and here among the believing Hebrews. No. We see the subtlety of the evil one. How grievous is this error. It has such an appearance of being right and yet was grievously wrong. The end of that departure from the truth is what Paul sets forth here: "A certain fearful looking for of judgment and fiery indignation, which shall devour the adversaries. He that despised Moses' law died without mercy under two or three witnesses: of how much sorer punishment, suppose ye, shall he be thought worthy, who hath trodden under foot the Son of God, and hath counted the blood of the covenant, wherewith he (and I believe that means Jesus Christ) was sanctified, an unholy thing, and hath done despite unto the Spirit of grace? For we know him that hath said, Vengeance belongeth unto me, I will recompense, saith the Lord. And again, The Lord shall judge his people. It is a fearful thing to fall into the hands of the living God."

Paul thus sets forth in these verses to the professed Hebrew believers the grievous end of those things he was warning against in his epistle to the Galatians. Now let me make this point plain. Paul says, "If we sin wilfully," if there is the turning away from Jesus Christ. Friends, how real is the temptation to this. You know, amid the difficulties and discouragements in the life of the believer, how often has that question of the Lord Jesus searched the heart. After the discourse he had given as recorded in John chapter 6 many that had professed to be his followers, said, "This is an hard saying; who can hear it? From that time many of his disciples went back, and walked no more with him" (vs. 60,66). Jesus turned to his disciples and said, "Will ye also go away?" Ah, what a searching word was that! "Will ye also go away?" There were those that "went back, and walked no more with him." True, they had openly professed to be his followers. They were described as disciples of the Lord Jesus Christ. They had been impressed with things outwardly but their departing from him evidenced that they were not the subjects of the sovereign, regenerating work of God the Holy Spirit.

Likewise in this Hebrew church, there were those that had outwardly professed faith in the Lord Jesus. But it is not the outward profession alone that will keep the soul in the hour of temptation, when troubles and distresses arise for Christ's sake. It is the inward possession of true and vital grace. In this, see how essential is that which Jesus declared to Nicodemus: "Ye must be born again" (John 3:7). Where there is the work of grace, then the same almighty grace will keep them to the end, though oftentimes they are oppressed and distressed and severely tempted to depart from him. This truth is confirmed in the text before us: "Now the just shall live by faith."

This is a big subject. Just a few thoughts in the light of what I have been mentioning this evening. "The just shall live by faith." Oh where is the child of God brought and kept as taught by the Holy Spirit? "Looking unto Jesus" (Heb. 12:2), seeking through his grace to live upon him daily in true faith. They do not find they are sinless—far from it. They are daily conscious of the workings of sin in their own heart and life. They are often beset with many fears and the temptations and suggestions of the enemy. But they are still looking and cleaving to Jesus. Is there anywhere else for them to go? Is there any other name given under heaven among men whereby we must be saved? (Acts 4:12). Is there anywhere else where true pardon and peace is to be found except at the foot of the cross of our Lord Jesus Christ?

Paul then warns here of the grievous error being taught in so many churches even in those days, the false teaching that would seek to bring the sinner off from wholehearted trust and confidence in Jesus Christ alone. Ah, to depart from him is to turn to utter ruin and black despair, to be under the curse and condemnation of the law. "But the just shall live by faith," yes, that faith which keeps them where Peter was brought when the question was put, "Will ye also go away? Lord, to whom shall we go? thou hast the words of eternal life. And we believe and are sure that thou art that Christ, the Son of the living God."

Friends, have you and I realised something of the truth of that, conscious of our unfitness and unworthiness? "Lord, to whom shall we go?" To whom else have we to look and cleave but to Jesus Christ, his person and his finished work. As Simon Peter wrote in his epistle, "Unto you therefore which believe he is precious" (1Pet. 2:7). We are brought to realise more and more that one thing is needful, even to live by faith in him. This is the blessed portion and experience of the sinner taught by God the Holy Spirit: "To live by the faith of the Son of God," as Paul says, "who loved me, and gave himself for me" (Gal. 2:20).

But I will leave the remarks there this evening. May the Lord add his blessing. Amen.

22

GALATIANS 5:1

Stand fast therefore in the liberty wherewith Christ hath made us free, and be not entangled again with the yoke of bondage.

As we have noticed over the past weeks, Paul is contending in this epistle against false teachers that were troubling the churches in Galatia and were teaching doctrines contrary to the gospel he had preached among them. He had received that gospel, not of man, nor by man, but by the revelation of Jesus Christ. In that gospel, God is exalted in the salvation of sinners through the person and finished work of the Lord Jesus Christ alone. As we have noticed many times now, the main error being promoted was joining obedience to the law with faith in Jesus Christ as the ground of the sinner's acceptance and justification before God. This false doctrine was causing much trouble and strife in the Galatian churches. Do notice this. Where error such as this was being promoted, it never led to real peace and unity among the brethren. It always resulted in contention which sadly manifested the working of the evil one whose whole desire is not to promote unity but disunity, not to bring into the liberty of the gospel but into the bondage of sin and guilt.

Now I do not want to go into those points again this evening, but to come to what Paul says here: "Stand fast therefore in the liberty wherewith Christ hath made us free." This verse is a most important gracious exhortation to the people of God, they who have been brought into gospel liberty. Paul's whole concern is that they be not moved away from the hope of the gospel which had been made known to them. You remember the subject I endeavoured to deal with last Friday evening out of Hebrews chapter 10. Paul speaks there of the solemnity of departing from Jesus Christ. He shows that to turn from Jesus Christ and his salvation of grace is to turn to condemnation under the wrath of God, as revealed from heaven against all unrighteousness and ungodliness of men. To turn from Jesus Christ is to turn to utter black despair. In this 5th chapter he sets the same solemn truth before us.

I mentioned in my closing remarks last Friday, the Lord's words to his disciples when many that had followed him, professing to be his disciples, "went back, and walked no more with him" (John 6:66). They could not receive his doctrine but said, "This is an hard saying; who can hear it?" Turning to his disciples Jesus said, "Will ye also go away?" Oh, those memorable words of Simon Peter! Is not this the language of the sinner taught of the Holy Spirit to know their own helplessness, ruin and need as a transgressor of God's holy law? Is it not the language of those whose whole hope of salvation is not in what they are or can do but in what Jesus Christ is and has done? How memorable are Peter's words, "Lord, to whom shall we go? thou hast the words of eternal life. And we believe and are sure that thou art that Christ, the Son of the living God." Oh, may that be the very language and portion of your soul and mine.

"Stand fast therefore in the liberty wherewith Christ hath made us free." Paul is writing to those who have been brought into liberty. What is this liberty of which Paul is speaking? This is the main point I want to deal with this evening. It is a most glorious liberty or freedom. Now there are varied understandings of this liberty. Some say it is a deliverance from all the ceremonies of the Levitical law imposed by God on the Jews through Moses. Though that is true, yet surely this liberty is far more than from merely outward ordinances or other outward restrictions. I do not want to burden you this evening with the differing views of men concerning this liberty. I want to come to what is most gloriously set forth in this scripture. I believe that the liberty wherewith Christ hath made us free is essentially liberty from the wrath of God. It is the deliverance of sinners from the curse and condemnation of the holy law of God against whom we have transgressed. I say that this liberty is a deliverance from wrath. "For the *wrath* of God is revealed from heaven against all ungodliness and unrighteousness of men" (Rom. 1:18) His wrath is set forth in the claims of his holy law and the condemnation it speaks to all transgressors. This then is a liberty, a freedom, a deliverance from the wrath of God.

What a solemn reality is the wrath of God! Indeed it is so as known in our conscience when quickened into spiritual life by the gracious teaching of God the Holy Spirit. Is not this wrath of God against all unrighteousness and ungodliness of men solemnly felt in the conscience of those taught by the Holy Spirit? Are we not brought to realise that we are ungodly sinners who have transgressed the law of God and are therefore under its just sentence and curse and exposed to the wrath of God? These are no trifling matters. They are most solemn realities. Oh, as felt in the conscience the sinner trembles before these things.

Is there not an apprehension of this wrath of God even in what we might term the natural man? We know that every particle of human nature was ruined in the fall including our conscience within us. Yet in that conscience there are apprehensions of wrath. We might say man has a very religious nature which is always seeking a way of deliverance from wrath, an escape from an accusing conscience. Oh, the many varied perverted ways by which the natural man seeks in his blindness of spiritual things and the deceivings of the great enemy of souls to quiet an accusing conscience and its apprehensions of wrath! Sadly and solemnly the accusations of conscience in many men have been so smothered that conscience seems almost dead.

But when God the Holy Spirit sovereignly and graciously imparts spiritual life to the soul, conscience is then truly awakened. Oh, the apprehension of wrath, as we are sinners and transgressors of God's holy law, is then a solemn reality. We realise that,

> "My sins deserve eternal death."

As taught by the Holy Spirit we will be brought to even justify God as one says,

> "If my poor soul were sent to hell,
> Thy righteous law approves it well."

Oh, we are brought to confess there would be nothing unjust if God dealt with us as our sins and iniquities deserve. What solemn apprehensions of the divine wrath of God are then known and felt in the conscience.

Now this liberty wherewith Christ hath made us free is essentially liberty from bitter bondage under the curse and condemnation of God's holy law. And remember that there is none but Jesus Christ can make us free from the wrath of God in the solemn condemnation and curse of his holy law which we have broken. Oh, there is no other way of deliverance and liberty but by Jesus Christ. But I will say more upon this point in just a moment.

As I have said, "The liberty wherewith Christ hath made us free" is liberty from wrath. Is not this a glorious truth set before us here? Let me just emphasise it in this way. Paul is contending in this epistle for the true liberty of the gospel, while those troubling the church were also promising the brethren liberty. They were saying the way of deliverance from the wrath of God manifest in the curse and condemnation of a broken law is truly by faith in Jesus Christ but also by obedience to the law of God. They were to signify their acceptance of this doctrine by submitting to the ordinance of circumcision. Paul shows that to introduce those things completely undermines the true liberty only to be found by the gospel. Instead of leading to liberty it brings sinners into bondage and under the curse and condemnation of the law. For the great truth set before us is that the "liberty wherewith Christ has made us free" is a liberty which is, as I have said, by Jesus Christ alone and his finished work. It is into the reality of this glorious truth that the Lord the Holy Spirit leads each one of his own people. They are those of whom we read in the closing part of chapter 4. "So then, brethren, we are not children of the bondwoman, but of the free."

This is a liberty through the propitiation of Jesus Christ which delivers us from the wrath we deserve as transgressors of the law of God. It is a liberty that consists in the free and full forgiveness of sins through the one atoning sacrifice of the Lord Jesus Christ alone. It is a liberty from wrath through that alone which reconciles us to God and wherein we stand before him as the objects of his love and the subjects of his saving grace. I am justified through the person and finished work of Jesus Christ alone. It is his obedience to the law and his atonement for my sin which meets all the requirements of a holy God and sets such a sinner as myself at liberty from the wrath revealed in the curse and condemnation of the law. It is in those things that the sinner is brought to stand before a holy and a just God through sovereign grace. Upon that ground alone is there acceptance before God and true access to him and deliverance from all wrath. As cleansed in the precious blood of Jesus Christ and clothed in his righteousness, what has the wrath of God, the curse and condemnation of that holy law of God, to do with me? It has nothing to do with me. It has nothing to say to me for Jesus Christ has answered its demands. He now stands in the very presence of God for me. As the word says, he is our great high priest who ever liveth to make intercession for us. There is the little stanza:

"My sins deserve eternal death,

But Jesus died for me."

What glorious truth is summed up there! Our sins truly deserve eternal death. We are subjects of wrath. But, oh, "the liberty wherewith Christ hath made us free"! This is what is made known in the truth of the gospel. It does not direct guilty, needy, burdened sinners to what they can do. It does not set them upon their own efforts to obtain acceptance by God. No. The gospel directs sinners to Jesus Christ only, and to his finished work. And it not only directs them to him, but oh, through the wondrous grace of God, that glorious gospel speaks peace to the sinner's heart through Jesus' blood and truly sets the sinner at liberty. "Stand fast therefore in the liberty wherewith Christ hath made us free, and be not entangled again with the yoke of bondage."

What a great contrast there was between what Paul preached and the teaching of those troublers of the church. True, they were teaching what was conducive to the natural man. As I have said many a time, the natural inclination of the human heart likes nothing better than to be set certain things to perform and achieve. You will find the whole religion of the natural man, whatever form it may take, is always a religion in which the sinner is supposedly doing something to make themselves acceptable to God. Oh, to what lengths will men go in these things! To what lengths did Paul go as Saul of Tarsus, as a very religious man under the bondage of the law! How particular he was in his whole life, circumspect and attending most zealously and religiously upon what he considered to be right and acceptable before God. Why did he give such attention? Why was he so strict in his life? Why did he watch every movement? Why was he so zealous? It was because he thought that by doing those things he would be acceptable to God. God would be pleased with him. He could thereby obtain a righteousness God would accept. But he was brought to realise the solemn truth that all his doings did not bring him liberty. They never brought him true peace of conscience. They never brought him into the realisation of the forgiveness of sins and acceptance before God. No, they left him under the curse of a broken law and instead of coming closer to God he was going further away. Instead of being brought into liberty he was left under the curse and bondage of a broken law. Though he promised himself deliverance from sin, his life abundantly evidenced that he was the slave of sin. So it is still with all that seek salvation and acceptance before God in any other way than by Jesus Christ.

Why! the word of God tells us that our righteousnesses, that is, our best things, "are as filthy rags" (Isa. 64:6). Take our most holy things as viewed by men, the best things you have ever done in which you might consider you have conformed the most closely to the demands of the law of God. We might think, well surely, do they not in some measure bring us nearer to God? By these things have we not some glimmerings of hope that we might be acceptable to him? I say, take our best things considered in that way, they are but what is abominable in God's sight. The prophet tells us *"all* our righteousnesses are as filthy rags." If our best things are such, then what about our worst things? Ah, does not this show how utterly ruined and lost we are? Does not this emphasise the bondage we are in, the guilt under which we are found, outside of Jesus Christ? But oh, to the sinner under the curse and condemnation of the law, apprehensive of divine wrath in a conscience awakened by the Holy Spirit, what a way of deliverance and glorious liberty is set before them in the gospel!

What a truth is opened up here! How full and free is that salvation!

Paul says, "Stand fast therefore in the liberty wherewith Christ hath made us free." He writes to those who have been brought into this liberty, those who truly apprehend the blessedness of it through the sovereign grace and mercy of God. Let me just give one or two illustrations of this. Take for example the well-known account of the Pharisee and the publican, who went up to the temple to pray. The Lord describes the case of the publican, who "standing afar off, would not lift up so much as his eyes unto heaven, but smote upon his breast, saying, God be merciful to me a sinner" (Luke 18:13). *There* was one with the solemn apprehensions of divine wrath in his conscience, one brought to realise his own unfitness and unworthiness before a holy God. Yet he is brought through sovereign grace to cry to the Lord for mercy. What is mercy? It is the undeserved favour of God towards a sinner. What did Jesus say? "I tell you, this man went down to his house justified." That sinful man with all the apprehensions of wrath in his conscience, truly feeling his own unfitness and unworthiness, was justified on the ground of sovereign grace and divine mercy. The grace that had awakened him to his need and had brought him to the footstool of divine mercy, also reveals the provision God has made in Jesus Christ for pardon, peace and eternal life. It reveals the true liberty of the gospel, the deliverance not only from all apprehensions of wrath but from all the reality of that wrath and from the curse and condemnation of God in his holy law.

Take the case of the dying thief. See there a man on the very verge of eternity. Oh, the solemn situation of those two dying men as they were both sinners. What had they to plead of lives lived in any way acceptable even to men, let alone acceptable to God? And there, in the last hours of their lives, what had they to look forward to? What are the consequences of unforgiven sin and the prospects of those under the curse of God's holy law? They have nothing to look forward to but hell, the solemn wrath of God to all eternity. And yet we see the sovereign gracious work of God the Holy Spirit in quickening that dying thief (Luke 23:40). His conscience is awakened in the last moments of his life to the solemn apprehension of divine wrath in the curse and condemnation of the law. Yet, what is more, the Holy Spirit reveals to him the way of deliverance from wrath, curse and condemnation, and the place of acceptance before God. See how grace brings that man to cry, "Lord, remember me when thou comest into thy kingdom." There we see the faith which is the gift of God, the faith which justifies by bringing the sinner to look to the Saviour and to receive out of his fulness.

"Stand fast therefore in the liberty wherewith Christ hath made us free, and be not entangled again with the yoke of bondage." Yes, everything apart from Jesus Christ is bondage. Everything that would bring the sinner away from looking to Jesus alone as the whole of salvation for time and eternity is nothing but bondage, whatever may be promised. This glorious liberty then, consists not in what we have done, not even what we still have to do, but in what God in Christ has done for us. "The liberty wherewith Christ hath made us free" is liberty from wrath, liberty from the curse and condemnation of the holy law of God, so that the believer is no longer under the law but under grace. It is full deliverance from wrath, from law, from curse, from all the reality of sin, death and hell. Yet the child of God still has a body of sin and death to the day of his death. As Paul brings out later in this chapter, there is a spiritual conflict within. The believer is conscious day by day of the working and defilement of sin. But how full is "the liberty wherewith Christ hath made us free!" One puts it well in this way:

> "Oft as sins, my soul, assail thee,
> Turn thy eyes to Jesus' blood;
> Nothing short of this can heal thee,
> Seal thy peace, or do thee good."

Even with every fresh apprehension of the guilt and defilement of sin, it is not to the demands of the law that we are to go, but to "the liberty wherewith Christ hath made us free." We are to go to the precious fountain of his blood, to that open way of access to God and of acceptance before him, through the person and merits of the Lord and Saviour Jesus Christ. As Paul says in an earlier chapter, we are to "live by the faith of the Son of God, who loved me, and gave himself for me" (Gal. 2:20).

To what does this liberty lead in the gracious outworking of it in the heart and life of a child of God? What are its fruits and effects in the believer's life? This is a most important point. Oh friends, it never leads to licentiousness as some would wrongly claim. Far from it. It ever leads and draws the child of God to Jesus Christ, with the real concern to know and do his will and to "show forth the praises of him who hath called them out of darkness into his marvellous light" (1 Pet. 2:9). The more this glorious liberty, this freedom from wrath, law, sin, death and hell is known, the more the soul will desire to glorify the Saviour. It is as Paul sums it up when he says, "If the blood of bulls and of goats, and the ashes of an heifer sprinkling the unclean, sanctifieth to the purifying of the flesh: how much more shall the blood of Christ, who through the eternal Spirit offered himself without spot to God, purge your conscience from dead works to serve the living God" (Heb. 9:13-14).

But I will leave the remarks there this evening. May the Lord add his blessing. Amen.

23

ROMANS 9:30-33

What shall we say then? That the Gentiles, which followed not after righteousness, have attained to righteousness, even the righteousness which is of faith. But Israel, which followed after the law of righteousness, hath not attained to the law of righteousness. Wherefore? Because they sought it not by faith, but as it were by the works of the law. For they stumbled at that stumblingstone; As it is written, Behold, I lay in Sion a stumblingstone and rock of offence: and whosoever believeth on him shall not be ashamed.

We noticed last Friday evening those words of the apostle Paul in Galatians chapter 5, "Stand fast therefore in the liberty wherewith Christ hath made us free, and be not entangled again with the yoke of bondage." He there sets forth the doctrine of true gospel liberty. And in this ninth chapter of the epistle to the Romans the apostle shows wherein that true liberty is found. He lays down the great distinction between the bondage of the law and the liberty of the gospel which is founded on the person and work of the Lord Jesus Christ.

We must look in some little detail at this chapter as a whole. In the opening part of it, Paul writes, "I say the truth in Christ, I lie not, my conscience also bearing me witness in the Holy Ghost, that I have great heaviness and continual sorrow in my heart. For I could wish that myself were accursed from Christ for my brethren, my kinsmen according to the flesh." Here is something that deeply affected the apostle. He lays great stress on the sincerity of the deep abiding concern he had for the spiritual welfare of his brethren, "his kinsmen according to the flesh." He is obviously referring to his fellow Jews, a people in covenant relationship with God throughout the old testament period. Paul considers their great privileges in what God had made known to them by his servants the prophets and how his hand had been on them in his preserving them throughout their generations. He considers the greatness of the privilege that of them the Lord Jesus Christ came according to the flesh in the fulness of time. As he says, "Who are Israelites; to whom pertaineth the adoption, and the glory, and the covenants, and the giving of the law, and the service of God, and the promises; whose are the fathers, and of whom as concerning the flesh Christ came, who is over all, God blessed for ever. Amen."

What was it then that so deeply affected the apostle as he looked on his fellow brethren the Jews. It was the hardness of their hearts, the grievous unbelief of this people who were very religious, who professed to have the knowledge of God and who were very zealous in their supposed worship of him. He was deeply grieved that with all their outward privileges they were far off from what saves the soul, even the saving knowledge of the truth as it is in Christ Jesus. How wilfully they turned away and rejected the person and work of the Lord Jesus Christ! Ah, Paul could not consider those things without deep distress in his soul. Does he not here reflect the very spirit of his Lord and Master who wept over Jerusalem, saying, "O Jerusalem, Jerusalem, thou that killest the prophets, and stonest them which are sent unto thee, how often would I have gathered thy children together, even as a hen gathereth her chickens under her wings, and ye would not! Behold, your house is left unto you desolate?" (Matt. 23:37-38). Oh, the solemnity of those things! See here the spirit of the Master reflected in his servant Paul.

Yet let us not overlook what he goes on to say: "Not as though the word of God hath taken none effect." He is deeply moved and grieved at the hardness and blind unbelief of the hearts of the Jews, his brethren according to the flesh. But has the word of God had no effect? Had the gospel been preached in vain? Is the word of God fallen to the ground? No, said Paul. He could rejoice in glorious, sovereign, electing, saving grace. Yes, his brethren according to the flesh were in hardness and unbelief of heart but the word of God was not without effect. The word has the effect for which God sends it in the hearts and lives of as many as the Lord our God shall call, to the praise of the glory of his grace. As he says, "For they are not all Israel, which are of Israel: neither, because they are the seed of Abraham, are they all children: but, In Isaac shall thy seed be called." Friends, there is a very important truth brought before us in this statement of Paul's. Though the Jews were the descendants of Abraham after the flesh through Isaac the promised seed, they were not thereby all the children of God. Though they were the descendants of Abraham and had all the privileges afforded them as a people in national covenant with God, it is evident they were not all the children of the promise. "In Isaac shall thy seed be called." And Paul glories in the fact that "there is a remnant according to the election of grace." Though the majority were solemnly left in unbelief, a remnant was saved, being called from among them and manifest as God's children by distinguishing grace. This remnant is not only from the Jews but also from the Gentiles as the Lord calls them by his almighty saving grace. Paul could rejoice at how the word of God had had effect and that "as many as were ordained unto eternal life believed."

He goes on to set forth the glorious reality of sovereign electing grace. He shows that even the unbelief of the Jews, as well as the saving faith of the remnant among them and of a great number of Gentiles, was not according to the will of man nor of the will of the flesh, but of God. God is here working out his own sovereign and eternal purposes. He sets before us this glorious doctrine which is so hateful in the eyes of unregenerate men and women. The natural man will not have, will not receive, and constantly cavils at what is stated in this ninth chapter of Romans. Paul proclaims God's sovereign grace in his choosing a people from before the foundation of the world and giving them in a covenant ordered in all things and sure to the Lord Jesus Christ. And this is manifest by his calling them in the fulness of time by irresistible grace. Oh, the wonders of electing redeeming love that Paul sets before us in this chapter. From this love arises the salvation of sinners to the praise of the glory of God's grace. Is not this borne out in the experience of every one of the living family of God? If he had not first chosen us we would never have chosen him. It is his grace that brings and draws us to the Lord and Saviour Jesus Christ. It never arises from the initiative of fallen human nature.

But I do not want to dwell so much this evening on this glorious truth but to come to these words of the apostle in our text. In verse 30 he says, "What shall we say then?" This follows from his saying that there was a remnant according to the election of grace even among the Jews. Among them there was a remnant brought through sovereign grace to repentance and saving faith in the Lord Jesus—a remnant to whom Jesus Christ was precious, even their "all, and in all" (Col. 3:11). I believe there is brought before us here a true distinguishing mark of the living family of God. I believe all taught of the Holy Spirit are brought into full agreement on this vital point. Oh, there is no difference between any of them here. There are differences in other things but never upon this essential point. And what is that? As taught of the Holy Spirit, all are brought to agree in this, that Jesus Christ is precious, that he is their all and in all. They are all brought through sovereign grace to trust in and rest alone upon Jesus Christ and his finished work as the one foundation of their hope of salvation.

What a vital glorious truth is this! And you know it was at the very heart of Paul's contention with those false teachers in Galatia. As we have endeavoured to consider over recent weeks, that false teaching fought against the very honour and glory of the Lord Jesus Christ. It aimed to dethrone him as the one in whom alone is salvation for sinners. True, as I have noticed, they were very plausible in their teaching. They said, 'We are not saying that faith in Jesus Christ is not essential, but something else is required also. You must keep the law as well to be accepted before God.' Such teaching is the utter rejection of Jesus Christ. It is the stumblingstone of which Paul is speaking here in this epistle to the Romans. He has taken great pains to point out in this chapter the wonderful manifestation of God's sovereign grace in bringing great numbers of the Gentiles to saving faith in Jesus Christ. Though the Jews who had all the privileges were left in the unbelief and hardness of their hearts, great numbers of the Gentiles were manifest as being among the true election according to grace. They had been brought through the teaching and power of the Holy Spirit, as the gospel was preached, to repentance and saving faith in the Lord Jesus Christ.

"What shall we say then" to this manifestation of the sovereign distinguishing grace of God? He says, "That the Gentiles, which followed not after righteousness, have attained to righteousness, even the righteousness which is of faith." Oh, the wonder and glory of this, that Gentile sinners have attained to righteousness, a righteousness that justifies them before a holy God, even the righteousness of faith. Ah, Gentile sinners are brought through grace into the place where they are justified and righteous before God. They have attained to the righteousness of faith. They are brought to know the blessings of the pardon of sin and peace with God through the person and finished work of the Lord Jesus Christ. Yet he says, "But Israel, which followed after the law of righteousness, hath not attained to the law of righteousness. Wherefore? Because they sought it not by faith, but as it were by the works of the law. For they stumbled at that stumblingstone."

Now what is essentially brought out in this statement before us here? It is that the Jews with all their profession and striving to keep the holy law of God, have not attained to the law of righteousness. They have not even come anywhere near being justified by those things. Paul here emphatically states the truths contained in the warnings he gives to the Galatians against the grievous error being taught there. He says that this error not only detracts from Jesus Christ but brings sinners under the bondage of the law, a situation wherein, strive as they may, they can never attain to the righteousness of the law. For as I have said so often, the law demands perfect complete obedience to all its claims, in thought, word and deed. Yet we see here the ignorance and foolishness, not only of Jews but of Gentiles also—all who hope to be justified by the deeds of the law. That is utterly impossible to be attained.

He says, "For they stumbled at that stumblingstone; as it is written, Behold I lay in Sion a stumblingstone and rock of

offence: and whosoever believeth on him shall not be ashamed."
What is the stumblingstone of which Paul is speaking, at which
the Jews stumbled and at which many still sadly and solemnly
stumble? It is Jesus Christ, the one who is revealed in the gospel
as God's "salvation unto the ends of the earth" (Acts 13:47). Is it
right for us to say that Jesus Christ is the stumblingstone, his
person and finished work being the only way of access and
acceptance before God? Yes, he is the stumblingstone at which
the Jews stumbled. He is the stumblingstone at which many still
stumble. Even though they may take the name of the Lord Jesus
on their lips, yet their trust and confidence is not wholly and only
in him. Even at best they are looking part to his finished work
and part to their own obedience. And to all that are in such a way,
Christ is a stumblingstone. He is still so to the natural man, to
men and women in the ignorance of their sinful fallen nature. Ah,
Jesus Christ and his finished work alone, is the only way unto the
Father. Men will not accept this.

"They stumbled at that stumblingstone; as it is written,
Behold, I lay in Sion a stumblingstone and rock of offence." Oh
the solemnity of this, *that what is laid in Sion as the one
foundation of salvation, is to many a stumblingstone, a rock of
offence.* This it is to all that would seek to be justified before God
by their own works whether in part or in whole. Whatever may
be said, Jesus Christ is a stumblingstone to them. For with us it
must ever be,

> "Jesus Christ as all in all,
> Or we perish in ruin, guilt and thrall."

Let us then just look at these statements of Paul from this
aspect. He says, "They stumbled at that stumblingstone."
Friends, how is it with you and I this evening? What is Jesus
Christ to us? This is no unimportant question. Oh, how we need
to be brought to true concern over these matters. Where is your
trust? Where is mine? Are we looking wholly to Jesus Christ?
Have we been brought through divine grace to look to him and
cleave to him as the only hope of salvation for our souls? As the
word of God declares, have we been brought to see our own
righteousnesses to be filthy rags, that is, our best, our most holy
things as stained and dyed with sin? Many would agree that their

sinful things can never be accepted before God, but oh, do they consider that their most holy things, their own supposed righteousnesses are but filthy rags?

Yet Paul knew this for himself. He says, 'There was once a time when I thought I possessed a righteousness. If any one was accepted before God for their own righteousness then I was one of those. I kept the law. I did what was right in God's sight. I was zealous for the traditions of the elders and fathers. Oh, I went to great lengths in opposing these new-fangled doctrines that were being taught. I fought against this Jesus of Nazareth. I was no whit behind any in contending zealously for the things of God.'

Notice this point. When Paul was Saul of Tarsus, what was the whole substance of his religion? This is not an insignificant question. He was a zealous bigot. His whole religion centred around his contending for the things he professed to hold and believe at that time. From whence did his religion arise? It arose from the pride and arrogance of his own heart. But oh the vast difference when sovereign grace laid hold on him! Then Paul was brought to see his own righteousnesses as filthy rags and to reject them and count as dung and dross all in which he had trusted. He desired to win Christ and be found in him, not having his own righteousness which is of the law (Phil. 3:8-9). And did Saul of Tarsus have such a concern over his brethren after the flesh as did Paul the apostle? Oh what tenderness in the fear of God was evident in Paul, what humbleness of mind and real concern for the honour and glory of God. True, Paul contended most earnestly for the faith once delivered to the saints, as we have noticed in his epistle to the Galatians. He was faithful in contending for the truth but was it in a spirit of arrogance, hardness and bitterness? No, the true spirit of Christ prevailed. Even in his contentions he could say, "the love of Christ constraineth us; because we thus judge, that if one died for all, then were all dead: and that he died for all, that they which live should not henceforth live unto themselves, but unto him which died for them and rose again" (2 Cor. 5:14-15).

"They stumbled at that stumblingstone." Solemnly, Jesus Christ was a rock of offence unto them. And so he is still to many. Friends, how is it with us? Are we brought through sovereign

grace to know nothing save Jesus Christ and him crucified? Do
we know daily what it is to flee from every supposed hope and
refuge to the one refuge the gospel makes known? Behold the
blessedness and truth in the hymn. It is something that is often
repeated but do we really believe it? Is there the true receiving of
it by us?

> "Christ is the friend of sinners;
> Be that forgotten never;
> A wounded soul, and not a whole,
> Becomes a true believer."

Friends, is Christ a stumblingblock to you who are truly
convicted of your sins to know the guilt and burden of them and
have many fears in your heart through a sense of your own
unfitness and unworthiness? All these convictions speak truth
and yet there is the cry in your heart to the Lord for mercy. Oh,
would it not be to the very joy and rejoicing of your heart if you
could truly lay hold on him as your all and in all? I say, is the
very language of your soul, "Give me Christ, or else I die?" To
such, Christ is not a stumblingstone. How precious he is, and the
scriptures speak to the soul thus brought to long, to look and to
seek after Jesus Christ under the sense of their own utter ruin
through sin. The scriptures set forth Jesus as an able and a willing
Saviour. Such souls never seek in vain. Oh for grace which brings
us to wait still upon him, as one well says,

> "Wait the appointed hour;
> Wait till the Bridegroom of your souls
> Reveal his love with power."

Yes, Jesus never rejects, turns away, or casts out one that is thus
brought to seek him through his sovereign grace.

"They stumbled at that stumblingstone; as it is written,
Behold, I lay in Sion a stumblingstone and rock of offence: and
whosoever believeth on him shall not be ashamed." As I have
said, though sadly and solemnly Christ is to many a
stumblingstone, yet to the sinner convicted and convinced of
their sin by the Holy Spirit, and thus brought to seek unto him, is
he not precious? I say, is not the longing of their souls that they
might lay hold upon him, coming as did that woman in the
gospel. She says, "If I may but touch his garment, I shall be

whole." And she "touched the hem of his garment" (Matt. 9:20-22). Oh, was she disappointed? Was she rejected and turned away by her Lord and Saviour? No! How he turns, how he speaks, how he claims her as his own, how he makes manifest the work of his grace in her heart and life, to the praise of the glory of his great and holy name. As he said to her, "Daughter, be of good comfort: thy faith hath made thee whole; go in peace." "And whosoever believeth on him shall not be ashamed."

But I will leave the remarks there this evening. May the Lord add his blessing. Amen.

24

GALATIANS 5

Stand fast therefore in the liberty wherewith Christ hath made us free, and be not entangled again with the yoke of bondage. Behold, I Paul say unto you, that if ye be circumcised, Christ shall profit you nothing. For I testify again to every man that is circumcised, that he is a debtor to do the whole law. Christ is become of no effect unto you, whosoever of you are justified by the law; ye are fallen from grace. For we through the Spirit wait for the hope of righteousness by faith. For in Jesus Christ neither circumcision availeth anything, nor uncircumcision; but faith which worketh by love. Ye did run well; who did hinder you that ye should not obey the truth? This persuasion cometh not of him that calleth you. A little leaven leaveneth the whole lump. I have confidence in you through the Lord, that ye will be none otherwise minded: but he that troubleth you shall bear his judgment, whosoever he be. And I brethren, if I yet preach circumcision, why do I yet suffer persecution? then is the offence of the cross ceased. I would they were even cut off which trouble you. For, brethren, ye have been called unto liberty; only use not liberty for an occasion to the flesh, but by love serve one another. For all the law is fulfilled in one word, even in this; Thou shalt love thy neighbour as thyself. But if ye bite and devour one another, take heed that ye be not consumed one of another. This I say then, Walk in the Spirit, and ye shall not fulfil the lust of the flesh. For the flesh lusteth against the Spirit, and the Spirit against the flesh: and these are contrary the one to the other: so that ye cannot do the things that ye would. But if ye be led of the Spirit, ye are not under the law. Now the works of the flesh are manifest, which are these; Adultery, fornication, uncleanness, lasciviousness, idolatry, witchcraft, hatred, variance, emula-

tions, wrath, strife, seditions, heresies, envyings, murders, drunkenness, revellings, and suchlike: of the which I tell you before, as I have also told you in time past, that they which do such things shall not inherit the kingdom of God. But the fruit of the Spirit is love, joy, peace, longsuffering, gentleness, goodness, faith, meekness, temperance: against such there is no law. And they that are Christ's have crucified the flesh with the affections and lusts. If we live in the Spirit, let us also walk in the Spirit. Let us not be desirous of vain glory, provoking one another, envying one another.

Two weeks ago I spoke at some considerable length on the opening verse of this chapter: "Stand fast therefore in the liberty wherewith Christ hath made us free, and be not entangled again with the yoke of bondage." Last Friday evening we turned to Romans chapter 9 and considered those last few verses where we read that "Israel, which followed after the law of righteousness, hath not attained to the law of righteousness. Wherefore? Because they sought it not by faith, but as it were by the works of the law. For they stumbled at that stumblingstone." As we noticed, that stumblingstone was the Lord and Saviour Jesus Christ, his person and finished work as the only way of access and acceptance for a sinner before a holy and just God.

Now I do not want to go over the same things that I have already mentioned in connection with the opening part of this chapter, except to remind you of the importance Paul places on the issues he is dealing with in this epistle. As I have said a number of times, they are not secondary matters of little concern but are as vital as life and death, as time and eternity. Paul is here dealing with spiritual eternal realities. He is setting forth the only way wherein sinners can be saved. In all his preaching he emphasises that Jesus Christ is the only way to the Father. He contends against the teaching troubling the church of Galatia, which said that though faith in Jesus was necessary for salvation, obedience to the law of God was also essential. And that was signified by attending to the rite of circumcision. Circumcision

was a part of the old covenant that God had made with Abraham
and had confirmed to his posterity and manifested most fully to
Moses on mount Sinai. As we have noticed, that covenant had
indeed a glory, yet a glory which is excelled in the new covenant
of grace and truth which came by Jesus Christ.

Paul emphasises this point. He says, "Behold, I Paul say unto
you, that if ye be circumcised, Christ shall profit you nothing."
What a solemn statement is that. He is not just referring to the
rite of circumcision itself. He is emphasising what circumcision
essentially signified. He says it is this: "For I testify again to
every man that is circumcised, that he is a debtor to do the whole
law." It was not the outward rite itself that was important but
what the rite signified. Every man that was circumcised was
under the covenant which required obedience to the whole of the
law of God. As I have frequently said, it is *perfect* obedience that
is required for a person to be justified. And the word of God
clearly testifies that it is impossible for sinners as you and me to
be justified by the deeds of the law, that is, by our own supposed
obedience to what a holy God requires. For that law demands
perfection and we, being transgressors, can never render that
perfection of obedience. We lost the power and ability to do so
when Adam fell in the garden of Eden. It is failure to recognise
what happened in the garden of Eden which leads men to
advocate (whether more or less) that the sinner's acceptance
before God is by the deeds of the law. No. The moment our first
parents disobeyed God in Eden they ruined themselves and all
their posterity. It was utterly impossible that any of the
descendants of Adam should ever render the obedience required
by the holy law of God. For such to think that by the deeds of the
law they can be justified before God is utterly vain and foolish.

He says, "If ye be circumcised, Christ shall profit you
nothing." The apostle is saying that these false judaizing teachers
appeared to make great play and emphasis on the person and
work of the Lord Jesus Christ. But they were denying him and
undermining the only foundation on which a sinner can be
accepted before God. Blessed be God, erroneous as this teaching
was, it can never undermine the one foundation laid in Zion.
Though it troubled the church at Galatia, yet it never undermined

the faith of the living family of God. Some may have been entangled for a time in that snare but they could not remain in it. The very teaching of Paul in this epistle was surely used under the Spirit's blessing to bring back those of the Lord's people who had become entangled in this snare of the false teachers.

He says, "Christ is become of no effect unto you, whosoever of you are justified by the law; ye are fallen from grace. For we through the Spirit wait for the hope of righteousness by faith." What an essential and blessed truth is brought out here in these words of Paul! Oh, where is the hope of the true believer? What does he wait for as taught by the Holy Spirit of God? What is his hope fixed upon? Where are his affections placed? We have it well stated in those words of Paul in which he testifies where his hope was and what he waited for, as we read in Philippians chapter 3. "We are the circumcision, which worship God in the spirit, and rejoice in Christ Jesus, and have no confidence in the flesh." He goes on to say that even the things that at one time he had gloried in, that he had put confidence in as the ground of his acceptance before God, he had been brought to count as dung and dross. He saw their utter folly as any ground of hope for him a sinner. His hope now was, "That I might win Christ, and be found in him, not having mine own righteousness, which is of the law, but that which is through the faith of Christ, the righteousness of God by faith."

The Holy Spirit ever brings the living family of God to not look to themselves but, as sinners, to look to, hope alone in and rest alone on the finished work of the Lord Jesus Christ. Oh! is not this the glory of the believer—not imparted righteousness but the imputed righteousness of Jesus Christ. Nothing else will avail us in that last great day. Nothing else will be of avail in the hour of death but the precious atoning blood and righteousness of Jesus Christ, as the ground of all our hope and salvation. The hymn writer could say,

> "Bold shall I stand in that great day,
> For who ought to my charge shall lay,
> While through thy blood absolved I am,
> From sin's tremendous curse and shame?"

Paul says, "For we through the Spirit wait for the hope of

righteousness by faith." And friends, that blessed hope and gracious waiting is a living vital reality in the life and experience of each one taught by the Holy Spirit. It evidences itself in the grace of living faith whereby the sinner is brought to true dependence, trust and confidence in the Lord and Saviour Jesus Christ alone. This faith is not a dead faith that just gives an intellectual assent to the truth of God's word. It is a living faith which has a real effect upon a person. Its fruits and effects are and will be seen. It is as Paul says, 'This is the thing that avails, this is the important matter, not circumcision or uncircumcision, *but faith which worketh by love.* For in Jesus Christ neither circumcision availeth anything, nor uncircumcision; but faith which worketh by love.'

He goes on to say, "Ye did run well; who did hinder you that ye should not obey the truth? This persuasion cometh not of him that calleth you. A little leaven leaveneth the whole lump. I have confidence in you through the Lord, that you will be none otherwise minded: but he that troubleth you shall bear his judgment, whosoever he be." Paul uses some very strong and searching language when speaking of those that trouble the church. He says, "They shall bear their judgment" and he goes on also to say, "I would that they were even cut off which trouble you." I say, Paul uses very strong language. See how he faithfully contends for the truth and stands against those who opposed the gospel he had received.

Let me just notice this here in passing, for it is not an unimportant matter. Paul is not just saying about those false teachers at Galatia, 'Well, they are mistaken. They are right at heart, but wrong in their head. Though we reject their teaching, yet we have a certain sympathy towards them.' No. The word tells us, "Try the spirits whether they are of God: because many false prophets are gone out into the world" (1 John 4:1). And John gives us some very clear criteria to judge and try these spirits. And are not *we* to judge them? Are they not to be tried by the things they teach? It is, "To the law and to the testimony: if they speak not according to this word, it is because there is no light in them" (Isa. 8:20). And such who resisted the truth and actively fought against the gospel Paul preached, he in no way counted to be brethren in Christ. He did not hold out the hand of fellowship to them. Speaking by the Spirit of God, he warns the church to have nothing to do with such false teachers. And he also says that they shall bear their judgment. God will bring them into judgment. It is a solemn thing to preach things contrary to the clear teaching of God's word. I know there are differences among the believing people of God on what can be considered secondary matters. There are differences between believers on church order. We are only too well aware of that and acknowledge it. But when it comes to the essentials of the gospel, to what it is that saves the soul, then all truly taught of the Holy Spirit agree. And it comes down to this—salvation is either by works or it is by grace through faith. It cannot be a mixture of the two. Paul teaches that "by grace are ye saved through faith; and that not of yourselves: it is the gift of God: not of works, lest any man should boast" (Eph. 2:8). Those are not to be received who come proclaiming salvation in any other way than through the sovereign grace of God revealed in the gospel. They are to be withstood, as Paul withstood those that troubled not only the church at Galatia but other churches also at that time.

He says, "For, brethren, ye have been called unto liberty; only use not liberty for an occasion to the flesh, but by love serve one another." Now I do not want to go over again what I have formerly spoken about that true blessed liberty of the gospel. Let me just emphasise this important point. Friends, it is only as we are brought into gospel liberty through saving faith *in the Lord Jesus Christ* that we know anything of the love of God shed abroad in our hearts by the Holy Spirit. True love to the Lord and to the brethren is never through the works of the law. Far from it. Where there is the advocating of the works of the law as the way of acceptance before God for sinners, what are its invariable fruits? It certainly does not lead to genuine love to Jesus Christ and the brethren. No, we sadly find that it puffs up the sinner. It is a way of pride. It is a way of self-exaltation. It leads to all manner of things that bring distress, division, strife, and contention.

But where will the true Spirit-taught liberty of the gospel in the receiving of the pardoning grace and mercy of God, bring us?

It lays us low at the feet of Jesus Christ. It brings us to realise our utter nothingness in self. The more we know of the love of the Lord Jesus Christ, the lower we shall lie. The real fruits are humbleness of mind and spirit, the esteeming ourselves as did the great apostle himself, as "less than the least of all saints" (Eph. 3:8) and the very chief of sinners. These are not expressions used just for effect. No, they were the genuine experience and feelings of Paul's soul as taught by the Holy Spirit. Grace always humbles. Its blessed effect is humbleness of mind, lowliness of spirit, and the desiring to exalt the Lord Jesus Christ alone. But everything else is that which puffs up the sinner.

What was being advocated at Galatia fed human pride with what is conducive to our own fallen carnal nature. One thing our old nature hates is to be dependent on another. As the ground of acceptance before God, it wants to be encouraged in the way in which there is something the sinner can do, even the least of things, to cause God to be favourable to us. Why, our old nature will seek after and clutch hold of any such thing with all tenacity. But what of the Holy Spirit's teaching of the grace of God in the gospel, which sets forth the utter inability and hopelessness of the sinner dead in trespasses and sins? This, the old nature hates, and will have nothing to do with it.

We find the illustration of this so clearly throughout the word of God. See the confrontations of our Lord Jesus Christ with the scribes, Pharisees and Sadducees. They were all very religious people. And Paul here was not dealing with pagans who were denying the faith but with very religious persons who even came professing the name of the Lord Jesus. But they hated and reacted against Paul's preaching of salvation which is wholly by the sovereign grace of God. This is still true. Proud nature will have nothing of this, nothing of the imputed righteousness of Jesus Christ. These things will never be accepted in an unregenerate heart. But the sinner taught of the Holy Spirit is brought to rest and glory in that which proud sinners despise and reject.

He says, "For all the law is fulfilled in one word, even in this; Thou shalt love thy neighbour as thyself." I believe that this statement is often misunderstood. Immediately, men set forth the importance of love one to another, because love is the fulfilling of the law. That indeed is true but from whence does this love come? Is this the easy thing some would make it out to be? Does this love grow on the barren ground of our fallen carnal nature? Is it that which we can produce of ourselves? Is it a work of the flesh? No, it is not. It is alone the fruit of the Spirit's work and teaching in the soul. It is the effect of the love of Christ as "shed abroad in our hearts by the Holy Spirit that is given unto us" (Rom. 5:5). Friends, this love is a very real and precious thing. It is a vital thing but it is not that which we produce of ourselves. It is the outworking of what John says, "We love him, because he first loved us" (1 John 4:19). Oh how we continually need the gracious renewings of the sense of his love in our own souls, to draw our hearts out after him in love to him, his truth, his ways and to the brethren.

You know, one of the real exercises so often of the child of God is their consciousness of the greatness of the love of the Lord Jesus to them and the felt weakness and coldness of their love to him. Oh how this brings forth, many a time, heart-cries that the Lord would revive, refresh and quicken them and lift up the light of his countenance upon them. They beseech him to come again and shed abroad his love in their hearts, that his word, his ways, his truth and his people may truly be the joy and delight of their souls.

He says, "But if ye bite and devour one another, take heed that ye be not consumed one of another. This I say then, Walk in the Spirit, and ye shall not fulfil the lust of the flesh. For the flesh lusteth against the Spirit, and the Spirit against the flesh: and these are contrary the one to the other: so that ye cannot do the things that ye would. But if ye be led of the Spirit, ye are not under the law." Now some essential things are brought out in this statement of Paul upon which there is much misunderstanding in the days in which we live. Paul is speaking here of the flesh and the Spirit. What does he mean by these things and what is the application in the life and experience of the people of God? I refer you to what I said the other week in reference to those words of the Lord Jesus to Nicodemus. He says, "That which is born of the flesh is flesh; and that which is born of the Spirit is spirit" (John 3:6). Remember he was speaking there of the new birth, the sovereign work of the Holy Spirit in regenerating the sinner. All born of God are brought into the possession of a new nature. They are made partakers of the divine nature. Peter sets this before us in his epistle, saying we are "born again, not of corruptible seed, but of incorruptible, by the word of God, which liveth and abideth for ever" (1 Pet. 1:23). In regeneration we are brought into possession of a new, divine, incorruptible nature which is born of God. It is a nature which is like unto the Lord Jesus Christ himself. It is without sin. This new nature is born of the Spirit.

Now this is the important point I want to stress here. Paul says, "Walk in the Spirit, and ye shall not fulfil the lust of the flesh." As I have said, in regeneration we are made partakers of that new nature which is born of God. It is incorruptible, it cannot sin, and it liveth in and upon the Lord Jesus Christ. But remember, we also possess what is termed here the flesh or the old Adam nature. I feel the misunderstanding so often on this point is that many think that in regeneration there is at least a partial reformation of the old nature. But I want to emphasise that in regeneration the old nature always remains the same. There is no alteration in our old Adam nature. In regeneration we are made a new creature, a partaker of a new nature, and these two principles of grace and flesh are found in everyone born again and led of the Holy Spirit. Our old nature is not regenerated, for is it not corruptible still? Will it not come to death and dissolution and be laid in the grave? It is at the last resurrection day "when this corruptible shall have put on incorruption, and this mortal must put on immortality. So when this corruptible shall have put on incorruption, and this mortal shall have put on immortality, then shall be brought to pass the saying that is written, Death is swallowed up in victory" (1 Cor. 15:54). It is at the resurrection day that what is sown in corruption at death and is buried, will rise again with that new body fashioned like unto the glorious body of our Lord Jesus Christ (Phil. 3:21). But the believer is made only too well aware of what the Lord states that, "that which is born of the flesh is flesh." And as Paul teaches here, these two natures always work and act according to what they are. That which is born of the Spirit ever seeks after the things of the Spirit, delighting in God, in his word of truth, and in his ways. While that which is born of the flesh acts according to its own nature.

He says, "Now the works of the flesh are manifest, which are these; Adultery, fornication, uncleanness, lasciviousness, idolatry, witchcraft, hatred, variance, emulations, wrath, strife, seditions, heresies, envyings, murders, drunkenness, revelling, and such like." These are the works of the flesh. This is what our old Adam nature ever seeks after and ever delights in—things which are opposite to God and godliness. Is not the believer, as he is in possession through grace of that new nature, only too well aware of these things? It is from this that arises the conflict in every believer, of which Paul speaks here. For that which is born of the Spirit ever seeks after the things of the Spirit, and that which is of the flesh, the things of the flesh. Friends, do not for one moment think that our old Adam nature, our flesh, is any different to anyone else. Even in every believer, what the flesh desires and seeks after is no different to the world around us. Is not this ever a source of distress, grief and sorrow to the believer? How powerful they so often find are the workings of their own fallen and carnal nature! But oh! though these things cause grief, yet Paul also writes here concerning that which is born of the Spirit. The new principle of grace within ever seeks after the things of God. Read again Romans 7. It well opens up this spiritual conflict and contains much instruction and also real comfort for the believer.

Paul is making the point here as well, that those who advocated the deeds of the law as the ground of their acceptance before God, were strangers to these spiritual conflicts. Knowing nothing of the new nature, nothing of the true liberty of the gospel, ruled only by fear, they knew nothing of the true going out of the heart in love to the Lord and his ways. Not being made partakers of the new nature and without gospel liberty, how could they do so? See the significant statement Paul makes. He says, "But if ye be led of the Spirit, ye are not under the law," no, not under its curse or condemnation, not under the fear and bondage it engenders, but made alive to God. Though, as I say, the believer is ever acquainted with the workings of his old fallen nature which causes so much grief and distress, yet he is "led of the Spirit," and is "not under the law."

Let us not overlook this important truth which the Holy Spirit sets before his living people. He says, "Ye are not under the law, but under grace" (Rom. 6:14). And again, "Even so might grace reign through righteousness unto eternal life by Jesus Christ our Lord" (Rom. 5:21). True, the flesh hinders and the believer is troubled and distressed by the workings of his fallen Adam nature. But is not the fruit of that which is born of the Spirit seen in the believer? He says, "But the fruit of the Spirit is love, joy, peace, longsuffering, gentleness, goodness, faith, meekness, temperance: against such there is no law. And they that are Christ's have crucified the flesh with the affections and lusts. If we live in the Spirit, let us also walk in the Spirit." This fruit is not only seen in the actions of a believer but it is seen in their reactions to situations into which they are brought in the outworking of God's providence. Here is one of the most powerful witnesses to the reality of the possession of the new nature through sovereign grace. The evidence of the grace of God is invariably seen more in the reaction of the believer than in what may be termed his outward actions.

What I am trying to say is well illustrated in the case of Job. When those terrible troubles came upon Job, overwhelming as they were in their nature, one after the other, what is the reaction of Job? Is it to curse God and die? Is it to rise up in rebellion against God? "The Lord gave, and the Lord hath taken away; blessed be the name of the Lord. In all this Job sinned not, nor charged God foolishly" (Job 1:21-22). Consider this principle in the testimonies the scripture gives to the people of God in their reactions to the various crises, troubles and distresses in providence into which they were brought. True, there were times when the first onset of those things seemed to knock them sideways, as it were. But we find them coming again to the Lord, their souls being drawn out to him. It was so with godly Hezekiah. When the land was invaded by the Assyrians, to whom did Hezekiah turn? It was to the Lord his God. But also when the prophet came with that heavy message, "Set thine house in order: for thou shalt die, and not live" (Isa. 38:1), we find Hezekiah turning away from everything else unto the Lord his God. We see it borne out in the affairs of the apostle as well. And is not this fruit of the Spirit truly evidenced with the believer in all the trials of faith? It is seen in his daily life and walk, not only in his outward actions, but in his reactions to the trying situations into which he is brought in the Lord's dealings.

But I also want to emphasise this point. He says, "If we live in the Spirit, let us also walk in the Spirit." Friends, the Spirit's teaching ever leads, draws and brings us daily to the Lord and Saviour Jesus Christ. The whole work of the Spirit is to glorify the Saviour. It is through the blessed work and teaching of the Spirit that Jesus is made precious—all and in all to us. "If we live in the Spirit, let us also walk in the Spirit," and so walk, as one has said:

> "To keep our eyes on Jesus fixed,
> And there our hope to stay,
> The Lord will make his goodness pass
> Before us in the way."

But I will leave the remarks there. May the Lord add his blessing. Amen.

25

GALATIANS 6:1-10

Brethren, if a man be overtaken in a fault, ye which are spiritual, restore such an one in the spirit of meekness; considering thyself, lest thou also be tempted. Bear ye one another's burdens, and so fulfil the law of Christ. For if a man think himself to be something, when he is nothing, he deceiveth himself. But let every man prove his own work, and then shall he have rejoicing in himself alone, and not in another. For every man shall bear his own burden. Let him that is taught in the word communicate unto him that teacheth in all good things. Be not deceived; God is not mocked: for whatsoever a man soweth, that shall he also reap. For he that soweth to his flesh shall of the flesh reap corruption; but he that soweth to the Spirit shall of the Spirit reap life everlasting. And let us not be weary in well doing: for in due season we shall reap, if we faint not. As we have therefore opportunity, let us do good unto all men, especially unto them who are of the household of faith.

We have considered the important themes that the apostle Paul deals with in this epistle to the churches in Galatia—his contentions against those who were teaching things contrary to the gospel that had been revealed from heaven and which he preached. These false teachers were saying that faith in Christ was not sufficient of itself to save the soul. Added to faith must be the works and obedience of the law wrought by the sinner himself. Now I do not want to go over again all the things that I have brought before you from this epistle over the past weeks but want to come to these verses before us.

We find that Paul very vigorously contends against the works of the law having any part in the salvation of the sinner. He proves most emphatically that salvation is by grace, "through faith; and that not of yourselves: it is the gift of God: not of works, lest any man should boast" (Eph. 2:8-9). The acceptance, or as the scripture puts it, the justifying of the sinner before God, is wholly on the ground of the person and finished work of the Lord Jesus Christ. The sinner is accepted for what Jesus has done in his holy life here on earth and his one offering, his atoning sacrifice of himself, on the cross at Calvary. Paul contends strongly against the works of the law as having any part in the justification of the sinner before God. But he also emphatically brings out in this epistle and in his other epistles that the life of God in the soul will be evidenced in a person's life. The work of the Holy Spirit in regenerating a sinner and bringing him to repentance and saving faith in Jesus Christ will be manifest in a walk and conversation consistent with the truths professed. He shows that the believer is justified by faith alone in Christ Jesus, yet genuine faith ever works by love in the believer's life.

Paul states this important truth in his epistle to the Corinthians. He says, "Now abideth faith, hope, charity, these three; but the greatest of these is charity" (1Cor. 13:13). "Charity" we understand as love in more modern language. Faith, hope and love are the fruit of the Spirit. Where one truly is, there also will the others be found. Thus one real characteristic of saving faith is that it works by love as he says in the previous chapter. It evidences itself in the reality of love, the love of the Lord Jesus Christ shed abroad in the heart by the Holy Spirit. And what is one of the most important outworkings of love? Love is ever drawn by attraction to the object of its affection, and for the believer that object is Jesus Christ. As Peter reminds us, "Unto you therefore which believe he [Jesus Christ] is precious" (1 Pet. 2:7). And so he is.

And where there is genuine love to the Lord Jesus Christ it surely evidences itself in concern to be obedient to his will revealed in the precepts he has taught and graciously commanded. Does not the child of God, the new man of grace as scripture puts it, ever desire to be found walking according to those things? Through almighty grace the believer possesses a new nature which evidences itself in love to the Lord Jesus, delight in his truth and in desires to be obedient to his ways. This is what Paul is coming to in these verses before us—the outworking of the life of God, the effects of grace, the reality of the love of God as shed abroad in the heart by the Holy Spirit who is given to us. It is as John reminds us when he writes to the people of God, "Beloved, let us love one another: for love is of God" (1 John 4:7). And again, "My little children, let us not love in word, neither in tongue; but in deed and in truth" (1 John 3:18). The outworking of this love is manifest in very practical ways, and it is in these ways that Paul instructs, exhorts and encourages the church.

One further thought before looking particularly at verses 1 to 10. In the closing part of chapter 5 he defines the fruit of the Spirit. He says, "But the fruit of the Spirit is love, joy, peace, longsuffering, gentleness, goodness, faith, meekness, temperance: against such there is no law. And they that are Christ's have crucified the flesh with the affections and lusts. If we live in the Spirit, let us also walk in the Spirit. Let us not be desirous of vain glory, provoking one another, envying one another." What were the sad fruits of advocating the law of Moses as a rule for the Galatian believers? What was the result of the contention brought into those churches by the false teachers? It produced vain glory, the "provoking one another, envying one another." This error did not produce the fruit of the Spirit but the works of the flesh. It highlighted the sad evidence of our fallen and carnal nature. Did what was being taught in the churches of Galatia lead to peace, spiritual harmony and union among them? Did it endear the Lord Jesus Christ to them and them to one another in desire to walk together in the bonds of love and union? No. What was being advocated sadly produced the very opposite. Paul says, "If we live in the Spirit, let us also walk in the Spirit." He warns against vain glory and the provoking and envying of one another.

He then comes in this sixth chapter to the practical outworking of the life of God in the soul—the fruits and effects of grace in the child of God. Let me just emphasise this point. Paul is here speaking of the fruit of the Spirit, the effect of grace. The things he here brings before us are not the cause of the Lord's love and favour to his people. That was where the problem in this church arose. They were putting cause for effect. They were advocating the works of the law to obtain the favour of God. Paul ever emphasises the glorious truth that the favour of God is never obtained by us through the works of the law but through "the hearing of faith" (Gal. 3:2). The mercy and favour of God to his people is wholly of his love and grace. Paul insists that the fruit of the Spirit is the effect of God's love, not the cause of it. This fruit is the outworking of grace, not the reason why grace is manifest in the first instance.

So then, coming to very practical things he says "Brethren." There is something very important and instructive in that word, *Brethren*. Is not this true of the people of God? As believers we are brethren in Christ Jesus. We are members of the same family. We have one Father. We are born again of one Holy Spirit. We have one elder brother, the Lord Jesus Christ, to whom we owe everything. *Brethren*. This is very expressive of the oneness and union of the people of God and indicates how we should ever view one another. Where faith is real, there is the accepting and embracing of believers as brethren in the Lord. We love them for Jesus' sake and account them the excellent of the earth in whom is all our delight (Ps. 16:3). Friends, how often we lose sight of the fact that believers are brethren in the Lord. As Paul shows here, how incumbent it is for us to act one towards another as those that are brethren, the children of one Father, who owe everything to his redeeming love and grace. We have nothing of our own in which to boast and glory but owe everything to our Lord and Saviour. "Brethren," he says. I repeat, may that truth be ever impressed upon our souls.

True, though through grace we are brethren who are one in the Lord we are also individuals. We have our own peculiarities, and being what we are while here below, we are subject to all the infirmities of human nature. But how incumbent it is on us to walk together in our relationships with one another as brethren in the Lord. Paul brings this principle before us in the following verses. What is at the root of true fellowship and communion one with another? It is love. As Paul writes in one of his epistles, "Touching brotherly love ye need not that I write unto you: for ye yourselves are taught of God to love one another" (1 Thess. 4:9). The fundamental fruit of the gracious teaching of God the Holy Spirit is to love one another. Ah friends, how vital, how essential is this love! How it is the very root of all true spiritual fellowship and communion and of the going forward together in the things of the Lord in the work and witness of his church.

It is true what the apostle Peter says, "And above all things have fervent charity among yourselves: for charity shall cover the multitude of sins" (1 Pet. 4:8). Now I know this will not always be accepted in some circles but one of the very fruits of brotherly love is not to be always seeking to expose the failings of others. It is not to be always in a critical controversial spirit in matters of church fellowship and communion. The word of God reminds us that fellowship requires much bearing and forbearing with one another. To illustrate this point, I personally have need to bear with the failings of others and they have as much need of grace to bear with my failings and infirmities as well. Is not this the very principle of the things Paul is bringing before us here? Is he not saying that we are never to lose sight of this?

He says, "Brethren, if a man be overtaken in a fault, ye which are spiritual, restore such an one in the spirit of meekness; considering thyself, lest thou also be tempted." Do not overlook the word he uses here, "Ye which are *spiritual*," not you that know the most but "ye which are spiritual." And friends, a real gauge of the spiritual standing and prosperity of any company of the Lord's people is how they react to brethren that are "overtaken in a fault." Yet remember, Paul deals very solemnly and emphatically with those that persisted in teaching false doctrines in the face of faithful rebukes against their error. Oh, I say, this verse does not condone false doctrine in the church. No, indeed not! But among the Galatians were those who for a time were overcome by the influence of those false teachers. And Paul here instructs the spiritual brethren how to deal with those who had been overtaken even in that fault but who were brought to realise their fall, to confess their sin and to show a spirit of true repentance. They are to "restore such an one in the spirit of meekness; considering thyself, lest thou also be tempted."

But does not this principle cover so much of the life and fellowship of the church of Jesus Christ and the reactions of brethren one to another. "If a man be overtaken in a fault." The spirituality of the church can indeed be gauged by the line taken towards him. Paul is saying, 'How are they to be dealt with? Are we to take a rod and beat them for their faults and failings?' Friends, when a brother or sister has failed, the church should rightly, prayerfully, carefully seek to deal with them and restore them even in the pointing out of their fault. But so often is there not rather the judging and condemning of the person? Often there is no spirit of kindness or real concern for the restoration and spiritual welfare of the erring one. At the time of failure in a brother or sister, when they most need the help and support of their brethren in the Lord, instead of receiving help they have received condemnation. We are not saying that evil or error is to be tolerated in any way in the church but oh may we have the spirit that Paul speaks of here in dealing with erring brethren. "If a man be overtaken in a fault, ye which are spiritual, restore such an one in the spirit of meekness."

What is the pattern set before us with respect to these things in the word of God? Is it not that of our Lord Jesus Christ himself? Is it not the way of the Lord's dealings with his own? Ah, is not this way of the Lord set forth in his word as we read in Psalm 103: "Like as a father pitieth his children, so the Lord pitieth them that fear him?" How very kind and tender hearted is the Lord in his dealings with his own, and no more so than when they are overcome in a fault! Does he then deal with them in a harsh way and manner? What is his whole concern? Is it not to restore them and bring them again to himself? You take the case of Simon Peter. See how Peter grievously denied his Lord and Master. What was the reaction of Jesus to him? Was it to have no more to do with him, to cut him off, to say, 'After all that I have told you, yet you still went and did the very thing you were warned against?' No, we read, "The Lord turned, and looked upon Peter." I believe that look broke Peter's heart. It says he "went out, and wept bitterly" (Luke 22:61-62).

"Ye which are spiritual, restore such an one in the spirit of meekness." Friends, meekness is not weakness. Is it not humbleness of mind, a sense of our need and our whole dependence on the Lord for his upholding and sustaining grace? As Paul says here, "Considering thyself, lest thou also be tempted." Have we anything to glory in over another? One may fail in one thing very sadly and grievously but am I to say that of myself I am any better or any less prone to fall into the same thing? Should not these considerations be a constant reminder to us of our whole dependence on the Lord for his upholding sustaining grace. "Considering thyself, lest thou also be tempted." This will not lead us to high mindedness but rather to true filial fear of the Lord.

He says, "Bear ye one another's burdens, and so fulfil the law of Christ." This likewise follows from verse one—the very practical outworking of the life of God in the soul, in the fellowship and communion of the people of God one toward another. What is the law of Jesus Christ? What is the commandment that goes forth from mount Zion? Look at what Jesus says to his disciples in that upper room shortly before he went forth to Gethsemane and Calvary. He says, "A new commandment I give unto you, That ye love one another; as I have loved you, that ye also love one another" (John 13:34). Is not that the sum and substance of the law of Jesus Christ? That new commandment is the essence of all that the Lord Jesus has revealed of his will to his true church.

"Bear ye one another's burdens, and so fulfil the law of Christ." This expresses the concern that believers should ever have, practically and prayerfully, for one another. True, we cannot enter fully into the path another has to walk. We cannot carry one another's burdens in that sense. Each have their own path to walk, which is appointed for them by the Lord. But as Paul sets forth here we can and should be prayerfully and practically concerned for one another, to help each other on the road, to seek each other's real spiritual welfare. Was not this borne out in the early church? Though Paul went forth preaching the gospel, he also engaged in collecting and carrying money from the churches of Achaia and Macedonia to relieve the needs of the poor saints of the Lord in Jerusalem. In his epistle to the Corinthians he exhorts and encourages them to be forward in this good and profitable work. The point I am making is that this bearing one another's burdens is both a prayerful and practical concern.

He says, "For if a man think himself to be something, when he is nothing, he deceiveth himself." Friends, what a warning is this to us against selfishness and self-importance and thinking that everything centres around ourselves. The Spirit's work in the soul never leads us to think of ourselves more highly than we ought to think. True, we all have the tendency to a greater or lesser extent to be very concerned with our personal affairs. But as brethren in the church, though we have our personal cares and responsibilities to attend to daily, Paul warns us here against the self-centredness which is so endemic in fallen sinful human nature.

He says, "For if a man think himself to be something, when he is nothing, he deceiveth himself. But let every man prove his own work, and then shall he have rejoicing in himself alone, and not in another." It is suggested by some that Paul is speaking particularly of the work of the ministry and of those that hold office in the church of Jesus Christ. Some in the church of Galatia were usurping the teaching office and were bringing in false doctrine. How highly they thought of themselves. How ready they were to promote their own ideas and pedal those grievous errors in the churches! Paul says, "If a man think himself to be something, when he is nothing, he deceiveth himself." One sad aspect of the work of those false teachers is always present where false doctrine is advocated. So much emphasis is placed on the individual who thus teaches. They seek to exalt or glorify themselves or the creature in some way or other. They do not essentially promote the glory of Jesus Christ and the spiritual welfare of the church.

"But let every man prove his own work, and then shall he have rejoicing in himself alone, and not in another." Paul writes similar things in his epistle to the Corinthians. He says concerning the ministry of the word, "For other foundation can no man lay than that is laid, which is Jesus Christ. But let every man take heed how he buildeth thereupon. Now if any man build upon this foundation gold, silver, precious stones, wood, hay, stubble; every man's work shall be made manifest: for the day shall declare it, because it shall be revealed by fire; and the fire shall try every man's work of what sort it is" (1 Cor. 3:11-13).

He says, "For every man shall bear his own burden." A solemn warning and truth is here set before those that minister the word or hold office in the church. We are reminded that we are not so much accountable to men as to the Lord. "For every man shall bear his own burden." Solemn and searching are these things. It was so with those who peddled false doctrine in the churches of Galatia. Oh, they would bear the burden of that. The Lord in his own good time would bring them into judgment for those things. Paul again in writing to the Corinthians warns with particular reference to the work of the ministry: "We must all appear before the judgment seat of Christ; that every one may receive the things done in his body, according to that he hath done, whether it be good or bad" (2 Cor. 5:10).

"Every man shall bear his own burden." Let us just notice here as well, the importance of being brought to realise where we stand as before the Lord our God. How vital it is, not only in the day of judgment but even now, to have the Holy Spirit's witness in our soul that we stand before God, not upon a foundation of our own making but upon the one foundation laid in Zion. How important that we have through his grace the testimony of the Holy Spirit in our own consciences that those things in which we are engaged are according to the will and word of the Lord our God.

"Let him that is taught in the word communicate unto him that teacheth in all good things." As I have said, some have suggested that the previous verses particularly apply to persons engaged in the work of the ministry. In these next verses the Lord addresses the brethren who are taught under the sound of the ministry of the word. He says, "Let him that is taught in the word." We have set before us here the responsibility of the brethren in the church to those raised up of God and set over them in the Lord as ministers of the word. "Let him that is taught in the word communicate unto him that teacheth in all good things." The care and responsibility of those that are taught is to see that those that teach them are provided for "in all good things."

Now this principle is clearly taught in the new testament scriptures. I know I may be partly inhibited in speaking on this, myself being one that receives those good things which are communicated by you that are taught in the word. And I do not bring this before you in any way as a criticism of the attitude of the church or the brethren here towards myself. No, I believe we can express our thankfulness as Paul did in his epistle to the Philippians: "Ye sent once and again unto my necessity. Not because I desire a gift: but I desire fruit that may abound to your account" (Phil 4:16-17). He received those things as "an odour of a sweet smell, a sacrifice acceptable, wellpleasing to God."

Let us not overlook then the important principle that Paul is laying down here. "Let him that is taught in the word communicate unto him that teacheth in all good things." The apostle, in writing to the Corinthians, unequivocally states that the Lord hath "ordained that they which preach the gospel should live of the gospel" (1 Cor. 9:14). He says also, "It is written in the law of Moses, Thou shalt not muzzle the mouth of the ox that treadeth out the corn" (1 Cor. 9:9). He shows that the Levites under the old testament law were provided for abundantly out of the offerings of the Lord. Doth God take care of oxen and Levites but sends gospel ministers at their own charges? No, indeed not. True, the renumeration they receive from the church for the ministry is not to be the chief concern of those who preach the word of God. As Peter reminds us, "Feed the flock of God which is among you, taking the oversight thereof, not by constraint, but willingly; not for filthy lucre, but of a ready mind; neither as being lords over God's heritage, but being ensamples to the flock" (1 Pet. 5:2-3). Paul himself showed in his epistle to the Corinthians that in the gospel dispensation it would have been right for him to receive renumeration from

the church for his ministry among them. For a particular reason he did not accept it of that church. But he shows that was not because he had not the right or power to receive renumeration.

Also, in his second epistle to the Corinthians, he writes

concerning giving not only to the work of the ministry but to the poor brethren in Judæa as well. He lays down the principle that, "If there be first a willing mind, it is accepted according to that a man hath, and not according to that he hath not" (2 Cor. 8:12). The importance of having first a willing mind is what Paul is dealing with in verses 7 and 8 of our text, I believe. These verses have much to do with what he is saying in verse 6: "Let him that is taught in the word communicate unto him that teacheth in all good things." They also concern the giving of the brethren to the wider aspect of the work of the Lord and to the poor brethren. In verse 7 he says, "Be not deceived; God is not mocked: for whatsoever a man soweth, that shall he also reap." Again in 2 Corinthians chapter 9 he says, "He which soweth sparingly shall reap also sparingly; and he which soweth bountifully shall reap also bountifully." That is true in nature. It is true of the church of Jesus Christ in what we might term the important responsibility of each church member to contribute to the service of the Lord according to the ability God has given them. As he prospers them, so the main principle is not to lay up things exclusively for themselves but in a right way to lay them out in the work and service of God.

And be assured that in this matter we find God is no man's debtor. That which is given to the Lord is not wasted. In that which is given to the Lord we are but giving out of what he has first given us. Paul, speaking the promises of God under the inspiration of the Holy Spirit could write to those Philippians who sent once and again to his necessity, "But my God shall supply all your need according to his riches in glory by Christ Jesus" (Phil. 4:19). None have ever been the poorer for their giving to the Lord, to his work, with a willing heart and mind. No. God prospers his people in these things. The promise is essentially that the Lord will supply our need and if we have our needs met what more do we require?

We are not to run away with the idea that the more that is given to the Lord's work the more we can expect back in material things. That is not the idea behind what Paul is saying here. But as this giving is a fruit of love, so we can expect the Lord's blessing on these things. Looking back to verse 6, "Let him that is taught in the word." Oh, does he not reap in receiving spiritual benefit under the teaching of the word as it is blessed of the Lord the Holy Spirit to his own soul? Then let him "communicate unto him that teacheth in all good things. Be not deceived; God is not mocked: for whatsoever a man soweth, that shall he also reap. For he that soweth to his flesh shall of the flesh reap corruption; but he that soweth to the Spirit shall of the Spirit reap life everlasting. And let us not be weary in well doing: for in due season we shall reap, if we faint not."

Is there not here the encouragement and exhortation to perseverance, to continuing to go forward in the things of the Lord, even in the face of the many discouragements we may meet with? Ah friends, those discouragements are not to divert the believer from the way the Lord sets before us. "We shall reap, if we faint not. As we have therefore opportunity, let us do good unto all men, especially unto them who are of the household of faith."

But I will leave the remarks there this evening. May the Lord add his blessing. Amen.

26

GALATIANS 6:11-18

Ye see how large a letter I have written unto you with mine own hand. As many as desire to make a fair shew in the flesh, they constrain you to be circumcised; only lest they should suffer persecution for the cross of Christ. For neither they themselves who are circumcised keep the law; but desire to have you circumcised, that they may glory in your flesh. But God forbid that I should glory, save in the cross of our Lord Jesus Christ, by whom the world is crucified unto me, and I unto the world. For in Christ Jesus neither circumcision availeth any thing, nor uncircumcision, but a new creature. And as many as walk according to this rule, peace be on them, and mercy, and upon the Israel of God. From henceforth let no man trouble me: for I bear in my body the marks of the Lord Jesus. Brethren, the grace of our Lord Jesus Christ be with your spirit. Amen.

We come this evening to the last part of this epistle to the Galatians which we have been considering from time to time over previous months at our Friday evening meetings. Now as we look at this sixth chapter from verse 11, we read, "Ye see how large a letter I have written unto you with mine own hand." I believe this verse sets forth the urgency and importance of the things the apostle wrote in this letter to the churches of Galatia. It shows his great concern for their spiritual welfare and for the honour and glory of the Lord and Saviour Jesus Christ. So concerned was he, that he emphasises it in this way, "Ye see how large a letter I have written unto you with mine own hand." He is referring not only to the length of the letter and the detail into which he had gone in dealing with the matters he wrote to them about, but that he wrote it with his own hand. He is saying that on this occasion he had departed from his usual way of communicating with the various churches of Jesus Christ. You will find that Paul usually dictated his letters—another person wrote them down. Thus you will find in the epistle to the Romans the various salutations in that last chapter, and we read there, "I Tertius, who wrote this epistle, salute you in the Lord." Though Paul used others to write what he dictated to them, he signed the letters himself. Thus we read at the end of 1 Corinthians, "The salutation of me Paul with mine own hand." His letters had authenticity as signed by himself. But on this occasion he says, "Ye see how large a letter I have written unto you with mine own hand." As I said, I believe this expresses the deep concern of the apostle and the weighty importance of the things he wrote to them. And I would emphasise again that the matters dealt with in this epistle are as important today as they were when the apostle first wrote this letter to the Galatians under the inspiration of the Holy Spirit. The same error that was abroad among those Galatian churches still raises its head among the churches of Jesus Christ. Sadly, its counterpart is seen to prevail in many places today.

Let us go a little further. He says, "As many as desire to make a fair shew in the flesh, they constrain you to be circumcised; only lest they should suffer persecution for the cross of Christ." He here distinctly touches on the motives of those who taught contrary to the doctrine they had received of the apostle, the doctrine which is according to godliness and in which Jesus Christ is set forth as the only salvation for sinners. Paul says they were not motivated by concern for the glory of the Lord Jesus Christ. How evident that was! Could it not be seen how detrimental their teaching was to the glory of the Lord Jesus, in that it added to the great work he had done. It was saying that the work of Jesus Christ was not sufficient of itself to save the sinner. How derogatory to the glory of Christ to say that something must be added to his work—that faith in Christ was needful but that those who would be saved must also keep the law themselves! Nothing more detrimental to the glory of Jesus Christ could be taught than that. Such teaching undermines the whole foundation on which the salvation of the church of Jesus Christ depends. And if that is taken away what hope is there for sinners?

But as I have mentioned a few times, what they were advocating was so conducive to sinful fallen human nature. That it appeals to the natural inclination of the human heart is not only evident here but in the history of mankind and religion down the generations. Nothing is more conducive to the natural inclinations of fallen man than a religion which puts great emphasis on the works, efforts and endeavours of men, whatever form they may take. I say again that the religion of the natural man is the religion of works. The gospel of God's grace being wholly contrary to those concepts will never be received by the unregenerate. It will never be received by those dead in a profession of religion. The natural reaction is a rejection of the glorious gospel, an enmity and hatred to it. In this 12th verse Paul puts his finger very clearly on the issue, "As many as desire to make a fair shew in the flesh." Sadly and solemnly, is this not the very essence of a religion of works? Is not this the concern of so many? They desire "to make a fair shew in the flesh." As long as things outwardly are all apparently fair then they have little concern over the inward workings of the heart. This was the whole religion of the Pharisees. Their concern was not how they appeared in the sight of God. Oh, they professed to have a concern for that, but their main concern was how they appeared before men. It was seen in their prayers. It was evidenced in their gifts and offerings. It was evidenced in the way they dressed and the manner in which they acted. Their concern in all their religious exercises was how they appeared in the sight of men. And you see how the Lord Jesus unmasks and brings to light these things and how he warns his disciples against them.

You read the sixth chapter in the gospel as recorded by Matthew. He said of the Pharisees, of the religious world of his day, that all they did in prayer, almsgiving and fasting, was to be seen of men. But the Lord instructs his own disciples completely opposite to this. "To make a fair show in the flesh" is not the vital thing. It is how we stand before God. Will not that be the exercise and concern of the soul truly taught of God the Holy Spirit? He will certainly not be unconcerned with respect to his outward conduct. No. But the great concern is 'how I stand before God, not whether I am accepted by men or whether they approve or disapprove. Ultimately, what does that really matter? What matters is how I stand before God. Am I accepted before him? Have I the favour of God?' And friends, this standing is only found in the gospel Paul preached. Yet these false teachers were denying the saving truth of the gospel.

He says, "As many as desire to make a fair shew in the flesh, they constrain you to be circumcised." Circumcision ensured conformity to the religious opinions and prejudices of that generation. And Paul brings out what was behind this. He says, "Only lest they should suffer persecution for the cross of Christ." These false teachers were true compromisers. They professed to hold the faith of Jesus Christ, yet they sought to fully conform to the prevailing religious fashion and opinions of those days. Though they professed faith in Jesus Christ they were very careful that they did not cross the religious opinions of the prevailing Judaism in those times.

We see also there was no real evidence that the things being advocated were ever of the working of God the Holy Spirit. Rather they were the very opposite. Souls were thereby sadly deceived and ensnared. As I have already said, the doctrines of the cross of Christ, of salvation by grace alone through faith alone in the Lord Jesus Christ, will never be conducive to the natural man. Where these doctrines are preached and held in faith and love, the religious world always evidences its opposition. It was so with the Lord himself and it was so with the disciples and apostles. What did their preaching of the cross bring them? It brought them into direct conflict with the professing religious world of their day, who rejected the doctrines the apostles preached because the gospel exposed the falseness of a judaistic profession. It showed the evils of the very things that they rested on. The doctrine of the cross cuts up, root and branch, all human righteousness and all the efforts of men as any ground whatsoever of acceptance before God or hope of salvation. And men will not have their cherished ideas and opinions so dealt with. Opposition was what the apostle proved. The preaching of the cross involved him in deep conflict. For it, he suffered persecution. And to avoid such suffering, these false teachers sought ways of compromise with the prevailing religion of the day. But as Paul shows here, to compromise on the essentials of the faith is to deny the faith and to be found in opposition to the work of God's Spirit.

He says, "For neither they themselves who are circumcised keep the law; but desire to have you circumcised, that they may glory in your flesh." Paul brings out a very important point here. And if we have but eyes to see it, what was true of those in Galatia who advocated obedience to the law as essential for salvation, is still true of those that join the keeping of the law to faith in Jesus Christ. These great advocates of the law never keep the law themselves. And by their opposition to those that will not accept their false doctrine, they show that they understand "neither what they say, nor whereof they affirm" (1 Tim. 1:7). The more they advocate the keeping of the law, the more they evidence their transgression of that law. It cannot but be so, and why is that? Because men and women are sinful fallen creatures and how can a sinful person ever keep the law in the way a holy God requires it to be kept? For as Paul shows, to be circumcised meant a person was a debtor to do the whole law, and not being able to keep that law they came under its curse and condemnation.

He says, "Neither they themselves who are circumcised keep the law; but desire to have you circumcised, that they may glory in your flesh." Ah, their glorying was in how many they could induce to follow them and take up with their opinions. It was so with the Pharisees. The Lord Jesus said of them, that they compassed sea and land to make one proselyte and when they had made him, they made him twice as much a child of the devil than they were themselves (Matt. 23:15). They spared no efforts in their proselytising, endeavouring to induce people to take up with their false opinions and come under their influence. You see it is as plain as ever today. Look at the many sects that are about—the Jehovah's Witnesses up the road—and their efforts to make proselytes, to bring people over to their ways and opinions, to bring them under their influence. This is not that thereby sinners may be saved but that they may glory in the adherents that they induce to come into their ways and under their influence. It is so with all false sects and ever is the tendency of fallen nature to glory in others being brought over to their opinions. Paul says here in effect that he desired to have nothing to do with such things. "God forbid that I should glory, save in the cross of our Lord Jesus Christ, by whom the world is crucified unto me, and I unto the world."

"God forbid." These words very strongly expressed Paul's abhorrence of the things he was warning against. 'God forbid that I should glory, save in the cross of our Lord Jesus Christ.' What does he mean? Did not the apostle desire to see souls saved? Did he not go forward in the preaching of the gospel? Was not his prayerful concern that the Lord the Holy Spirit would call out his own elect? Did he not rejoice to see sinners called by grace and added to the church? True he did, but he did not glory in that as the work of men or as his own achievements, as if *he* had converted men to the Christian religion. No, there was nothing of that in Paul. Paul's desire was to see the work of God the Holy Spirit manifest in the hearts and lives of sinners. It is as I believe I mentioned on Sunday, speaking out of Ezekiel chapter 36. Those words left a very deep impression on my spirit: "I will yet for this be inquired of by the house of Israel, to do it for them; I will increase them with men like a flock" (Ezek. 36:37). The blessing on the preaching of the word of God, by which as many as are ordained to eternal life are added to the church, is not through pleading with men but as we are brought to plead with our God. We are brought to have our eyes up only to him and not to go forward in our own strength but in his strength, not dependent on an arm of flesh but seeking the Holy Spirit's blessing on his own word. The work of calling the sinner and of imparting spiritual life is the work of God alone and to him be all the praise and all the glory.

"God forbid," says Paul, "that I should glory, save in the cross of our Lord Jesus Christ." What are we to understand here by the cross of our Lord Jesus Christ? Friends, I believe it is expressive of the very person and all the work of the Lord and Saviour himself. Here is the glorying of the church and people of God. It is not in what they are or in what they have done. Paul does not

glory even in the fact that he was the instrument in the Lord's
hands for many being called by divine grace. He seeks to give
the honour where it is due—not to himself but to the Lord Jesus
Christ, who he is and what he has done. I believe "the cross of
our Lord Jesus Christ" embodies the whole of the person and
finished work of the Lord and Saviour Jesus Christ, all that the
gospel reveals and makes known of him. All the apostle's
glorying, as a servant of Christ, as a sinner saved by divine grace,
is in the person and finished work of the Lord Jesus Christ.

"God forbid that I should glory, save in the cross of our Lord
Jesus Christ." And the person and the finished work of Jesus
Christ was ever the central theme of the apostle's preaching and
teaching. This was sadly being beclouded and undermined by
those false teachers and preachers in the churches of Galatia. Ah,
I said that what deeply concerned the apostle were the sad
attempts being made to eclipse the glory of the Lord and Saviour.
The work of salvation is his from beginning to end. He is to have
all the glory of it. I believe a few weeks ago I spoke concerning
the song of Moses and the song of the Lamb (Rev. 15:3). The
very theme of that sacred song and hymn of praise is the giving
all the glory to God for the salvation of his church and people.

"By whom the world is crucified unto me, and I unto the
world." The apostle knew in his own soul the blessed power of
the cross, that is, the finished work of Jesus Christ. He knew daily
the sanctifying influence of it in his life, in dying to sin and living
to God through his Lord and Saviour. It is often suggested that
we can put too much emphasis on the doctrine of justification by
faith. We can put too much emphasis and encouragement on the
sinner looking alone to Jesus Christ. We have to be careful to
maintain the right balance between justification and sanctification. People who say things like that have no real idea of what
the apostle is saying here. For friends, the more the soul learns of
Jesus Christ as taught by the Holy Spirit, the closer we are
brought and kept to him. These things can never lead to
licentiousness. The more we know of the preciousness of the
salvation which is all of grace from beginning to end as
proclaimed by the apostle, the more will we live to God. The
more the love of God in Christ is shed abroad in our heart by the

Holy Spirit, the more will we live in love to God. If we ever live to God it is as these truths are deeply impressed on our hearts and we are brought through grace to live on them daily. A free full salvation always has a true sanctifying effect on the soul. True sanctification is found at the cross of Jesus Christ. The more I know of true spiritual fellowship and communion with him as taught by the Holy Spirit, the more will I die to sin and the more shall I declare what Paul says here: "the world is crucified unto me, and I unto the world."

"For in Christ Jesus, neither circumcision availeth any thing, nor uncircumcision, but a new creature." Let us not overlook the essential truth Paul is bringing out here. There were those that were advocating circumcision in the churches in Galatia. There are those today who advocate this, that and the other and put great emphasis on the ordinances of God. Now all those things have their place but Paul shows here that "Neither circumcision availeth any thing" because it has been done away. Neither does "uncircumcision," that is, it is not outward things or even the most assiduous attendance on the outward matters of religion that avails anything. The essential thing is "a new creature." As the Lord Jesus said to Nicodemus, "Except a man be born again, he cannot see the kingdom of God" (John 3:3). What are all outward religious exercises without the new birth, the new creature, the soul made alive unto God? I can attend assiduously on the outward duties of religion all my life and yet what are we and what do we have without the regenerating work of God the Holy Spirit? Friends, those outward things of themselves avail nothing. Even the proper exercises of religion as you might put it, the attending on the ordinances of the Lord's house convey no real and lasting good of themselves. They are not to be attended upon as a work of the flesh but as the fruit of the new birth in the soul of the sinner made alive to God. They must be attended to in the true exercise of a God-given faith. "Neither circumcision availeth anything, nor uncircumcision, but a new creature."

He says, "And as many as walk according to this rule." What is this rule he is advocating? What he says here particularly relates to his contending against those who were troubling the churches of Galatia. Yes, they had a rule to which they said men must conform to be saved. They were very strict in laying down that rule. They said that the rule which must be observed for people to be saved is the keeping of the law as well as faith supposedly in Jesus Christ. Without going over the things I have said already such ideas are very conducive to fallen nature. Many are ensnared by those things still. But he says, "As many as walk according to *this* rule." It was the very opposite of the rule advocated by the false teachers. It is the rule of the new creature in Christ Jesus. And what is that rule? It is what proceeds from what we might well term mount Zion. It is the will of God as revealed in the person and work of the Lord Jesus Christ. It is the revealed will of God found in the entire scriptures of truth as those things centre in Jesus Christ.

This rule of the new creature is emphasised in what Paul writes in his epistle to the Romans chapter 7. He says there, "Know ye not, brethren, (for I speak to them that know the law,) how that the law hath dominion over a man as long as he liveth?" Using the illustration of marriage, he says, "For the woman which hath an husband is bound by the law to her husband so long as he liveth; but if the husband be dead, she is loosed from the law of her husband...if her husband be dead, she is free from that law; so that she is no adulteress, though she be married to another man." And when she is married to another the law of the first husband obviously cannot apply to her. She is now under the law of her second husband. And so the apostle goes on to say, "Wherefore, my brethren, ye also are become dead to the law by the body of Christ; that ye should be married to another, even to him who is raised from the dead, that we should bring forth fruit unto God." And the law of the new creature is that true subjection in everything to Jesus Christ our Lord and Saviour. His word and will is the rule found in Zion of which the apostle James could write, when he speaks of the perfect law of liberty. "But whoso looketh into the perfect law of liberty, and continueth therein, he being not a forgetful hearer, but a doer of the work, this man shall be blessed in his deed" (Jas. 1:25).

"And as many as walk according to this rule, peace be on them, and mercy, and upon the Israel of God." Yes, he desires the blessing of God to rest on all who walk according to this rule, this law of liberty. And they *shall* be ever blessed. All others are under the curse and condemnation of the law from mount Sinai.

"From henceforth let no man trouble me." What does he mean by that statement? He contends here most earnestly and faithfully for "the faith that was once delivered unto the saints" (Jude 1:3). And he is no longer prepared to debate these things in any way. There is no question of his debating them. What he is stating here is the very truth of God and he will no longer be troubled with those that want to debate those matters. 'Let them do so, but I Paul will not be involved in any debates.' Here is the truth which he faithfully preached and taught and would do so even to his dying day.

He says, "For I bear in my body the marks of the Lord Jesus." Now I know there have been various ideas put forth as to the meaning of this statement. We can interpret it in this way. This was why I read chapter 11 out of the second epistle to the Corinthians. There Paul speaks of the things that he suffered for Christ's sake and what he bore in his body of the marks of the Lord Jesus. As he went forward upheld and sustained by grace in the work of the ministry, see what sufferings, afflictions, privations and persecutions it involved him in for Jesus' sake. Paul is here saying, 'I have not suffered and gone through all these things, now to deny and reject what I have preached.' Did he not verily believe and rest in dependence on what he here advocated? Was not the gospel he preached the whole hope and ground of his salvation?

"I bear in my body the marks of the Lord Jesus." We might say they were honourable scars that Paul bore, yet what can he say of all that he had suffered in the path the Lord had appointed for him? He could view it in this way. He says, "Our light affliction, which is but for a moment, worketh for us a far more exceeding and eternal weight of glory; while we look not at the things which are seen, but at the things which are not seen: for the things which are seen are temporal; but the things which are not seen are eternal" (2 Cor. 4:17-18).

"Brethren, the grace of our Lord Jesus Christ be with your spirit. Amen."

May the Lord add his blessing. Amen.